My
Friend
Anne
Frank

My Friend Anne Frank

*The Inspiring and Heartbreaking True
Story of Best Friends Torn Apart and
Reunited Against All Odds*

Hannah Pick-Goslar

with Dina Kraft

Little, Brown Spark
New York Boston London

Little, Brown Spark
Hachette Book Group
1290 Avenue of the Americas, New York, NY 10104
littlebrownspark.com

First North American Edition: June 2023
Published simultaneously in Great Britain by Penguin Random House UK

Little, Brown Spark is an imprint of Little, Brown and Company, a division of Hachette Book Group, Inc. The Little, Brown Spark name and logo are trademarks of Hachette Book Group, Inc.

The publisher is not responsible for websites (or their content) that are not owned by the publisher.

The Hachette Speakers Bureau provides a wide range of authors for speaking events. To find out more, go to hachettespeakersbureau.com or email hachettespeakers@hbgusa.com.

Little, Brown and Company books may be purchased in bulk for business, educational, or promotional use. For information, please contact your local bookseller or the Hachette Book Group Special Markets Department at special.markets@hbgusa.com.

ISBN 9780316564403
LCCN 2023933313

Printing 1, 2023

LSC-C

Printed in the United States of America

Contents

Prologue   1

1.   Berlin   5
2.   Amsterdam   16
3.   New Friends   23
4.   Arrivals   36
5.   Invasion   52
6.   Aftershocks   71
7.   The Noose   96
8.   Deportation   118
9.   Westerbork   128
10. Limbo   148
11. Bergen-Belsen   164
12. Anne   189
13. The Lost Train   208
14. Liberation   223
15. Beterschap   241
16. Switzerland   252
17. Ghosts   265
18. The Promised Land   275

Afterword   295

Dina Kraft's Acknowledgments   306
Elegy for Hannah and Anne's Classmates   308
Selected Bibliography   311

Prologue

Spring, Jerusalem 2022

Thank goodness I can still see the path outside my door, framed by purple bougainvillea, palm trees and clay pots of pink and white impatiens. It gives me some peace, knowing who is on their way to my door and who is just walking by. From this chair in the living room of my garden flat where I spend most of my time these days, I look out to a large window which allows me to see my family and friends as they come down the path.

Most of all, I'm grateful to see Tali, arriving as she does every afternoon on the dot at 4.15. This youngest granddaughter of mine is now a young mother herself. She's only ever lived five minutes away from me by foot. Even after getting married, she insisted on staying in the neighbourhood. She wants to be close to me, she says. Not necessary, I answer back, not really believing my words. Luckily, Tali knows better.

We share a kind of unspoken language. I find it hard to describe why, but I feel she understands me, and I her. She was just a toddler when her father was killed in a car crash on a rainy afternoon years ago. I stepped in as a second parent of sorts to help my daughter Ruthie, her mother, who became a widow and single mother to eight children that terrible day.

'Wait!' Tali calls out to her eldest daughter Neta whose hair is the colour of dark honey, just like Tali's. She's a beautiful, vibrant girl, now going on four. She's already barrelling down the path, Tali trailing behind her, hands steady on the pushchair. It holds her youngest, Shaked, who was born at the height of the Covid pandemic. Even in lockdown, Tali would still come every day, but we would speak at a distance – me from the balcony, her down in the garden below, one arm wrapped around Neta, Shaked strapped into a baby carrier.

Buzz goes the doorbell. In sails Neta, in full pre-school glory, announcing herself to me and the world. 'Savta!' she bursts out, Hebrew for grandmother. Whatever is going on that day, whether it's more bad news in the world or another ache and pain, I feel a warmth rising inside whenever I see her and break into a smile. She presents me with a drawing filled with hearts, balloons and the occasional Mickey Mouse sticker. Her eyes grow wide when I tell her Mickey Mouse and I are the same age, both born 93 years ago, in 1928. And then she settles down at my feet and, as she spreads out her shape-matching game, my mind travels back almost 90 years.

When I was only a little older than Neta, I had just arrived in Amsterdam with my parents, escaping Berlin after Hitler came to power and fired my father, a deputy cabinet member in the Prussian government during the Weimar Republic. We moved into a two-bedroom apartment in a residential neighbourhood, overlooking green trees and neat squares.

One day, not long after our arrival, I walked hand in hand with my mother to a local grocery. There, my mother noticed another woman talking in German to her dark-eyed daughter, who was about my age. The two mothers spoke briefly to one another, smiling, clearly relieved to find some familiarity in this foreign place. I was a shy child and I clung to my mother's leg, unused to other children but curious about the little girl looking back at me.

She was to be my very first friend. A childhood playmate, neighbour and school friend. Our families became close as they navigated life as refugees in a new city, sharing their fears as the war, occupation and all that would mean for us moved inexorably closer. That little girl, so full of life, would become the most famous victim of the Holocaust. A symbol, in many ways, of all the hope and promise that was lost to hatred and murder. Talking about her story, our story, would later become a thread that bound me to her and kept our friendship alive long after she was gone. But from when we first met to when she abruptly disappeared from my life not long before my fourteenth birthday, to reappear fleetingly in the strangest and most tragic of ways, she was simply my friend, Anne Frank.

Chapter 1

Berlin

In one of my earliest memories, I am sitting on the parquet floor, watching some men wrap our blue velvet sofa first in blankets and then in brown paper. They tie it with string, making it look like a huge, ungainly birthday present. To my surprise, they then lift it up and, with some difficulty, carry it out of the front door of our apartment, leaving a large, dusty space where the sofa has always stood. I wonder what we will sit on now.

In other rooms, the dining room set was being packed up and paintings taken down from the walls, leaving yet more conspicuous empty spaces where our things used to be. Even the bronze bust of Otto Braun, the Prussian prime minister and leader of the Social Democrat Party, whom I vaguely understood to be an important man and my father's friend and boss, was lowered into a wooden crate.

My mother – the far more practical of my parents – bustled around our home, trying to sort out the family silver. Meanwhile, my father stared unblinkingly at his beloved books on the shelves that lined the wood-panelled wall of our living room. He had carefully packed some away into boxes but there were many, many more, both still on the shelves and in piles around his feet.

'You can't take all of them, you know,' Mama told him in a low, gentle voice.

We were preparing to leave our home, on Den Zelten 21A, Berlin, opposite the big Tiergarten park where fat yellow roses grew along iron gates and my parents would take me to play and sometimes to visit the elephants in the zoo. We were leaving our country too, but this was too hard for me to understand, aged only four. I was aware, I think, of the marching boots, the noise and the red-and-black flags that were now a regular sight in Berlin. And I would have noticed that my father – who used to be a busy man who left the house early every morning to go to his office – now stayed at home all day. But my memories of our home in Berlin are mostly fragments: the crunching sound my shoes made on Tiergarten's pebbled pathways, the way the apartment vibrated from the tolling of the bells from the church across the road built in memory of Kaiser Wilhelm and the soft sounds of our grand piano being played by mother.

Our apartment, my first home, on a tree-lined street is not there any more. It was bombed by the Allies some years later. But I know that it was spacious and elegant, with high ceilings, thick Persian rugs and Art Deco wooden chairs and tables. My mother, Ruth, (or Rutchen, as she was known to family) had an eye for beautiful things and our home was filled with art and fine porcelain. She had the help of a cook and a maid to run the house and we enjoyed a comfortable life of relative privilege.

Mama had been an elementary school teacher, but as an upper-middle-class wife of a government official she had regretfully left the profession according to the convention of the day. She loved working with children and being in the classroom, but it was not thought correct for a married woman, with a husband to support her, to take a job from a single woman. Mama would get on the floor and play games with me and delighted in my stories and questions about the world, which she would answer with patience and detail. I liked to watch her get dressed in one of her tailor-made silk or velvet gowns, ready for one of the many evening outings to concerts, cabarets, receptions and even formal balls to which my father was invited as a high-ranking government official.

As an only child for many years, I basked in the attentions of both of my parents. I believe their marriage was a happy one, though they were quite different people. Whereas my mother, who was 12 years my father's junior, was fun and outgoing, witty and a smart observer of people, my father was more serious and could be preoccupied, even brooding – but he also had a charisma that drew people to him. He was a natural leader who could inspire and connect to others. Though a pessimist – of course he preferred to call himself a realist – somewhat in contrast to my mother's can-do pragmatism, he was still a warm man, known in our community as someone who enjoyed helping others. His talents as a communicator, both in the written word and as a speaker, took him far professionally in his chosen field of politics. He always had the patience to answer my questions and make me feel like the most important person in the room.

At the start of the Great War, my father, Hans, had recently graduated from university with an economics degree and begun his career as a business and economics reporter. In 1915, aged 25, he was drafted as a foot soldier to serve in the German army and sent to the Eastern front to fight the Russians. Thankfully, a year later, he was transferred to Germany's general headquarters of the Eastern front in Kaunas, Lithuania. He later said how grateful he was to emerge not only alive but uninjured from his time in the icy mud of those death-filled trenches fighting the Russians, where so many lost their lives.

In Lithuania, two things happened that would change the course of his life. First, to his great relief, he was removed from frontline duties and his journalism skills were tapped for the war effort by none other than General Erich Ludendorff, the celebrated war hero of that time, known as the 'brain' of the German army. Ludendorff gave him orders to edit a Lithuanian newspaper, even though my father knew nothing about the country and did not speak the language. He joked years later: 'I was probably the only journalist in the world who was unable to read the newspaper he edited.' Instead, Lithuanian-speaking German soldiers translated what he wrote.

As the war went on, Ludendorff's prowess as a military strategist turned disastrous when he stymied and then outright refused all attempts at making peace. His ambitious push for victory in the final stages of the war backfired. When post-war Germany staggered under the weight of resentment and shame from the Versailles Treaty that ended the war in the harshest of ways for Germany – lost territory, reparations it could never hope to pay and the hyperinflation and hunger that followed – Ludendorff acknowledged no missteps of his own. Instead, he promoted the 'stabbed in the back' theory, which blamed Jews for Germany's defeat, claiming Jews had conspired against Germany from within during the war. Captivated by conspiracy theories, he was among the first of the German elite to endorse Adolf Hitler. He argued that for Germany to recover, a massive new world war was needed, one that would forge a new German empire beyond anyone's previous imaginings. Ludendorff's actions helped enable Hitler, with catastrophic results for my family and for all of European Jewry. During the First World War, though, by keeping him off the battlefield, Ludendorff may well have saved my father's life.

The second thing that changed for my father – which had a profound impact on him and, by extension, on the life of my family – was that, while serving in Eastern Europe, he encountered and became enchanted with the world of religious Judaism. My father was the son of a banker who had grown up fully assimilated, with little connection to Jewish tradition. On Christmas Eve, his family even put up a Christmas tree, aglow with candles. He had encountered devout Jews back home in Germany, and no doubt some from Eastern Europe, but I believe that like most secular Jewish Germans, he would have likely viewed them negatively, in accordance with the prejudices of the day – backwards, loud, unmannered. This was a time when many Western European Jews were abandoning any trappings of Jewish ritual life and intermarrying with non-Jews at record rates, with some even choosing baptism as a way to get ahead professionally and to help ensure they would not be a target of antisemitic bullying and violence. So my secular father's embrace of Orthodox Judaism was highly unusual. Nonetheless, during his military posting to Bialystock, he became besotted with the tenderness and closeness of the Hassidic religious Jewish communities and their culture. He met rabbis, studied Hebrew and got to know large, warm, devout families, which changed his attitude to religion for the rest of his life. He learned how to pray for the first time, sang spiritual songs, attended Sabbath services and then stayed on for Sabbath meals in modest but close-knit homes, enchanted by the melodies and spiritual life infused in them. He decided to take on observant Jewish life himself.

In 1919, after returning to Germany, my father joined the Social Democrat Party – which played a key role in forming the Weimar Republic with hopes of seeding a new democratic culture – and took part in negotiations for a new government in Prussia. He became the head of the Prussian state government press office and a deputy cabinet minister. He was prized by his colleagues, who described him as having exceptional levels of energy, knowledge and a conveniently long memory that came in handy in political sparring. He was a proud German and one of the highest-ranking Jewish officials in the government, probably the only observant one. If called into the office, close to the Reichstag, the German parliament, for a meeting on a Saturday, he could walk there and still not break the Jewish Sabbath. In his ornate, high-ceilinged office he'd read a daily page of the Talmud, an overview of rabbinic discussion of Jewish law over the centuries. On Sundays, he'd go to his office to read his letters and get a head start on the week's correspondence. Sometimes he'd take me along; I have a memory of walking there with him, hand in hand.

My father had a front-row seat to the internal workings of the government and the country and fumed when, in January 1933, President Paul von Hindenburg, the former general and war hero, relented to advisors who said making Hitler chancellor would appease his ego while allowing cooler minds to rule behind the scenes. 'How blind they are,' Papa railed. After the Nazis took power, my father was put on 'indefinite suspension'. His offence was never put into writing, but he had been known for speaking on radio programmes and in newspaper columns about the importance of safeguarding democracy. I imagine being Jewish also made him an easy, early target for firing at the beginning of Hitler's ascendance in the German government. Several other Jewish government officials and employees lost their jobs at the same time. Many of his fellow members of the Social Democrat Party, which was outlawed by the Nazis, along with all other political opposition, were arrested. Some were sent 300 miles away to Dachau, near Munich.

In April 1933, laws were brought in to exclude Jews and anyone who spoke out against the Nazi party from government and the civil service. A number attempted to sue. In their lawsuits, they proudly held up their Germanness, their deepest loyalty and love for their country, with many pleading their steadfast service to the state and, in some cases, their Iron Cross medals, won fighting for Germany in the First World War. Many of the 100,000 Jewish men who served had willingly volunteered, thinking this most essential declaration of life-or-death dedication to the fatherland would lead to their final full acceptance and integration. But their words were lonely protests, doomed defences in a world where the extinction of reason had already begun.

Of course, I was too young to understand the terrible changes that swept through our country in the earliest years of my life. And I know my parents would have tried to shelter me from any fear. But I sensed their anxiety; I became clingy and protested against sleeping alone. Most often, the sound of change came from the radio, usually accompanied by my mother hissing to my father to lower the volume so I would not hear. But by our last year in Berlin, 1933, the noise of political upheaval came floating through my bedroom window and it became increasingly difficult for my parents to carry on as normal.

First, there was the cacophony of trombones, clarinets and SS men's marching boots: a torchlit parade throughout Berlin celebrating Hitler's appointment as chancellor, as they sang out about being soldiers for a 'new era' committed in blood to 'the racial struggle'. Torches lit up the street below like a glowing river, illuminating the billowing swastika flags, white and black against red.

Then, a few weeks later, in February 1933, we were woken by the noise of sirens and fire trucks. The sky was bright and full of smoke. The Reichstag – only a five-minute walk from our apartment – was on fire. I went running to find my parents but my mother quickly tried to shoo me – and my questions – back to bed. I can only imagine the expression on my father's face and the depths of his feelings as he tried to absorb the symbolism of democracy aflame.

More fires burned in May. In the name of 'purifying Germany', students had met with professors to decide which books were 'un-German' and should be confiscated from the nation's libraries and incinerated. Books were crammed into trucks and cars, and young people carried armfuls to a square between the opera house and the university, before feeding them to the flames. In our apartment, we could smell the smoke rising from the many thousands of volumes.

*   *   *

All over Germany, Jewish families were asking themselves the same impossible questions my parents were – what shall we do? How will we make a living? Is it only a matter of time till saner minds prevail? Or must we leave our home? Where can we go? In a country where protestors were punished by being sent to a concentration camp, non-Jewish dissidents – writers and artists among them – were facing similar dilemmas and were among the first to flee.

It was incredibly painful for my mother and father to face up to the increasingly apparent truth that we would have to leave. My mother was especially devastated by the idea of abandoning a country she loved fiercely. She adored the vibrant cultural and intellectual life of Berlin, its concert halls, art museums, the discussion of books and ideas. She gave me the middle name Elisabeth in tribute to Goethe, her god and Germany's too. Both my parents were products of interwar German intellectualism and liberalism, shaped by the previous 150 years of growing social acceptance for Jews. Our home bridged German philosophy and literature with Jewish tradition; among those books my father so reluctantly packed into crates, some never to be seen again, were volumes on German politics and literature and Jewish thought. Some of them he had even written himself.

But my father feared that his past government position and his warnings and criticism of the Nazis on the radio and in newspapers marked him as an enemy of the state, and that he could face possible arrest. He prided himself on his sober, realistic assessments and he simply did not see a future for our family as Jews in Germany with so much hostility and violence simmering beneath the surface. My family had called Germany home for a thousand years. Among my ancestors were rabbis, philosophers, journalists, economists, professors, lawyers, bankers and teachers. But I was to be the last of my family to be born there when I arrived in 1928. We were no longer safe.

My extended family, like so many Jewish families across Germany, were scattering to various countries around the world. Mama was the middle child of three siblings who were good friends to one another and all equally devoted to their parents. Her family, the Klees, were extremely close, making the decision even harder to take. Their parents wanted to stay in Germany, as did my father's mother; they could not imagine starting their lives again in a foreign country. But my mother's brother, my uncle Hans, a lawyer like their father, was trying to decide where he might go, ultimately choosing Switzerland so he could continue to practise law in German. Their sister, my aunt Eugenie, was fired from the Institute for Cancer Research in Berlin, even though she was a leading expert in tissue engineering. She and her husband, Simon Rawidowicz, tried urgently to find academic posts for themselves abroad, sailing first to Leeds, England, and later to Chicago before settling in Boston.

It was finally decided: the three of us were going to England. My father had managed to secure a job in London at Unilever. And so our Berlin apartment was emptied until only our own voices echoed in its vacant rooms. On the morning we left, the boycotts, the Brownshirts beating people up in the streets, the Nazi marches and chants no doubt echoed in my parents' minds, but I thought mainly of my beloved Tiergarten. As I turned my back on the park for the last time, I could hear the sounds of children chasing after one another in games of tag. Balancing suitcases and trunks, we made our way to the station to board a train to Hamburg, the first leg of our journey to England.

* * *

We arrived safely in London under grey, leaden skies. This metropolis of eight million people, twice the size of Berlin, built of limestone and brick, where we had few contacts and no family, felt overwhelming. Luckily, both my parents spoke English, although my mother was the more proficient of the two – she was a talented linguist who also understood French, Greek and Latin. London was the capital of the British Empire and so I saw faces from around the world for the first time and watched in awe as ships from Asia, the Caribbean and Africa steamed up the mighty Thames.

Papa, an economist by training, had been offered a good job at the Unilever corporation. But our stay in England was to be brief. Only after arriving in London to start in his new role was he informed the position included working on Saturday, the Jewish Sabbath.

'In my government job in Germany my Sabbath observance was respected, but not here in England?' he railed, flabbergasted, reporting the news to Mama.

When he told his employers he was not prepared to break the prohibition against work on the Jewish Sabbath, his contract was rescinded.

For my father, being a committed Jew went beyond being the deeply spiritual person he was. It meant being fully bound to the 'mitzvot', Hebrew for commandments, with Sabbath observance being one of the most central tenets. It was through observing these rules and rituals that he found purpose, a gateway to living a good and meaningful life. These values he found in his Judaism were not something he was willing to abandon, even if they were sometimes painfully inopportune.

It was a fateful decision, one that would reverberate in ways we could never have imagined. England was and would remain safe ground. Meanwhile, Europe was only getting more dangerous as the Nazis continued their rise to dominance. But for all his wisdom and understanding of the politics of the time, my father could not have dreamed of what was to come. No one could have foreseen the horror that was to descend a few short years into the future. So we were again on the move, this time to Amsterdam, in search of refuge.

Chapter 2

Amsterdam

'Neutral' is not a word most five-year-olds know, but I did.

Even in 1934, there was growing talk of another war but, like Switzerland, the Netherlands had been neutral throughout the First World War. No matter what happened, everyone reassured themselves, neutral countries don't get involved in wars and are certainly off limits for invasion. The Dutch had a reputation of being fair-minded and liberal, and the country did not have the entrenched antisemitism seen in so much of Europe. Importantly, we would be just across the border from Germany. It was also close enough for my mother and me to visit my grandparents and other family and friends still there (though my father thought even a visit would be too risky for him). These are the reasons I believe my parents chose the Netherlands as a new home for our little family of three. In Amsterdam, we could lay low and let the madness hopefully burn itself out. My mother especially harboured hopes that we would only be temporary exiles and that, with time, we would be able to return home.

So it was that on 20 December 1933, the city of Amsterdam registered my father's arrival by emblazoning Goslar, our family name, across an entry form in sprawling, elegant cursive. Father's full name followed in the line below with his date of arrival and the address of the hotel where he stayed those first weeks as he tried to get his bearings and establish himself in yet another new country, while we stayed with my grandparents in Berlin. Three months later, a clerk added my mother's full maiden name, Ruth Judith Klee, followed by my own, and the date of our arrival: 19 March 1934. A simple piece of paper, a tool of officialdom. But one which would change everything for us.

The tulips were starting to bloom when my mother and I disembarked from the train in Amsterdam. Our shoes tapped against the cobblestones and we tried to stay out of the way of hurrying cyclists. After weeks of separation from my father, I was so happy the three of us were together again. I felt safe walking hand in hand with both my parents. Still, I let go and walked ahead, briefly lost in how the golden light spilled on the canal, magnifying the reflections of the barges skimming by. But then I felt my mother suddenly yank my arm back as I stepped too close to the water. For a moment, I was scared, my feeling of calm shattered.

'We are now in the Jerusalem of the West,' my father declared, trying to sound enthusiastic, as we took those first steps through the city as a family.

He harboured hopes this Jerusalem would be a stopgap until we could get to the real one, nearly 3,000 miles east in the Levant. Zionism at the time was the movement to establish a Jewish homeland in what was in biblical times the Land of Israel, where Jewish statehood had once existed 2,000 years earlier. Its proponents saw it as an answer to centuries of exile and struggle in the diaspora: a safe haven and movement of Jewish rebirth. But with Arab–Jewish tensions brewing, the British, who ruled what was then called Mandatory Palestine, were making it increasingly difficult for Jews to immigrate. Getting a visa took time, luck and money. My father was told he'd need to declare a large amount of capital to even apply for a visa, which he did not have.

Although my mother's father, Alfred Klee, was a leader of the Zionist movement in Germany – as was my own father – Mama didn't share her husband's dreams of immigration to the Middle East. She had travelled with her parents and brother and sister to British Mandate Palestine on a family visit as a young woman of 20 and witnessed the hardscrabble lives of Jewish pioneers on early kibbutzim and settlements. It was not an easy life and she had promptly decided it was not for her.

'I can't work that hard,' she said, only half-joking.

After the months of uncertainty, there was at least a reassuring solidity in the brick and stone buildings and bridges linking Amsterdam's criss-crossing streets and canals. Even more snug and secure was the feel of the Rivierenbuurt, Dutch for River District, the name of our new neighbourhood in the southern part of the city, wedged between the Amstel River and two major canals, where most of the streets – including ours – were named for Dutch rivers.

We climbed the stairs to our new apartment at the top of a flight of stairs on Merwedeplein 31. My father pushed open the big bay windows in the living room that overlooked the square. 'Welcome home!' he announced. It was a lot smaller than our Berlin home. No more high ceilings, wide balcony or extra rooms. There was also no maid or cook to help my mother with the housekeeping. As the wife of a senior official in the Prussian government who'd always had domestic help, this was entirely new territory.

Looking out of the bay window, I could see below us a triangular-shaped expanse, filled with sand, its edges marked by a low hedge and flowerbeds where children of different ages were playing and riding bikes. The apartment blocks all around were in the same light brown brick as ours, although a number seemed to still be under construction when we arrived. Trucks full of cement, plaster and tiles were parked on street corners and I was surprised to see construction workers walking along scaffolding planks high up in the air. Towering over the neighbourhood was a 12-storey building. 'The tallest building in all of Holland – right here!' neighbours proclaimed. We would learn to call it, as everyone did, 'the skyscraper'.

We were the tenth Jewish family from Germany to move in on our street when we arrived in early 1934. But we were just the beginning of a tidal wave of increasingly desperate Jews looking for refuge. Eventually, Tram Line 8, which ran between our neighbourhood and the Jewish quarter in central Amsterdam, would be nicknamed the 'Jerusalem Line' and the 24 tram, linking the Beethovenbuurt neighbourhood, another area in which many German refugees settled, to downtown was called the 'Berlin Express'. There were also Jewish immigrants from Russian, Belgian and Czech backgrounds. The global economic crisis had not spared the Netherlands and some apartments had stood empty since they were completed two years previously. So our landlord was happy to have Jewish refugees from Germany like us arrive, anxious for a place to live and able to afford the rents that were considered relatively high for what were billed as 'luxury' apartments, since they featured modern perks of running hot water and central heating.

In the first few days Mama focused on unpacking and trying to make our apartment feel like home. Out came the dark green bedspread that covered my parents' bed back in Berlin, and the chair upholstered in the same fabric. On the wall in the living room she hung a Van Gogh print of a red and black fishing boat beached on a sandy strip, lapped by the waves of the Mediterranean Sea. She said it made the room feel bigger. Looking back, I wonder if she identified with that boat, washed up somewhere she had not intended to be, hovering in the in-between, the invisible line between sea and shore.

French doors made of glass divided the dining room from the living room. Our walnut formal dining room table and chair set never did arrive from Germany. But the patio furniture for a patio we no longer had did. So we ate our meals at that wicker table, sitting on its matching chairs, covered in white pillows with tiny red flowers. Every week, my mother would buy flowers and place them in a white ceramic vase, one of her many tasteful touches to our life. And I immediately loved my new room, fascinated by my Murphy-style bed that folded into the bedroom wall between a pair of built-in bookcases every morning after I woke up.

Wanting us to settle in as soon as possible, my father talked enthusiastically about the bookstore around the corner, the handful of cafés and shops all within walking distance. But we were in a leafy, quiet area on the edge of the city, so there were no fine shops or department stores along smart, tree-lined streets, or café-crammed squares overflowing with people like those on our doorstep in Berlin. My mother never got over her homesickness for the city of her birth. It clung to her even on that first day of new beginnings in Amsterdam, the three of us finally back together after those months apart, although she tried hard not to show it. She was 32 years old to my father's 44. She had loved her life in Berlin and did not relish starting over. Neither did he, but he was so gloomy about the situation in Germany that I think it was easier for him not to dwell on my mother's nostalgia for what until recently they had both cherished as their homeland. I wonder now how much I absorbed of my parents' anxieties as newly displaced people.

Learning Dutch was our first obstacle. Mama, who so loved languages, dismissed guttural Dutch as a 'throat condition, not a language'. On the one hand, it was close to German, on the other, a slightly different arrangement of words created – sometimes comically – entirely different meanings. My parents were confused at first when they read signs that meant one thing in Dutch and another in German. For example, a sign on a front door instructing visitors on how to summon attention. In Dutch, the word '*bellen*' means to ring a doorbell, whereas in German it means to bark like a dog. At first we were insulted – did it mean they thought we barked like dogs?!

And most Dutch people had a sign next to their door to deter travelling salesmen: '*Aan de deur wordt niet gekocht*,' meaning 'No purchases at the door.' However, to a German eye, this reads as 'We are cooking at the door.' This sort of thing made for funny misunderstandings in our early days in Amsterdam. But unfortunately, it was about the extent of Dutch I was exposed to before I started school.

Mama was finding her way around the neighbourhood, learning which shops carried which produce and household supplies for cleaning and organising our new apartment. For someone like her, accustomed to domestic help, this alone was challenging, but she was also doing it as a newcomer and in a foreign language she did not yet speak. She gradually grew her cooking repertoire, becoming a competent cook, but not a natural one.

One morning, I went to pick up some groceries with my mother. I loved venturing out with her, hand in hand, to get another glimpse of our new surroundings. In one of the aisles of a local shop we overhead German and turned our heads to see who was speaking. A woman was talking to her young daughter. The two mothers began chatting, relief in their voices to have found someone familiar in this foreign place.

The little girl with the dark pageboy haircut and I just eyed one another shyly. We did not say a word. Timid around other children, I took a step backwards, half hiding behind my mother, clutching her skirt. But the little girl and I kept staring at one another in shared silence and a measure of shared comfort.

Chapter 3

New Friends

I was shy on the best of days, but setting off for my first day of nursery school at the 6th Montessori school on Niersstraat, I was positively petrified. I cried leaving our apartment and, though usually an obedient child, tried to hold onto the front door handle as I begged to stay home. For months, my main company had been my mother or other adults. And I hardly spoke a word of Dutch.

'Enough, Hanneli,' Mama said sternly, using the name most of my family called me, while peeling my fingers off the door. 'It's always difficult to start anything new. We are going now and you are going to be fine. You'll see.'

The pep talk continued as we walked down our street to a three-storey brick building with a façade of narrow floor-to-ceiling windows. I understood that this was where I was to be left by my mother and I felt my stomach drop. I whimpered but she cut me off with a look that said she was not tolerating any more fuss. She opened the large wooden door of the school and, once inside, I clutched Mama's hand even harder and dragged my feet slowly down the tiled hallway, even though that meant scuffing my new patent leather shoes.

We went into a classroom where there were lots of children looking extremely busy. Some sat at small desks, playing with wooden blocks; others traced letters or sat on mats working on their writing. I spotted a girl with glossy dark hair that was almost black. I couldn't see her face as her back was turned towards me. She was playing on a set of silver bells. In that moment, she turned around and looked at me. In a flash, we recognised one another. It was the girl from the corner grocery store! We instantly rushed into each other's arms as if we were long-separated sisters, sentences in German flowing between us like a volcano of connection. My clenched stomach released; my anxiety vanished and I smiled.

'My name is Annelies. You can call me Anne,' said the girl.

As two little girls who didn't know Dutch, we were thrilled to find one another and I didn't even notice when my relieved mother tiptoed her way silently out of the door. Anne was also a new girl at the school. Her family had recently arrived from Frankfurt, another big German city. We both had liberal-minded parents who had decided that the modern Montessori approach, which promised children freedom to follow their own curiosity, was right for us. Instead of grades, learning was child-centred, with pupils choosing what they were interested in.

I was instantly dazzled by Anne, this first friend, though I quickly understood that we were very different. I had a habit of hunching into myself, tilting my head sideways and thinking about what I wanted to say before saying anything. I wasn't used to being around other children and was easily intimidated. I was gangly and tall for my age. Anne had pale olive skin and was shorter than me by about a head – a slip of a girl, almost fragile, with large, flashing dark eyes that seemed to laugh when she did. But her slightness belied her big personality. She was excellent at initiating ideas for games and leading other kids. She was confident, even with adults. She would ask an adult anything; in fact, she always seemed to be asking questions. I marvelled at how she came up with so many. When we met, her dark brown hair was cropped into a short bob swept to the side. I also wore my hair short, like most girls our age did then, but mine was chestnut brown with a little wave. Sometimes my mother fastened it to the side with a big bow. But I always made sure my hair covered my ears. I detested my ears because I thought they were too big.

Anne and I were thrilled to discover we were also next-door neighbours. Our side-by-side apartment buildings had identical flights of concrete stairs that led up to the front doors. It took me less than a minute to swoop down from my apartment and race up to Anne's. Her place was a floor above ours, so I'd ring the brass doorbell, she'd answer and then we'd bounce up the steep, carpeted staircase inside, holding onto the cream-coloured painted railings that led to a hallway with light blue patterned wallpaper.

Soon we were walking the ten minutes to school every day together, sometimes with Anne's big sister Margot, who was three years older than us. She was exceptionally bright and kind, and had a more serious nature than Anne. Even though I was younger, she never spoke down to me. How wonderful to have a sister, I thought. Margot went to a more traditional school called Jekerschool on Jekerstraat, just a few blocks away from our school.

Every day, with the help of patient teachers and the will of children desperate to fit in, Anne and I learned new Dutch words and phrases. Very quickly we were speaking fluently (and teasing our parents for their mispronunciations). But of the two of us, I was the only one to retain a slight German accent. With time, we felt like Dutch girls. Our friends came from various backgrounds, some Dutch, some of whom were Jewish too. Others were refugee children, like us. But we did not think much about the differences between us, nor did we feel them. Our memories of Germany were dim and we quickly embraced our new country, rushing headlong into wanting to be like everyone else.

Anne and I soon found a way to communicate from our apartments whenever we wanted. All we had to do was put our heads out of our front windows and call out to one another – me from the second floor, her from the third.

'An-nah,' I would call out in a singsong voice in the mornings from my window when it was time to set out for school (Anne was pronounced 'Anna'). We chose the Dutch national anthem as our personal whistle, so we knew who it was calling out when we wanted to meet up to play outside or go to one another's home. Anne had trouble whistling, so sometimes she'd just hum the tune. Once the whistle exchange was completed, we'd meet on the pavement below for the ten-minute walk to school. A stream of non-stop chatter would ensue.

'Hanneli, did you hear about the new Popeye film?' Anne might ask, and then recount to me the entire story arc of the film she had seen with her family over the weekend. She'd tell me about her mother fretting over her latest ailment – she stayed home sick quite often – or about her excitement over an upcoming visit from one of her grandmothers. She did a lot of the talking, I did a lot of the listening, but there was plenty of back and forth too.

We liked to have sleepovers, to which Anne would bring a small suitcase. I remember her sitting on my bed, brushing her hair and – as young as we still were and despite the fact that our trips were mostly limited to the three yards between our apartments and going to school – talking about wanting to travel the world.

As an only child who longed for siblings, I looked up to Margot. I thought she was beautiful, with her large bright eyes and clear skin. Later, when she needed glasses, I even thought they only added to her sophistication. She radiated a calm, quiet kindness and liked to help people in need. I would have enjoyed having a big sister like her. She had a head for learning and discipline and was quiet, an introvert to Anne's spirited, talkative self. She was also athletic, and later on would become a rower and a good swimmer. I observed with the intense interest of an only child as Margot played the role of peacemaker in her family. She was extremely obedient and never talked back to her parents. 'Anne, do calm down, take it easy,' she'd coax when Anne got agitated. Margot was her mother's pet (and Anne her father's) and she wanted to preserve the peace and quiet in the house she knew her mother prized.

I knew right away after meeting Anne that she loved being the centre of attention. She was full of life and lit up the room. Though as a reserved child myself, I also admired Margot's quieter grace and poise. I wanted to be like Margot: smart, beautiful, good hearted. I also liked to see how protective she could be of Anne. If I ever get to be a big sister, I told myself, I wanted to be like Margot.

Anne had lots of self-confidence, much more than I did. We argued sometimes – not serious things, typical childhood disagreements, forgotten moments later – but her opinions and energy could ocasionally feel exhausting to me, accustomed as I was to a quiet house and being around adults. Sometimes when we played games, Anne would get restless, especially if she wasn't winning. She was so bright and far less unquestioningly obedient than me. 'God knows all, but Anne knows better,' my mother joked when I returned home with details of another 'know-it-all' Anne moment.

One day, on the way to school, Anne and I rounded a corner to see chairs and tables dangling in the sky. We watched open-mouthed as they descended from the windows of the apartment of a girl named Juliane. She too was from a German Jewish family, who also lived on Merwedeplein Square. Our parents explained that in Holland people move houses with ropes, lifting heavy furniture through windows with them. That's because the narrow houses were built on stilts, as anything at sea level here was at risk of flooding. For us, it was great entertainment. Juliane's family was moving to New York City. 'You should come to America too,' Juliane's mother urged Anne's mother, Edith.

* * *

As my friendship with Anne deepened, so did the bond between our families. They often came to our home for Shabbat dinners and Jewish holidays like Passover and we spent New Year's Eve every year at the Franks' home, the adults talking into the night and the children trying to stay up as long as we could. New Year at the Frank home became a tradition and always included a sleepover. I loved being in their house on Merwedeplein 37, Apartment 2. It felt an extra notch more elegant with its green velvet curtains, Persian rugs in rusts and reds and always the aroma of something sweet wafting in from the kitchen. Mrs Frank, Anne's mother, was a wonderful baker. To me, the apartment smelled like vanilla and books.

Mrs Frank, her dark hair tucked into a matronly bun, was kind, if a little reserved with us children. She and my mother got along very well and were thrilled Anne and I were so close, 'like sisters', they would say. They were both 12 years younger than their husbands, and both terribly homesick for Germany and their loved ones there. I know that Mrs Frank also felt the loss of the relative ease of her former life, just like my mother did, especially with her husband working long hours.

It's never easy being a refugee, especially for mothers, charged with keeping homes and young children afloat, and Mama and Mrs Frank leaned on one another for help and moral support. They could complain to one another about the burden of doing all the shopping, cleaning and cooking with little or none of the domestic help they were used to back home. Everything was new and perplexing. They could not understand their children's homework; it was hard navigating cultural clues and their accents in Dutch were thickly German. They exuded the German penchant for order and manners and wanted us to love Beethoven and Bach and German poetry as much as they did. I noticed a certain sadness clung to the mothers in our lives – my mother, Mrs Frank and also Mrs Ledermann, the mother of our good friend Sanne. It was a longing you could almost smell.

The Ledermanns had fled Berlin with their two daughters around the same time we did. Mr Ledermann had originally baulked at the idea. He had a prosperous law practice in Berlin representing large companies, and it's hard to be a lawyer when you don't speak the local language and are not trained in the specific laws of the country. Both Ledermanns were reluctant to give up their weekend outings to museums, fine restaurants and concerts, but Ilse Ledermann, who was Dutch-born and had family in the Netherlands, kept pressing her husband Franz to make the move. Mrs Ledermann had a brother-in-law who was a journalist for a Dutch newspaper. He had been sent to cover Hitler's trial back in 1923 when he was charged and convicted of treason in Munich. The memory of Hitler's courtroom antics, the raging diatribes and, perhaps even more than that, how the judges did not even try to silence him, left an indelible impression. It made him certain that, now Hitler was in power, he would act on his threats against the Jews. He called Hitler an unstoppable danger. Leave, he urged them, as did Mrs Ledermann's other Dutch relatives. Mr Ledermann, a proud German, continued to reject the idea of immigration, until the Nazi boycott laws made it virtually impossible for lawyers to practise and he relented.

The family moved into an apartment just around the corner from Merwedeplein, on a parallel street called Noorder Amstellaan. Mrs Ledermann had to adjust to life without nannies for her two little girls, nor cooks and maids. A pianist, she'd had two grand pianos in their large Berlin apartment, but both were sold ahead of the move to Amsterdam. Her husband was a musician too, and they would host classical music concerts in their living room on Sundays.

Mr Ledermann and my father decided to run a two-man refugee relief agency out of our apartment, with my mother assisting as secretary. The two men would sit on opposite sides of a writing table passing documents back and forth between them. My mother was the only one who could type their correspondence and her black typewriter sat in our living room, put away only for Shabbat. They mostly assisted fellow German Jewish refugees as they resettled in Amsterdam. They helped them sort out their economic and legal matters, including trading real estate they might own in one country for property in another. My father brought his expertise in business and economics and Mr Ledermann his legal background. For three years, Mr Ledermann went back to law school to get his Dutch law degree – we were all so proud and impressed. His family threw him a wonderful party when he graduated.

My father did not have the heart to charge much for their services, with everyone feeling the financial stress of the upheaval and the times, so he and Mr Ledermann did not scratch out much of a living. But it was my father's only source of income at that time. I would have liked to have a bicycle or ice skates, like Anne and my other friends had, but my parents did not have extra money for what in our new circumstances were considered luxuries. Making a living in a new country was a struggle for all of our families, but any difference between us and our Dutch friends was lessened thanks to the Dutch penchant for thriftiness. They shunned showiness and preferred not to talk about money.

The Dutch Jews we encountered felt themselves to be very Dutch and they were not entirely sure what to do with 'us'. So while they were horrified by the political violence and persecution that had sent Jewish families like mine scurrying to the Netherlands, they were wary of upsetting the delicate balance of acceptance they had found in Dutch society, especially the more wealthy and established Jews, many of whom were Sephardic. There was also a certain resentment among some Dutch Jews, especially the working-class ones (many with Eastern European origins), who thought the German Jews looked down on them as less cultured and educated. And when refugees started arriving in larger numbers, some feared their more brash, outspoken style was upsetting the equilibrium they had carved out for themselves in low-key, modest Dutch society. Although there was less of a cultural history of antisemitism in the Netherlands than other parts of Europe, there was still an undercurrent of it among some. So Dutch Jews as a whole did little to absorb the influx of German Jews, which is why my father and Mr Ledermann's services were essential. They helped many people in our community, help that would be remembered in the future.

While my father and Mr Ledermann were serious and occupied with their work and events unfolding in Germany, Mr Frank was a different sort of man. Distinguished-looking at about six feet tall, with a salt-and-pepper moustache and sparkling eyes he had passed on to Anne, he was the kind of father who would sit down at bedtime and spin stories with his children. We all adored him; he seemed like a novelty to us – a father who was fully accessible, not shooing us away to read the newspaper or attend to more worldly affairs. Mrs Frank would lose her patience sometimes, especially with Anne who needed a lot of attention, but Mr Frank delighted in her bottomless curiosity and seemed to genuinely like hearing what we kids had to say. And he could be very silly. He taught Anne and me a nonsense song that he told us was in Chinese and for years we believed him.

Jo di wi di wo di wi di waya, katschkaja,
Katscho, di wi di wo di,
Wi di witsch witsch witsch bum!

We'd beg him to sing it for us again and again. The song was one of our own private jokes we'd laugh about even when we were older. Another favourite activity of ours for some reason was watching him pour his beer into a tall glass. We'd watch the foam rise and rise over the cup's edge, waiting for it to spill over – but it never did.

When we were young, Mr Frank's companies, Opekta and Pectacon – one for making jam preserves, the other a spice company – were located along the Singel canal, though they later moved to a larger location on the Prinsengracht canal. Sometimes Anne and I would take the tram there on Sundays with her father, to explore and play in the maze of offices and spaces of the four-storey seventeenth-century canal house while he got in a few extra hours of work. It felt like a huge adventure. There were spice mills and a warehouse, pungent with the scent of spices packed in crates. Upstairs, we sat at empty desks and played on the telephones and intercom, and sometimes, when the adults were out of sight, we'd spill cups of water out of the window, surprising the occasional passer-by. We thought our pranks were hilarious and had a good laugh over them.

Mr Frank was also patient with me. Once, when I was a little older, he valiantly tried to teach me – an uncoordinated and anxious girl who had trouble remembering the steps of dances and was bad at sports – how to ride a bicycle. Everyone got around by bicycle in Amsterdam and though I still didn't have my own I really wanted to learn. So I decided to face my fears and I borrowed Anne's. Mr Frank offered to help.

'Hold on, hold on, you can do it,' he reassured me as he held on to the back of the bicycle, running alongside me on the pavement in front of Merwedeplein Square. Neighbourhood children watched and cheered me on.

'Go, Hanneli, you can do it!' Anne said, as I tried another round. But it was no use. I was terrified of getting hurt and I couldn't bear to have Mr Frank let go. I eventually ceded defeat. Mr Frank tried to cheer me up through my frustrated tears, but I felt terrible, like I had failed both myself and Mr Frank.

* * *

In August 1935, my grandmother, Ida Goslar, died in Berlin. She was my father's mother and he her only child. He was grief stricken, but so worried he'd be arrested by the Nazi authorities as a political dissident if he returned that he sent my mother and I in his place. I was happy to revisit some of my favourite old spots, like Tiergarten, though they had already started to fade in my memory, consumed as I was by then by my new life and my friends in Amsterdam.

One day, we walked by a public pool in our old neighbourhood and I puzzled over the words on the sign on its gate. I was new to reading but could still make out the words slowly, *'Juden Zuttrit Verboten.'* No Jews allowed. No Jews allowed? To the pool? I could not understand why, even after my mother tried to explain it to me. It just made no sense.

Just a month later, the Nazis imposed the Nuremberg Laws which stripped Jewish citizenship rights and citizenship itself in the name of 'preserving the purity of the German nation'. That meant German Jews were officially stateless, the full impact of which I would understand only later. It also meant that if my grandmother had died a month later, we would not have been able to travel to her funeral. The laws defined who was Jewish and who was Aryan. It was now officially legal to discriminate against Jews. Professors were dismissed from teaching at universities, actors banned from the stage, Jewish journalists and authors struggled to find publishers or newspapers who would use their work, intermarriage was now illegal and Jewish merchants were driven out of business. Our old family friends and relatives struggled to earn a living.

Seeing how desperate things were, even before these anti-Jewish laws were announced, was hard on my mother. Her nostalgia for life in Germany was tarnished; things were indeed bleaker than anyone could have imagined.

It felt good to return home to Amsterdam, to our neighbourhood.

Rivierenbuurt was a warm bubble of friendship, school and community. Nestled in the centre of this cocoon was Merwedeplein Square – a place of our own creation, where we counted down backwards in big boisterous voices for epic games of hide and seek, squealing in delight when someone was found. With other friends from the neighbourhood, Anne and I rode scooters, played hopscotch and pushed hoops with a stick. Round and round the hoops whirled. We'd run and giggle alongside them, trying to keep up. We were focused as only children can be in the moment: that hoop *must* keep spinning. We felt invincible. We felt free. We thought our cosy, contained, protected world would keep spinning onwards. We thought it would last forever.

Chapter 4

Arrivals

'What are you doing here, Opa?' I squealed.

I couldn't believe it. Walking back from synagogue between my parents, we had spotted a man in the distance sitting by himself on the front stairs that lead to our apartment building. He was wearing a bowler hat and tailored wool coat, a small suitcase at his feet. When I realised it was my grandfather, Alfred Klee, I looked up at my parents, but they seemed as surprised as I was. He lived in Berlin and none of us were expecting a visit.

I took off at a run and, reaching him, I jumped into his arms.

'I hear someone has a birthday today,' he said, eyes twinkling behind his pince-nez glasses.

It was Saturday, 12 November 1938, my tenth birthday. But despite what he told me, that was not the reason he was sitting on our steps in Amsterdam. Three days earlier, he had set out from his home in Berlin to go to Hamburg. My grandfather had been invited there to give a lecture about Zionism. The mood in Germany was tense. A 17-year-old Polish Jew had shot the German ambassador to France in a bid to garner attention to the plight of Polish Jews in Germany. On 9 November, the day of my grandfather's trip, the ambassador died of his wounds and the Nazis used the incident as a pretext to attack Jews in the name of protecting Germany's honour.

In Hamburg, my grandfather saw packs of Nazi Brownshirts, the paramilitary of the Nazi party, storm Jewish-owned shops in the centre of the city, shattering glass storefronts, hurling merchandise onto the pavements and beating Jewish residents. Hordes of people screamed and chanted while hurling stones through the stained-glass windows of synagogues and setting them alight. Some Jews tried to rescue Torah scrolls from synagogues before they caught fire. Across Germany, between 9 and 10 November, similar scenes of chaos and destruction played out. Our former synagogue in Berlin was burned to the ground along with 1,000 others across the country. Firefighters were instructed by the authorities not to put out the fires of burning synagogues unless they endangered adjacent buildings. It was first referred to as a pogrom, the name used for attacks on Russian Jews during the time of the czars. But soon it was called *Kristallnacht*, 'the Night of the Broken Glass'.

On the morning of 10 November, my grandfather called his son, my uncle Hans, to ask if he thought he could safely make it home to Berlin. Uncle Hans answered cryptically: 'You have a granddaughter who has a birthday in two days.' He immediately understood the coded meaning of his words: go to Amsterdam. So that's how he ended up on our doorstep, with the same small overnight suitcase he had packed for Hamburg – suddenly a refugee, my grandmother still back in Berlin.

My grandfather had silver hair and a moustache. He always wore sharply tailored suits and carefully placed pince-nez on his nose to read. He was a well-respected lawyer, known for representing Jews in racially motivated libel cases against them. One of his best-known legal successes was winning the libel trial against

Count von Reventlow who promoted the Protocols of the Elders of Zion, an infamous antisemitic document which purported that Jews had a secret plan to rule the world. Like all other Jewish lawyers in Germany, my grandfather had been officially barred from the profession just two months earlier. As a young man, he had become an early disciple and aide of Theodor Herzl, the famous founder of Zionism. Herzl, celebrated as a hero and visionary in our circles, sent a silver baby rattle when my aunt was born. A gifted orator, my grandfather was the chairman of the main Zionist organisation in Germany and was active in other Jewish causes as well. He found out later that, while he was on his way to us in Amsterdam, the Gestapo had come looking for him at his office.

That night, we heard President Roosevelt on the radio condemning the attacks. He said: 'The news of the last few days from Germany has deeply shocked public opinion in the United States. Such news from any part of the world would produce a similar profound reaction among American people in every part of the nation. I myself could scarcely believe that such things could occur in a twentieth-century civilisation.'

My German friends and I heard our parents discussing Kristallnacht, reeling from what felt like a blow to their last shreds of hope that Germany might wake up from its stupor and return to being the decent, cultured place to which they felt so deeply connected. We learned that around 100 Jews had been killed or died later of injuries inflicted by the mobs. We were all very worried for our family and friends who had remained.

On a wet cold, day soon after Kristallnacht, Anne and I walked home from school with Iet Swillens, one of our Dutch friends. We were up to our usual giggling and gossip until suddenly, as we entered Iet's apartment, Anne lowered her voice to tell us: 'Something terrible has happened to my Uncle Walter.'

'What? What?' we clamoured. Bits of a story spilled out. Uncle Walter had been arrested. Anne's mother did not know where he was being held.

As we found out soon after, Walter Holländer, Anne's uncle, had been arrested and sent to a concentration camp just ten miles outside of Berlin for about two weeks, where he and his fellow Jewish prisoners were treated like criminals and worked to exhaustion. He had been caught in a sweep of Gestapo-ordered arrests of upwards of 30,000 'well-to-do' Jews across the country. Walter was released a few weeks later, thanks to intensive efforts and financial guarantees made by his brother, Julius. Both of Anne's uncles managed to flee Germany and procure visas to the United States, eventually settling in an industrial town outside of Boston where they subsisted on low-paying factory jobs.

The welcoming atmosphere my family experienced in 1934 was beginning to shift now that the numbers of Jewish refugees were swelling so quickly. In our family, we were happy and relieved when my grandmother came to join my grandfather, moving into an apartment close by. Meanwhile, Mrs Frank's mother, Rosa Holländer, had arrived from Aachen, Germany, and was living at Anne's home. Our neighbourhood felt like it was overflowing with the new arrivals. In the buildings on Merwedeplein Square alone there were over 100 Jews, many of them German refugees. In addition to us and the Franks, there were the Hamburgers, the Jacobs, the Heilbruns, the Lowensteins and so many more.

We moved around the corner to a slightly larger apartment on 16 Zuider Amstellaan. There was a room there for a young woman named Irma whom my parents helped immigrate to the Netherlands. She was a Jewish refugee from Germany, intellectually disabled and in need of a home and work, so my parents took her in as our maid. Every life we could help bring in from Germany was considered a *mitzvah* – a good deed. She was good-natured, though rather hapless as our maid, but my mother did her best to help and give her direction.

My parents and grandparents talked about how worried they were for friends and relatives still in Germany, who sent harrowing accounts of their attempts to find refuge anywhere in the world that might take them. No country was too remote – China, New Zealand, Argentina. It was becoming difficult to get visas anywhere, in particular to the United States. The Netherlands was safe for Jews but, because of restrictive immigration policies, for many it could only be a way station, rather than a place to settle. Having a passport and therefore citizenship for any other country at all was a very useful asset for anyone escaping Germany. I learned after the war that as many as 50,000 German Jews applied to enter the Netherlands. Only 7,000 were permitted entry, most given only temporary refugee status, with the understanding they were to find other countries to settle in.

* * *

My parents and the other parents who had arrived from Germany felt the increasing anxiety of the deteriorating situation there, and we did pick up on it. But we were still children, and school and birthday parties and friendships and fallings-out loomed just as large, if not larger, in our world than dictators and pogroms. And so my relatively sheltered life sailed on. Anne and I had formed a firm trio with the Ledermann's youngest daughter, Susanne – Sanne for short – who was the same age as us. Anne, Hannah and Sanne – our names even rhymed. Sanne had a sweetness about her. Sensible and sensitive, she liked to write poetry and had small, delicate features and a wide, easy smile. When we met, she wore her brown wavy hair in a short bob like Anne's and mine.

We'd do gymnastics in the Frank or Ledermann living rooms, pushing the furniture back against the walls. We loved Monopoly and could play for hours, even days, until someone won. But Anne did not always have enough patience to play to the end of any game. There was a restlessness about her that frustrated Sanne especially. Anne didn't seem to be able to help it – her mind was just always on to the next thing. We liked to read the same books, including tales of Greek and Roman mythology. We collected trading cards of the European royal families, featuring the British Princess Elizabeth, who was just a year older than us, and Princess Juliana of Holland. We looked up to the Dutch royal family, swooning over their clothes and wondering which eligible royals might marry who. We also liked collecting postcards of Hollywood stars. And we loved going to the pictures, especially anything featuring Shirley Temple or Popeye the Sailor Man. Sometimes, to my slight surprise, my otherwise very serious father would accompany us, saying he was there to 'improve his English'.

Sanne idolised her big sister Barbara, who was three years older than us, the same age as Margot, with honey-coloured curls and blue eyes. She was cheerful and dreamy and wanted to be a ballet dancer. The two older girls went to school together and became good friends, although they were quite different – Barbara was fun-seeking and light-hearted compared to the more bookish

Margot. Barbara credited Margot for study sessions that she said helped get her through school.

The three of us were always hungry for the older girls' attention, which they occasionally gave into. Anne especially would ask Barbara what books she was reading, what she was thinking about, what games she liked. I think she admired her because she was more 'girly' than Margot and Anne was always interested, even as a younger girl, in all things feminine.

At school, Anne was still a livewire with endless energy, who found creative ways to get attention, including showing off one of her tricks – popping her shoulder out of her socket. But there was one place she did not want attention: anyone looking at her writing. At recess she'd carry around a notebook, scribbling down stories or thoughts, known only to herself. She refused to show anyone what she was writing, even me, holding the notebook close to her chest if anyone approached. Adults often seemed half amused, half exasperated by Anne. Some mornings we would walk to school with our teacher Mr Van Gelder and, much to his delight, she'd share with him the silly stories she said she had made up with her father.

The Jewish holidays helped anchor us against the growing tide of fear and anxiety. Neither the Franks nor the Ledermanns were observant like us but they would still join us for a festive meal. I think they liked learning about the holiday traditions and perhaps found the cycle of the year, the old customs reassuring. We were living in modern times, yes, but also followed the lunar Jewish calendar, rooted in the ancient accounting of the seasons. We marked every holiday with its accompanying foods and traditions. There were apples dipped in honey for a sweet new year during Rosh Hashanah, the Jewish new year, and cheesecakes on Shavuot, when it is customary to eat dairy to mark this harvest holiday. In the narrow garden space behind our apartment block, we built a make-shift shelter each autumn to mark the week-long holiday Sukkot. We are instructed to have our meals there during the holiday as a way to remember we were once a people wandering in the Sinai Desert. My father would tell us to look through the branches covering the *sukkah* so we could see the stars. 'Look up,' he told us. 'This is how we remember that as challenging and frightening moments in life can be, just as the Children of Israel found their way through the wilderness, with God's help, so will we.'

We hosted a party every year for Purim, the Jewish version of a carnival holiday where we would dress up in costumes and celebrate the eleventh-hour rescue of the Jews of ancient Persia by their own queen from a plot to destroy them, a story that must have resonated a bit too closely for the adults. One Purim, before the party began, my father pranked Mr and Mrs Frank. Wearing a small black moustache, his hair combed to one side, he rang their doorbell. I watched from the bottom of the steps as they opened the door, momentarily confused and a little concerned by this strange man who looked like Hitler giving them such a menacing glare. 'Hans?' they ventured, and we all burst out laughing.

As an observant Jewish family, the Sabbath was central to our life, the day the whole week built up to. This day of rest and ritual, which begins at sundown on Friday and lasts till night falls on Saturday, is heralded not just by darkness but also the spotting of three stars. In Hebrew, Shabbat means 'to cease' and for our family, like so many others, it served as a shelter from the demands of everyday life. God rested on the seventh day after creating the world and when we too rest every seventh day, we are also living the idea that we are more than our workday selves – the divine dwells within us too.

But of course, it took a lot of work to prepare for 24 hours of non-work, mainly for my mother. All the food for the evening and the next day had to be cooked by the time it got dark. All the cleaning had to be done in advance. We also wouldn't turn the electricity on and off.

Sunset comes early in Holland in the wintertime and it is dark by 4.30pm. So when I walked in from school on a Friday afternoon in December or January, very often the first thing Mama said to me as I put down my satchel was: 'We have just one hour till sunset!' If we were hosting Shabbat dinner at our apartment, which we often did, it meant there was no time to waste. With the countdown upon us, and the apartment smelling of the chicken soup simmering on the stove, I would immediately set to my chore of helping to lay the table with the finery we had managed to bring from Berlin. In the cupboard lived the white linen tablecloth with ornate handstitched embroidery that my mother had brought to her marriage as part of her trousseau. I would retrieve it and cover the patio table in the dining room with it, my mother appearing from the kitchen to help me smooth it over the bumpy wicker edges, lamenting for the hundredth time the loss of our actual dining room table that never made it from Berlin. Atop went the porcelain plates and bowls for each table setting. Then we put the flowers for Shabbat at the centre.

My next job was to lay out the good silver, kept in a velvet-lined wooden box. Each spoon, knife and fork was engraved with a Gothic 'G' for Goslar. I liked to feel its weight and coolness in my hands as I counted out the silver for my mother, my father and me, and the extras for our guests. I quickly arranged it on the disguised patio table before Mama and I looked out over Merwedeplein Square to see the sky glow tangerine with the sunset and got ready to stand before the pair of heavy silver candlesticks and recite the Hebrew blessing:

Blessed are You, Lord our God, King of the universe, who has sanctified us with His commandments, and commanded us to kindle the light of the holy Shabbat.

The first set of footsteps approaching the front door would be my father's, returning from Friday night prayers at the synagogue. He would take off his coat and hat, give me a big smile and, as he did every Friday evening, say, 'Shabbat Shalom, Hanneli.' Next, he would put his hands over my head as I looked downwards and blessed me with the prayer Jewish parents have given their children for generations, every Shabbat. For daughters it begins recalling the foremothers, for boys the forefathers. Papa would incant in Hebrew:

May God make you like Sarah, Rebecca, Rachel and Leah.
May God bless you and keep you.
May God shine light on you and be gracious to you.
May God turn towards you and grant you peace.

The Franks were our regular guests for Shabbat dinner. Mr Frank, fully secular, never learned Hebrew, but in all the time the family came to our house, he heard the prayers so many times at our table they became part of his own memory and he could join in. He felt little towards religion, but Mrs Frank, who grew up in a more traditional Jewish home, keeping kosher and attending synagogue, appreciated the ritual and familiarity of these Shabbat meals.

So often, the next set of footsteps I heard outside the door belonged to Anne, who would usually come through the door first, entering like a whirlwind of energy and cheer. 'Hanneli!' she'd exclaim, as if weeks had passed and we had not just seen one another at school that day. She'd give me a big hug and then her parents and Margot would come in too, Mr Frank smiling widely, shaking my parents' hands, pressing flowers into Mama's hands.

At the table, set with shimmering silver candlesticks, a silver wine goblet and the traditional challah – a braided egg bread set under a white satin cloth – Anne and I always sat next to one another, giggling about something until we rose together when my father recited the Kiddush, the blessing for the ritual wine. After Kiddush and the blessing over the challah she bought from a kosher bakery, Mama, almost on cue, would let out an audible sigh. Another Shabbat eve sunset deadline met. The food was always good – my mother may have been a reluctant cook but she had got to grips with it during our time in Amsterdam, even if she drew the line at baking the challah.

This was a time to try to unwind from the stress of everyday life and the gathering storm of anti-Jewish violence and perse-cution in Germany, which we followed anxiously through radio and newspaper reports and was detailed in letters from relatives and friends still there. I know that, for the adults, it was hard to forget about it for long, but the closest they came was here in our snug Amsterdam apartment, Shabbat candles glowing, the crys-tal wine glasses clinking a toast of 'L'chaim' – to life. It was good to be in the company of close friends and it was good to be in Holland, everyone agreed, as we passed around the roast chicken and noodle kugel.

'Otto, how is business, how are your partners?' my father would ask Mr Frank – ever the business reporter. He was curious to hear the economic ramifications of Hitler's growing strength in Germany.

As the two men spoke business, trying not to talk politics and dread in front of the children, my mother would attempt to shift the topic. 'Margot, how are your studies? What books are you reading now?' she would ask.

Margot became most animated talking about school; she was a real scholar and Anne and I longed to know as much as she did.

'Anne and Hannah, how are your maths lessons coming along?' Mrs Frank would ask.

The two of us would blush; maths was rarely going well for either of us.

*   *   *

The next morning, Saturday, my father and I would stroll hand in hand to synagogue together for services on 63 Lekstraat, about a ten-minute walk from our home. My mother, who was less religious than my father, also preferred the liberal synagogue services. The Franks were not big synagogue goers; if they went it was to the liberal Reform synagogue and it was usually Edith and Margot who would go. I cherished these quiet walks with just my father, our neighbourhood still sleepy and still. We'd see other Jewish friends trickling like a small stream towards the synagogue too. My father would nod and say '*Gut Shabbos*', wishing them a good Sabbath. Sometimes he'd tell me the story of that week's Torah portion, which we would hear read aloud that day, breaking down the possible interpretations and, in some cases, how we could apply these ancient Biblical dramas and dilemmas to our own life. I was proud of how much Papa knew about so many things and how he could paint pictures with his words. When he told me the story of Joseph, now a viceroy to the mighty Pharaoh, testing his brothers who once threw him in a pit to see if they had truly transformed, I felt like I was there in ancient Egypt waiting for the moment of truth, not on an Amsterdam street corner under a grey, dreary sky.

I was proud of my father's status in the community. Papa was one of the founders of the newly built synagogue. At its consecration, I was part of a group of girls who laid flowers on the pulpit. We were all so proud of this new sleek, modern building with its large brass front doors, milky coloured walls and flat roof surrounded by a spacious, grassy lawn. Written in large Hebrew letters on its facade is a line from The Book of Kings: 'And I will dwell in the midst of the children of Israel, and I will not forsake my people Israel.'

The synagogue was an outer visage of our community's confidence that we were putting down roots. I loved going to the kids' service that was run and led every week in a separate room by the teenagers. After it finished, I would slip into the main sanctuary, into the women's section upstairs, and look below at the men. I'd watch my father, wrapped in a white prayer shawl, swaying, lost in prayer and intention. He stood out from some of the other men who seemed more interested in swapping gossip and political news in low voices towards the back of the sanctuary. My father had chosen to be a religious Jew; watching him I felt his deep connection to the tradition. That impression would stay with me.

Back home on Saturday afternoons, after lunch, my parents and I would often sit in the living room together reading. Much of our home life revolved around books. My parents had a very liberal reading policy and let me scour their bookshelves for new books to discover and then discuss with them.

While Saturday mornings were a chance to spend time with my father, Wednesday afternoons were just for Mama and me. It was our own sacred space in a way, marked by a different sort of standing ritual: a trip downtown by tram to De Bijenkorf, a luxury department store on the edge of the Dam Square, the very heart of Amsterdam. I'd come home from school and we'd head straight for the tram, sitting close together, watching as the streets became less leafy and more dense and urban the closer we got to our destination. Mama would point out her favourite flower shops and boutiques and ask about my day.

To me, she was beautiful and elegant. I admired her perfectly applied deep red lipstick, her razor-straight posture and tailored clothes. She always looked put together. I often felt clumsy and unathletic and I studied how she moved, hoping to pick up on the way she appeared to float lightly, but with purpose.

I think that for my mother, it was important to carve out space for just the two of us that was free from the stress of being a foreigner living in extremely anxious times, much as she and my father tried to protect me and hide their own stress. She also simply relished being a mother; she saw it as her central and most important role and was genuinely interested in me – and my friends – as people. Even aged 10 or 11, I understood on some level that these weekly dates were her way for us to escape our everyday surroundings and obligations and for her to check in with who I was and who I was becoming.

Tree-lined, cobblestoned Dam Square lay at the historic centre of Amsterdam. It felt like the most exciting place in the world to me. Church bells would toll from Nieuwe Kerk, which looked like a castle to me with its spires and stony, stained-glass facade. We would stroll hand in hand amid the rush of shoppers, pigeons and day trippers and walk towards the towering De Bijenkorf building, topped with its trademark yellow flags fluttering in the wind. De Bijenkorf's high ceilings, parquet floors and displays of French perfumes, bolts of satins and silks and the latest fashions in eveningwear and ballgowns must have reminded my mother of her more carefree, pampered Berlin life. Almost everything sold in De Bijenkorf would have been beyond her means now.

I'd have a hot chocolate and she'd have a cup of strongly brewed coffee and we'd share a slice of cake. She'd lean forward, listening closely to my stories of school and friends. I'm sure some of my stories sounded tedious to her ears, but if so, she never let on. I felt safe and spoiled by her on those Wednesday afternoons.

* * *

I started to overhear discussions between my parents about a plan to try to immigrate to Argentina. But when I asked them about it, they said not to worry, we were staying put. On school days, I'd return home briefly for a hot lunch and afterwards scan the pages of *De Telegraaf*, the main Dutch newspaper, while lying on my belly on a Persian carpet in our living room, next to the blue velvet couch my family brought from Berlin, where much of the news in the paper was coming from. I asked my mother questions and she'd do her best to answer me honestly, but also gently. She reassured me that Holland was safe from Hitler.

Towards the end of August 1939, the newspaper headlines were full of news that Joseph Stalin, the Soviet leader, had signed a non-aggression pact with Hitler. My parents were concerned, they told me, because everyone knew Hitler wanted to invade Poland, a move he knew could trigger war.

'Germany might be emboldened to invade now that the Soviets won't fight them if they do,' my father explained. Great Britain and France had already said they would help protect Poland should Hitler dare to cross its borders.

It was the end of the school holidays and I was enjoying the long days outside, playing with Anne and Sanne and our other friends in the neighbourhood. But when, on 1 September 1939, Germany invaded Poland, it was impossible not to feel the tension and dread. We all followed the news closely, fearing what might come next. Two days later, Britain and France declared war. I had hoped war could be avoided; so did everyone I knew. But we also wanted Hitler stopped. The Netherlands declared itself neutral. We were going to stay out of this, just like during the First World War. Ours was a tiny country with a small army, with limited equipment and fighting power. There was no chance that, even if the Dutch wanted to do their part and fight the Germans, they could hold up for long against such a massive foe. Our script, as much as we had one, was the same as that of the last war – no one could think beyond it. We would sit tight while this frightening new conflict unfolded around us.

Chapter 5

Invasion

I woke up in the pre-dawn darkness of my bedroom, confused by a low rumbling sound, growing louder, building to a roar. *Is it thunder?* I thought. *It must be thunder.* But I was frightened. At nearly 12, I was perhaps getting a little old to run to my parents when I was scared in the night. Particularly now I knew I was going to be a big sister. My mother was pregnant with a much longed-for second child, due in the autumn. But still I darted out of bed and raced to their room. I curled up close to my mother. 'Shh, shh,' she said, pulling me close. The morning light was just beginning to seep in. My father pulled back the curtains to look outside. The noise was not thunder.

'It's planes,' he said.

I looked at my parents. They were people of action. Yet in that moment, they appeared paralysed. This was almost as frightening to me as the noise of the planes. Eventually, one of them turned on the light and then the radio in the living room. There were messages from the government: stay indoors, close the curtains, do not stand by the windows.

I was still only half awake but I could feel my heart pounding, full of fear.

It was Friday, 10 May 1940. The three of us, like people across the country, were waking up in shock. The German Luftwaffe was attacking Schiphol Airport, the main airport in the country, both a civilian and military airfield, 15 miles southeast of us. The roar was warplanes swarming low in the sky, seeming to hover one above the other. They flew so low in some areas that people could see the swastikas on their wings. It was a massive show of force. No declaration of war had been received by the neutral Dutch government; the Germans simply started bombing, paratroopers following immediately after the aerial bombardment. They wanted to show us they were here. The dreaded invasion dismissed as far-fetched by most Dutch had come.

'Do I have to go to school?' I asked my parents.

'No, I'm sure there's no school today,' my mother replied, her voice flat.

My father was afraid that, as a former government official who had opposed the Nazi party, he would be a specific target once the Germans arrived. He started sorting through the folders he had brought with him from Berlin, his eyes scanning through various pages and documents for articles he wrote critical of Hitler and the Nazis and any other potentially incriminating material. 'We have to get rid of these,' he said to Mama. My mother joined him and they began piling papers together in a stack and then ripping them in small pieces. There were soon so many pieces of ripped-up paper my mother brought out several bowls to gather them.

'Hanneli, we need your help. It's going to be your job to flush these pieces of paper down the toilet,' Mama instructed me. 'Not too many at a time though.'

I nodded, baffled by my mission but determined to help.

I took the ripped-up pages, some of them embossed with stamps and calligraphy, others crammed with typewritten words, and with a trembling hand dropped them into the toilet basin. I tried to focus on my job, but my mind raced. Could my father be arrested? Would he be punished severely? We knew of concentration camps for political prisoners, like Dachau. We did not know what happened there exactly, only that it was nothing good.

'Oh no,' my mother groaned. 'Otto Braun.'

She was pointing to the large bust of Otto Braun, my father's former boss and once one of the most powerful men in the Weimar Republic, perched in a corner of the living room. It had come with us from Berlin six years ago, a physical reminder of another era, but it now appeared to my parents as incriminating evidence.

My father, mindful of my mother's pregnancy, told her to stop trying to move it by herself. 'No, no, I'll do it,' he said. I watched as he bent his knees to lift it and started hauling it out of the apartment.

'If the Germans searched our home and found this, we'd definitely be in trouble,' Papa told me, noticing how startled I looked.

So Braun's likeness – bald head, bushy eyebrows, round glasses cast in bronze – was dragged down two flights of stairs by my father, my mother assisting, and I looked on with confusion as this symbol of a revered figure in my father's life was unceremoniously shoved onto the street. I wondered what the neighbours would think of this behaviour. But when I looked around I was stunned to see the pavements piled up with destroyed papers and discarded books. People were pouring out of their apartments and onto the streets with armfuls of whatever they thought might get them into trouble.

'Anything the Germans might find suspect or forbidden, it all has to go,' one man said as he dumped his trove into a bin.

Mr Ledermann also joined in the frenzy. He piled his German books into a basket and lit them all on fire, embarrassing Sanne and Barbara who watched on.

The sun was rising into a brilliant blue sky. It was an especially beautiful spring day after another seemingly endless wet, windswept winter, and completely out of place as a backdrop to the rising sense of shock and fear felt by people all over the Low Countries, now under German bombardment, but especially by my parents and other German Jewish refugees, who understood what the Nazis might be capable of.

We were glued to the radio. It became clear that the Dutch military, outgunned and outmanned, was having an impossible time staving off the overwhelming force of the German assault. Rotterdam was under heavy bombardment that day and it sounded like it would be completely flattened. A whole city. There were reports of casualties and even a rising number of dead. All of the Netherlands shuddered. Black smoke curled into the sky from oil supplies at the port in Amsterdam being destroyed by Dutch authorities before the Germans could capture them. We could smell the smoke in south Amsterdam.

My parents' anxieties were compounded as they glanced at my mother's rounding belly. They had always wanted more children and, despite everything, hoped their dream of a big family might still come true. I had always wanted to be a big sister and had been thrilled at the news. But also I understood that the future suddenly looked especially uncertain.

By the next day, we were plastering blackout paper on the windows as the punishing air raids continued on Rotterdam, which had by now injured hundreds. Two days later, on 12 May, we were devasted to hear that first Queen Wilhelmina and then her daughter Princess Juliana and her husband Prince Bernhard with their two young daughters, Beatrix and Irene, had sailed to Britain. The security establishment determined they could no longer guarantee their safety. So they fled. Fled! It felt like a betrayal. I thought of the trading cards of the royal family that Anne and I collected. They felt like people we knew, people we trusted. Within hours, it emerged that the Dutch government – the prime minister and his cabinet – had also escaped to Britain by boat. Like everyone in Holland, we were overcome to hear they had left us alone in the clutches of the Germans.

Panic was rising and rumours circulated of a boat waiting to bring Jews across the English Channel from the port city of Ijmuiden. We heard there was a British consul general in the city issuing visas! But how to get there? It was 20 miles away and most people we knew didn't have cars. Some of our neighbours decided to head out on bicycles for the coast. My father, so convinced the Germans would arrest him, decided to try to catch this boat, or any boat to England. I watched as he hurriedly packed a suitcase. The plan was that we would try to follow in a couple of days, but the fact that he left us behind – me and my pregnant mother – only reinforced the seriousness of the situation for me. His taxi joined the crush of traffic on the roads, a trail of exodus.

It was a few days before we heard from him. He had found a frantic scene awaiting him, of some 30,000 people who also fled to the coast, desperate to catch a boat of any kind – a ship, a tugboat, a fishing boat, anything. Some who had arrived early or could afford to pay vast sums for spots – payment in cash or jewellery – were able to take one of a small number of boats at the harbour to safety, but the vast majority were out of luck. And even if you got a spot, the passage was dangerous: the Channel was mined and German aircrafts were strafing ships. That boat we had heard was waiting to take Jews to England did not exist, and neither was the British consul handing out visas. Another flood of refugees tried their luck further south, but those few who made it safely around the fighting in France and into Spain were not allowed to stay there and were left to find a way to cross the Atlantic or try their luck in the still-unoccupied part of France.

Unable to leave the country, Papa stayed with a Dutch Jewish family outside Amsterdam for six weeks before returning home. Only with time did we understand the Germans were not looking for specific Jews, like my father, as he feared. But we didn't know this at first. So on the Tuesday following the start of the invasion, my mother, thinking Papa may have found passage to England, hired a taxi to take us to the British Consul in Amsterdam in the hope we might secure a visa and join him there. We arrived to see the massive lines to get into the consulate, and it was just then we heard the news. It rippled through the crowd: the Dutch had surrendered. Five days was all it had taken for our small country with its insufficient army to be overrun. Rotterdam had been practically destroyed by air attacks and the Germans offered an ultimatum: surrender or we flatten your other cities too. The commander-in-chief had made the decision, we were told, and the Netherlands had capitulated.

'Does this mean we are now part of Germany? We aren't free?' I asked my mother. I saw she had tears in her eyes. She looked like she'd just seen a ghost. This was not the mother I was used to seeing. I felt like the ground was shifting underneath our feet. I was terrified seeing her so afraid. I looked around at the hundreds and hundreds of people who, just like us, had come to the consulate seeking a way out. I saw other anxious mothers, some with young children in their arms, everyone clamouring to leave before the Germans arrived. *But we are trapped*, I thought to myself. *And I have to be strong, especially with Papa gone.* He had told me before he left that I had to be brave. My mother seemed too distraught to even talk. We silently climbed back into the taxi.

The next day, we heard sirens and saw an ambulance had come to Merwedeplein 12. We found out that a couple named Benjamin Jessurum Lobo and Jeanette Theresia Maria van de Coolwijk had asphyxiated themselves. Other stories of suicide in the neighbourhood and across the city followed: by hanging, drowning, sleeping pills. I heard the words 'suicide epidemic' whispered by adults. But the most common escape route seemed to be the gas from kitchen stoves. Stories spread of families sitting around their dining room tables, talking out their options, among them suicide. Sanne and Barbara told us about their neighbour who had tried to kill himself in this way. A German Jewish refugee, he was standing on the balcony of his apartment across the street from theirs, shouting, 'Don't save me. I want to die.' Two neighbours broke down the door of his apartment and an ambulance arrived and took him away. Many of those who died this way were German Jews who had, like my family, escaped once from Nazi rule and had hoped they would be safe in neutral Holland. They now felt their persecutors catching up with them and, fearing the worst, decided to end their lives on their own terms. Jewish cemeteries in the Netherlands have a disproportionately high number of gravestones dated 15 and 16 May 1940.

For the Germans, controlling the strategically located Netherlands – and Belgium – was essential to their plan to conquer France and make Europe into its very own fortress. Occupying that territory also prevented the area from becoming a launching ground for the British. Germany's plan – successfully executed – was to swiftly defeat Belgium, the Netherlands and Luxembourg in a Blitzkrieg (lightning strike) attack. A month later, they added France to their crown. The seemingly bulletproof German army had already swept through Poland, Lithuania, the Czech Republic, the Slovak Republic, Austria, Denmark and Norway.

I felt sick to my stomach when I saw the first German soldiers on our streets, some careening around corners in motorcycles with sidecars, kicking up clouds of dust. I rushed back inside and, from the window, I stared at the rows and rows of young men – grey-uniformed, helmet-wearing Wehrmacht soldiers, rifles in hand, marching through Rivierenbuurt in precise step. There were so many of them. They seemed so tall and strong. Among the choruses of war songs, they sang, 'We will soon be marching into England.' I understood what they were saying and felt ashamed we came from the same country.

There was a feeling of unreality to the days after German soldiers filled the streets. We felt their presence everywhere but at the same time, life went on. To our surprise, and cautious relief, the weeks following the invasion were quiet and fairly uneventful, and we resumed daily life with less anxiety. Anne and I returned to the Montessori school, now in the sixth grade. My parents continued working with Mr Ledermann but with no new refugees arriving from Germany now, there was little demand for their services, so they began seeking out other forms of income, such as translation work. At one point, they even brought in some extra funds by making ice cream in our kitchen for an Italian man with an ice-cream business.

Some people (though not my ever-pessimistic father) even began to speculate that things might not get as bad as we feared. My father thought he would be arrested and sent to a concentration camp, like those in Germany in which some of his former colleagues had been incarcerated. He imagined the Germans crushing any kind of dissent, anti-Jewish laws being implemented and the violent targeting of the Jewish population of the kind that had been taking place in Germany. He didn't trust the feeling of things being oddly quiet.

Despite the eerie normality, there was an air of desperation among everyone in our community. The adults were all working every lead, every connection around the globe, hoping to find an exit route. They also did not trust that the situation would remain safe. We stayed in touch with the wider family, although of course it was harder than before. Because Britain and Germany were at war, postal service was cut off between the countries. So Uncle Hans relayed updates he received in Switzerland from their father in Amsterdam to his sister Aunt Eugenie in Leeds, England.

My grandparents, using my grandfather's connections in the Zionist movement across the world, were trying to emigrate to British Mandate Palestine. But getting an immigration certificate was even more difficult now. Uncle Hans was working hard to get permission for them to get there via Switzerland. But the Swiss authorities told him at the end of May that permission would only be granted to those who could prove they had a place to go next. So in June, Uncle Hans sent a telegram to Louis Brandeis, the recently retired US Supreme Court judge and most prominent American activist for the Zionist cause who knew my grandfather. He thought someone of his status could help advocate for his parents and get them a visa to British Mandate Palestine. (Unlike the majority of American Jews at the time, Justice Brandeis felt that the creation of a Jewish national homeland would be a key way to solve the problem of antisemitism and persecution of Jews in Europe.) Uncle Hans desperately hoped such a high-level connection might be able to help his parents.

Brandeis cabled him back: 'Matter receiving attention communication Holland most difficult.'

My grandfather was at least good at keeping himself busy as the question of where we could go and how we could get permission to get there went round and round. He was steeped in his own study of the history of philosophy, history and Jewish topics and spent his mornings in the library. Among my grandparents' tight-knit circle of intellectual friends from Germany, new and old, were doctors, scholars, composers and musicians. Opa sometimes gave lectures to young Zionists who were preparing to work as farmers in British Mandate Palestine, hoping they would all be able to immigrate there. It was the one place, they imagined, they might finally find safety for themselves and future generations.

Hope for escape via Argentina flickered briefly when my grandparents were informed that the Argentinian government would grant them six-month tourist visas. Uncle Hans tried to procure visas for my parents and me as well. The International Migration Service in Geneva even wrote to the Committee for Jewish Refugees in Amsterdam in September to see if there was a possibility both families could make the necessary travel arrangements 'under the present conditions'. But no such visas to Argentina ever materialised for us.

Emigration appeared increasingly impossible. We knew that except for a handful of what were called 'special cases', there was a blanket rejection of anyone requesting emigration permits. So although my grandparents had been delighted they had been granted Argentinian travel visas, what good were they if the Germans would not let us out?

'Can nothing be done?' I heard my grandmother ask. No one had an answer for her.

The uncertainty and stress was hard, especially on my parents and grandparents, much as they tried to shield me from their worry and distress. At least we had our community, the cocoon of support among the Franks and other good friends and neighbours. Mr Frank was fond of saying the Allies were going to win – we had to hold on, they'd certainly defeat the Germans. He was the clear-sighted, calm optimist in our circle, a foil to my father's less sunny outlook. I hoped, like we all did, that the whole war would be over in weeks, maybe months, and was encouraged by Mr Frank's assessments.

What I didn't know until after the war – but my parents did – is that while Uncle Hans, my grandparents and parents were scrambling for a way to get out of Holland, pulling every well-placed connection they had, so were the Franks. 'I think every German Jew must be combing the world in search of a refuge and not finding one anywhere,' Mrs Frank wrote to a German-Jewish friend in Buenos Aires. They had applied in 1938 to emigrate to the United States and waited. And waited. The American consulate in Rotterdam, which processed the visa applications in the country, was among the buildings bombed and burned down during the German invasion. That meant all applicants, the Franks included, had to resubmit their paperwork. Like other Jews, they were walking a difficult line, trying to create the impression they could support themselves financially in America, while also trying to get across how dire their situation was in Holland. Those with connections in the US also had to work out how to express themselves in letters requesting help from family and friends there. German Jews from well-educated backgrounds tended to be extremely proper and did not like to get too emotional. But as the situation worsened, their letters reflected their desperation.

Mr Frank reached out to his old friend Nathan Strauss Jr, son of the co-owner of Macy's department store, to enlist his help to immigrate. The two had become close friends in their college days when Strauss, at the time a student at Princeton University, studied for a semester at Heidelberg University in Germany. In April 1941, Mr Frank wrote to Strauss, 'I would not ask if conditions here would not force me to do all I can in time to be able to avoid worse … It is for the sake of the children mainly that we have to care for.' He would not be an economic burden to anyone, he assured him: 'I feel still young enough to work and I trust that I shall find the means to get along.'

But the US State department officials were stonewalling, informed both by their own antisemitism and anti-foreigner outlook. They hid behind claims that refugees might include Communists and spies; the Jews could, they said, become a destabilising force within America. US consular offices in Europe, like the one in Rotterdam, denied hundreds of thousands of people who applied from 1933, when Hitler was put in power, to 1945, when the war ended. American Rabbi Stephen Wise, who oversaw lobbying efforts for immigration from within the United States' Jewish community, called this 'death by bureaucracy'.

Mrs Frank's brothers, now settled in Massachusetts, were also trying every option. Their application for a Cuban visa for Mr Frank was cancelled on 11 December 1941, the same day the US entered the war.

In July 1941, all US consular offices in German-occupied territory shut down. Another hurdle making immigration look increasingly like an impossible dream. The closest US consular office for most Jews trapped in Occupied Europe was now in Spain. Had they reached this office, the application process would have to be restarted. Over 80 years later, I look back at this Byzantine, cruel system and want to shout out in protest. How could someone get there without German permission to leave the country? And to embark on a journey across Nazi-occupied Belgium and France, partially by foot over the Pyrenees, with only the help of the underground resistance movement, was a risk most families understandably decided not to take.

*　*　*

For us, at least, the autumn of 1940 brought the most wonderful of distractions: in October, my baby sister was born. A beautiful pink-faced girl. My parents named her Rachel Gabrielle Ida. We called her Gabi, sometimes by the endearment Gigi. My mother had worried I'd be jealous but nothing could have been further from the truth. I was besotted. I finally had the sibling I had so wanted and it was like having a living doll in the house. My parents, grandparents and I were entirely focused on Gabi and her arrival. It helped lift the gloom we'd been feeling. There were so few babies being born at the time so Gabi was a complete novelty – practically a celebrity.

However, despite our joy, there was no escaping that things in Amsterdam were getting worse. The same month Gabi was born and five months after the German invasion of the Netherlands, the first anti-Jewish restrictions were ordered. The strange, surreal calm was broken as we started to realise the Germans' so-called 'velvet glove' approach in Holland was by design, intended to deceive us into thinking there was such a thing as a benign German occupation. There was a ban on kosher slaughter, which meant in our observant household we could no longer eat meat. Jews were not permitted in hotels, restaurants or other 'recreational facilities'. We were also given a two-month deadline with which to register with the authorities. Our identity cards were now marked with a large J on them, identifying us at a quick glance as Jews. Most people complied, fearing retaliation if they did not.

The Germans declared it illegal for the Dutch to listen to foreign or Dutch broadcasting organisations, including Radio Free Orange, the radio station of the Dutch government in exile in England. As my parents were both English speakers, like many others, they had relied on the BBC for up-to-date information. They felt suddenly cut off, imprisoned in a harrowing new reality. Soon, most of what there was to listen to was Nazi, or so called 'Aryan' programming. Propaganda. But upon hearing of the ban against listening to foreign radio my ever-practical mother said, 'I don't want to give the Germans any excuse to give us any trouble.' And with that, she picked up our sleek, modern radio and left it outside on the kerb. It seemed like a terrible loss but it was just as well. Soon, Jews were no longer allowed to own radios at all.

Without radio and now that Dutch newspapers were under German control – publishing only censored, approved reports and Nazi propaganda – people had to rely on word of mouth for information. Some of it was based on illegal listening to British and American broadcasts, or reading underground, uncensored papers. That was the only way to try to glean what was really happening around us. We felt the significant shift underfoot: the process of identifying and isolating Jews within Dutch society had begun.

* * *

When Gabi got a bit bigger, Anne and Margot would come over to help with her baths and we'd take her for walks in her pram. They seemed almost as taken with her as I was. 'Gabi is so sweet,' Margot said as we powdered and dressed her. Gabi wriggled as we tried to get her into her pyjamas but rewarded our efforts with a stream of smiles. Anne and I started making funny faces at her while Margot fastened the buttons of her pyjamas. All of a sudden, Gabi started giggling. Over and over again the peals of giggles came. Then we all broke out laughing and could not stop.

'What's going on here?' my father said, walking in. Then he too got the giggles.

When it was time for Gabi to start eating solid foods, she turned out to be a terribly picky eater. She spat out much of what we spooned into her mouth. Feeding her became one of my main jobs to help lessen the load on my mother. Irma, our maid, had no success in getting Gabi to eat. But aside from being a misery to feed, she was whip-smart and seemed to understand everything we told her. That included the game I played with her, trying to coax her to eat: 'One bite for Margot, one for Sanne, one for Oma.' If I dared repeat a name she clamped her mouth down, on strike, till I came up with a new one.

To our delight – and relief – Mr Frank had the magic touch with her. 'Hello, Gabi,' he cooed, sitting down at our table, next to the latest bowl of mashed sweet potatoes or apple sauce she'd rejected. 'Open wide,' he said, his eyes twinkling, a big smile on his face. She squirmed delightedly and opened her mouth. My parents and I were astonished anew every time.

A new law came out which decreed that Jews were barred from going to cinemas. 'Cinemas?' I groaned, hearing the news. How could that be? What did we do wrong? Anne, Sanne and I, and our other friends, adored going to the pictures. We could rattle off the names of Hollywood movie stars and swooned over their photos in magazines: Ginger Rogers, Greta Garbo, Rudy Vallée. We especially loved Deanna Durbin, just a few years older than us, who always played the kind of spunky girl who could fix whatever had gone wrong – even in the world of adults. The films were our escape to other worlds of gauzy musicals and unlikely heroines finding true love. Anne – ever ready with grand plans and big ideas – talked about wanting to be a famous actress herself one day, though she also talked about being a famous journalist or writer.

* * *

At home, our parents continued to try to buffer us from the full brunt of their own horror at what was going on, and dread that things could get even worse. But at my house I was long accustomed to being candid with my parents and asking questions about world events. Perhaps that was the benefit of being the only child in the house for so long. Now, though, my parents struggled to answer my questions, especially when they were about things I had heard – for example, that Jews were getting beaten up and attacked at cafés and dance halls in the Jewish quarter in central Amsterdam. I knew the area well; I liked its gritty, vibrant streets packed with grocery and delicacy shops, an open-air fruit and vegetable market full of the sing-song sound of 'sweet potatoes for sale'. Jews of all backgrounds lived there: secular, religious, Zionists, socialists. Some even spoke a dialect called Amsterdam Yiddish. I liked to go to the Portuguese Synagogue in the heart of the quarter with Mama and Papa. The massive building, hundreds of years old, felt like a magical place to me and I was awed by its soaring ceilings, stone columns and brass chandeliers that glowed with thousands of candles. It was so different from our modernist, minimalist synagogue. It felt shocking that this sort of violence could be happening here, so close to where we lived.

By early February 1941, things started feeling even scarier. Public buildings in the Jewish quarter in Amsterdam and other cities like the Hague and Rotterdam were being targeted regularly for harassment by members of the Weerbaarheidsafdeling, or the WA, the paramilitary arm of the Dutch Nazi party. There was more violence in our city's Jewish quarter when WA members, backed by German soldiers, forcibly entered a café called Alcazar on 9 February. That night, in spite of new rules barring Jewish musicians, Jewish jazz musicians were on stage, including the famous trumpet player Clara de Vries. A massive fistfight broke out, leaving over 20 injured. Another riot followed in the area two nights later, and a Dutch Nazi was injured so severely he died from his wounds shortly afterwards. The Jewish quarter was sealed off by the Germans in response. Overnight it became Amsterdam's Jewish ghetto, ending its residents' freedom of movement beyond its confines.

Closer to home, just 15 minutes from our apartment, Koco, an ice-cream parlour popular with German Jewish refugees, which my parents sometimes went to, was raided by German police. The customers were so sick of the Dutch Nazi taunts and harassing visits that they decided to douse them with ammonia the next time they came. But they miscalculated, as the next raid was by German soldiers who opened fire in return.

It was horrifying. I was shocked when I heard the 'punishment' that followed: the Jewish owner of Koco was executed by firing squad. And the Germans decided to make a sweep of arrests of men in the now sealed-off Jewish quarter. It did not matter to the authorities who specifically they were arresting. We heard that Jewish men were plucked off bicycles at random, or dragged from apartments, then pushed to the ground, beaten, sometimes in front of their children. Over 400 men were arrested and forced to assemble on Jonas Daniël Meijerplein, a central square in the Jewish quarter, and were loaded onto trains across the border to Germany to the concentration camps of Mauthausen or Buchenwald. I felt terribly for them and their families. I could not sleep after hearing about the arrests.

'A general strike has been called,' my father told us at dinner the next night. I didn't know what that meant, so he explained it was a collective protest by the non-Jewish Dutch against the violence and arrests of fellow Jewish workers. Most Dutch did not support the Germans and referred to them as the 'uninvited guests'. My father, still a socialist, was especially proud and moved by the nationwide strike called for by the (now-outlawed) Dutch Communist party. 'Strike! Strike! Strike! Shut down Amsterdam for the day,' read leaflets distributed across the city.

On the appointed day, 25 February, drivers of the trams that kept the city in motion stopped working, joined by dockworkers and sanitation workers. Factories shut down. Employees of companies, including my beloved De Bijenkorf department store, and schools went on strike. Activists went into the streets asking people to join the struggle. Others knocked on doors, trying to drum up support. Some 300,000 people took part in this act of solidarity. At home, we were heartened by their bravery, and grateful for this show of humanity and decency. It gave us hope.

But the Germans, initially caught off guard, responded by firing into crowds and throwing hand grenades. In the end, nine strikers were killed, over 70 wounded and scores arrested. The strike did not lead to a mass uprising, as the Germans at first feared it might and we so desperately hoped it would.

In its aftermath, a Jewish Council was formed, comprised of community leaders, to represent Jewish interests to the German occupying government. People hoped some sort of order might be restored and things would get better. At first, it included only Dutch Jews, but later on a subcommittee of German Jews was attached to it. My father and grandfather became members.

The deportations and arrests were disorienting to digest. The only information we had was that people were being sent to work camps in 'the east' – either Germany or Poland. What exactly a work camp entailed we didn't know. Factory work? Farming? We hoped they would return soon and that there would be no additional deportations. But weeks turned to months, and the hundreds of Jewish men who had been arrested and deported in February didn't come home. By summer, some relatives had finally received letters – nine lines allocated to the prisoners on a Mauthausen-embossed form. They sent no news, but they did send declarations of their love. In one letter, a man told his pregnant wife what to name a child he would never meet.

We heard of more rumours of people trying to smuggle themselves over borders but that sounded hugely dangerous and difficult. What if you got caught? Could it be worth the risk?

There was no way to get out of Holland. Not for the Franks, not for us. Not for any of our Jewish friends and neighbours.

Chapter 6
Aftershocks

'All Jewish schoolchildren will be excluded from public schools,' my father said, reading the latest anti-Jewish measure by the Germans, just before school summer holidays were set to begin. The pronouncement was published in *Het Joodsche Weekblad*, the Dutch Jewish newspaper which kept us updated on all regulations. It was where we had read that Jews were no longer allowed to employ non-Jewish servants and new Jewish students were banned from starting at universities. From the pages of *Het Joodsche Weekblad*, we learned we were forbidden to go to playgrounds, parks or even public beaches. I was aghast to learn that we were even banned from just sitting on the edge of a park on a bench! There would be no more trips to the zoo or to museums or sports clubs, which was especially bad news for athletic Margot who rowed and played tennis. Even our neighbourhood swimming pool, where we had spent so much of our last summers, was off limits. Anne joked that at least we wouldn't get sunburned this summer. At 12 years old, I was still grieving for the loss of my beloved movies. We sometimes watched films at the Franks' house, as Mr Frank would hire a projector. This was great fun but I still felt the injustice of the real cinemas being closed to me and my Jewish friends.

And now school too? Papa let out a long, sad sigh. He looked up from his paper at me, pressing his lips together as if to say he was sorry. I felt my anxiety rising as my stomach dropped. 'What does this mean? No more Montessori?' I asked, hearing panic in my voice. It was the only school I'd ever known. I had one more year of primary school. 'What about my friends? What about our teacher? Where are we supposed to go instead?'

Reading further, Papa explained there were going to be certain schools designated specifically and solely for Jews, taught only by Jewish teachers, by the start of the new school year in the autumn of 1941. I would have to apply to one of them. I thought about my shaky maths skills. Anne struggled too, but at Montessori the teachers were relaxed and we didn't have to bother with tests and assessments, so it had not been a major issue. But what if we didn't get accepted? What if we had to take a maths exam to get in and failed?

On our last day of school, which was as much a home as a school for Anne and me, Mrs Kuperus, a kind woman who always wore her greying hair swept into a bun, who was both our teacher and principal, seemed even more distraught than we were. She cried when she said goodbye to the Jewish pupils, tears streaming under her wire-frame glasses. She invested so much in us and I got the feeling she really enjoyed being with us. We had all been so well integrated that I didn't even know which students were Jewish until we were forced to leave. It turned out almost half my class was Jewish. A total of 91 from the school of us had to scramble to find new places to study.

Summer holidays began and with them the long summer days, when the sun only fully set after 11 at night. I wondered if the ducks floating by on the tree-lined canals minded the drone of German planes overhead, on their way to bombing raids in England. I found it impossible to get used to. Anne, Sanne and I still spent time together over that summer, but I also saw a lot of Ilse Wagner, who was a friend of Anne's too. Her family had also fled to Amsterdam from Germany; she lived with her mother and grandmother in the neighbourhood. She wore her brown hair in a short bob, like mine. Anne's hair had now grown longer and she spent a lot of time fussing over it. On Saturdays, Ilse and I went to synagogue together, where we attended the youth services led by the teenagers and a Zionist youth group afterwards. I liked that Ilse was smart with a sensible outlook; I found her easy to talk to. I was still on the shy side with people I did not know well, and I found comfort in Ilse's easygoing nature.

It was at this time that I got to know Alfred Bloch, another friend from synagogue. We spent time together on Saturdays and I wouldn't say I was in love with him, but I can say my cheeks flushed when we spoke. He was sweet and had a seriousness and intelligence about him I found intriguing. He said he liked me too, so in our world that made him my boyfriend. He was two years older than me and, like me, he came from Germany. He had pretty almond-shaped dark eyes and brown hair he slicked down to the side. He was a good artist. He gave me two paintings he made, one of the Western Wall in Jerusalem. I think he was rather alone in the world. He lived with relatives in Amsterdam but his mother had stayed behind in Germany and his father had died a few years ago. I was flattered by his attention and liked our conversations, even if I did get butterflies in my stomach when I saw him approaching. I was friendly with boys in school but I lacked Anne's easy confidence and always felt a few steps behind her and some of our other friends with regard to their interest in boys, clothes and other typical teenage pursuits. Alfred was the first boy I was beginning to know well.

Another new regulation had been brought in by the occupying Nazis: Jews could not visit the homes of non-Jews. So we could no longer play at the homes of our non-Jewish friends. We felt almost entirely separated from them. My social scene was definitely shrinking because of the German occupation. One of the girls we didn't see any more was Lucie van Dijk, a Montessori school friend. Anne and I were shocked when we found out that Lucie's parents had joined the Dutch Nazi party, the NSB. Lucie had stopped inviting us to her birthday parties in recent years – at least now we understood why. There's a photo of all of nine of us neighbourhood and school friends, standing arm in arm at Anne's tenth birthday party in our patent leather shoes and short summer party dresses. Lucie is the girl with a pixie haircut, next to Anne. We found out later that Lucie joined for a time the Jeugdstorm, the Nazi youth group, the name of which meant 'Youth Storm'. I saw her once in the neighbourhood in uniform: knee-length belted black skirt, red-topped black cap, long-sleeved sky-blue button-down shirt. I couldn't tell if she saw me but I hurried on, not stopping to say hello.

After some wrangling, and thankfully without the need to take any exams, Anne, Ilse and I were assigned to the same school as Margot: the Jewish Lyceum. There was a scramble to set up enough new schools to cater for all the Jewish students in Amsterdam after the decree that we had to leave the ones we went to before the Occupation. My parents were pleased as this was to be a large public Jewish school with high academic standards. Sanne's parents, however, decided to send her to a private school, while her big sister Barbara, a talented dancer, began attending a ballet school.

On the first day, Anne, Ilse and I were nervous. We didn't know what class we would be placed in and if we would know anybody in it. Anne and I crammed ourselves onto the busy tram, heading in the direction of the Amstel River. At the school entrance on an alley just off the river, dozens of other boys and girls were already there. I looked out for any other familiar faces but didn't see any. At 8.30, the whole lot of us were swallowed up into the three-storey red-brick building. I was so relieved that Anne and I had both been assigned to the class 12 I. We found places to sit and our teacher, a woman in a long dress and flat heels, called out our names and told us which books we'd need to buy. Then, 'Class dismissed!' she announced abruptly. We were disappointed we had not met our other teachers, or the principal, or received a full schedule. I was homesick for our cosy Montessori classroom, predictable in its routines we knew so well, at a time when everything seemed to be changing, but it still felt like a relief to be in a school setting after a long summer under all those restrictions.

Rain was pouring down the next week when the school term began properly. Anne and Margot rode in on their bicycles but I still couldn't ride a bike so I went by tram. The first thing I saw was a big sign posted at the entrance with the names of 20 pupils, including Anne, who had been assigned to new classes. Anne had to go to 16 II! My heart sank – she was the only person I knew in my class. Now I would have to walk into 12 I all by myself, without Anne's confident presence at my side. I suddenly felt very much alone. But that afternoon, the teacher came to tell me I'd been reassigned to 16 II too. I was stunned and relieved. I walked down the hall towards my new class, saw Anne and gave a shy smile as the teacher introduced me. It turned out that my class move wasn't random – Anne asked the gym teacher, who she decided seemed like a very nice woman, if she could help get me transferred. Who knows what the kind teacher did, but whatever it was, it worked. I slid into my newly assigned seat at the desk right next to Anne, grateful and feeling much better.

There was a good energy at school. The teachers were excellent, drawn from the top tier of high schools across the city. The curriculum included a lot of German language and culture study, courtesy of our occupiers. But we also learned more about subjects we might not have learned in a non-Jewish setting. For example, we studied the Spanish Inquisition in depth, and of course the students and teachers couldn't help but connect that period of anti-Jewish persecution to the one we were currently living through.

One of the girls in our class we got to know was Jacqueline van Maarsen, a tall, pretty girl with shoulder-length light brown waves and big blue eyes. As she was leaving school one day, Anne had spotted Jacqueline just ahead on her bicycle and called to her. Jacqueline was surprised she even knew her name. They went off together, crossing Berlage Bridge over the Amstel River, chattering all the way. No doubt Anne asked endless questions about Jaqueline's life, as was her way, and gave her a crash course on her own. By the time they reached Merwedeplein Square ('the Merry' as Anne liked to call it), Anne had invited Jacqueline home and then for dinner, sealing a new and close friendship.

Dutch-born and half Jewish, half French, Jaqueline was an anomaly in our German-Jewish refugee circle. Thanks to a certain divide between our communities, we still knew few Dutch Jews. Jacqueline's father was a Dutch Jew and her mother was a Catholic from France, who had converted to Judaism when they married, though they were not an observant family. When all Jews had been required to register with the authorities – which meant anyone with even one Jewish grandparent, according to the Nazi race laws

– her father had registered Jacqueline and her sister Christiane as Jews. Her mother had urged her father not to do it but, like many others, he feared the consequences of disobeying the Germans. He was also proud of his Jewish heritage and did not want to feel like he had to hide it.

Before she met us, Jacqueline had lived in a lavish apartment surrounded by domestic help, accustomed to fancy holidays. Her father's thriving antiquarian books and prints business had made them a good living. But the business was hurt badly by the anti-Jewish laws and the family was now struggling financially. They had moved to our neighbourhood, which was less affluent than the one where Jacqueline had grown up.

At first, as Anne and Jacque, as we came to call her, became increasingly close and shared conversations that felt beyond my reach, I felt insecure and frustrated. Anne was my best, my first friend, after all, and it wasn't a good feeling to be left behind. But, despite my slight feelings of jealousy, I could see they complemented one another well. Jacque was more reserved than the ever-exuberant Anne but they had lots in common, too. For example, both especially loved a book series by Cissy van Marxveldt about a plucky teenage girl named Joop ter Heul. We all read it but they could talk about Joop for hours. They shared a sophistication and curiosity about boys and the mysteries of love and adult life and our changing bodies that I did not yet have. After a while, my observant mother noticed that I sometimes felt left out of their conversations and took me aside to explain some of these mysteries to me, which helped a little. And eventually, Jacque and I also became close. In her, I found a thoughtful, intelligent friend and confidante. Anne and Jacque had lots of sleepovers, which could also pique my jealousy, but Ilse and I were also spending a lot of time together too – and so it all settled down, as is the way with childhood friendship, and our original trio of 'Hannah, Anne and Sanne' expanded to include Jacqueline and Ilse. We did not have a lot of social options because of the anti-Jewish laws, but we were hungry to hang out with one another as much as possible.

One of our favourite things to do was play ping pong at Ilse's home. There was no fancy ping-pong table, just our paddles, a ball and a net that stretched across her large dining room table, which her mother kindly let us colonise. We played so much we decided to make a ping-pong club, based on the 'Jopopinoloukicoclub' in the Joop series. At first we called our club 'The Little Dipper', inspired by the Little Dipper constellation, which we mistakenly thought had five stars. When we realised it was actually seven, we tweaked the name to 'The Little Dipper Minus Two'. A little awkward, but it worked for us! Ping-pong tournaments on Ilse's dining room table and playing Monopoly and other board games was almost all that was left to us by the autumn of 1941. Jacqueline used to joke that soon we would not even be allowed to breathe the air any more.

One thing we could still do was stroll over to one of the nearby Jewish-owned ice-cream parlours – we couldn't go to ones that were not owned by Jews because of the new laws, which left Oase ('Oasis' in English) or Delphi. Oase was also a tea house and we could get ice cream for 12 cents. It was owned by Max Gallasch, also a German Jewish refugee, and a friend of Anne's family. If there was a group of boys hanging out at the tables outside Anne would find a way to flirt with them. Thanks to her, the boys often ended up offering to pay for our scoops of ice cream. Anne and Jacque were more comfortable flirting with boys than I was, and sometimes Anne teased me about that. She liked to tease me about Alfred too and I was annoyed and felt self-conscious. Teenage life still felt somewhat mysterious and daunting to me, so I tried to observe what I was missing. After school, I watched as girls and boys headed off on their bicycles, shyly playing close attention to those 'riding hand in hand', signalling a new crush in bloom.

By the approach of winter break, with exams hanging over our heads, I felt the pressure of just how hard we had to study at the prestigious Jewish Lyceum. Aside from maths, I was a good student and, as a conscientious sort, I always did my homework. There was in fact a lot of homework and exceedingly high expectations of us. But there was also a palpable sense of camaraderie between the students and teachers. It was as if there was an unwritten pact between us to make the best of the situation now that we'd all been thrown into this experience together. There was an undercurrent of anxiety outside, but inside the classrooms, where soft light poured through the pane-glass windows, we felt like normal seventh to twefth graders. There was a lot of laughter, a lot of chatting in the hallways, and the passing of notes, just like in any school, anywhere, at any time.

However, after the open, free-wheeling approach to education of Montessori, the more rule-based setting of our new high school was something that Anne, Ilse and I had to adjust to. We now had to study for tests and weren't allowed to talk during class, something that Anne found especially challenging. Mr Keesing taught us algebra and geometry. He was a kind, older and exceedingly patient man who liked to mix in riddles with his lessons. But he became increasingly exasperated with Anne's chatting and assigned her a series of essays to try to cure her of it. It didn't work! Anne loved to write, of course, and the essays she turned in became ever funnier. Sanne liked to write poetry and so Anne asked her to help write her final response in rhyme. Mr Keesing read it aloud to the class and everyone fell over laughing.

A less amusing turn in school left me mortified. One day in French class, feeling underprepared for our test, I stole a quick glance at Anne's paper. It was the briefest of glances and I don't know why I did it, but at that very moment the teacher happened to be looking over and caught me. As punishment, both of us were given zeros. Anne too, though it was my fault for looking and it was only for a moment. We thought this was unjust so we went to the principal to appeal. But sitting across the desk from him, I felt increasingly nervous and, before I could stop myself, I blurted out, 'Mind you, sir, the entire class had open books under their desks!' Anne glared at me. We'd argued before because she thought I was something of a tattletale to my mother. And now this. I wanted to be swallowed up by the floor.

The headmaster saw how distraught we both looked at my snitching and told us he wouldn't punish anyone as long as they admitted to doing it. But of course, when he came to our classroom and asked our classmates who had been cheating, only ten hands rose in the air, even though we were a class of 30 and at least 20 people were culpable. We were given the same test two days later in reprisal, but the worst of it was that Anne and I were deemed traitors for telling and iced out by our classmates. I felt awful, sick to my stomach. I didn't know what to do but Anne, as usual, had a plan. She took action by writing a letter we both signed, asking for our class's forgiveness. We appealed to their empathy, explaining that anyone in the heat of the moment can slip up, even if they don't intend any harm. 'We hope that 16 II will regard the incident in that light and repay evil with good,' Anne wrote. 'Nothing can be done about it, and the two guilty ones can't undo their misdeed. We wouldn't write this letter if we were not genuinely sorry. We ask those who have "cut" us until now to reconsider, for after all, our act was not so heinous that we have to be looked upon as criminals for all eternity.' Luckily our classmates were a good-natured bunch and all was eventually forgiven.

* * *

Even after the Nazis arrived and we were full of fear as to what life would be like under the Occupation, we didn't predict the draconian rules to segregate us from our non-Jewish friends and neighbours that it seemed were constantly being brought in and made harsher. In the spring of 1942, the walls of separation grew higher when we were ordered to sew a mustard-coloured Star of David with the word '*Jood*' (Jew) written in its centre onto our clothes.

We were told to pick up the star-imprinted fabric from our synagogue, so we walked over to Lekstraat. We had to pay for it – four cents for four stars – and if we were caught without this mark to identify us as Jewish, we were told we would be sent to prison. My mother sat down to start sewing them onto our jackets and other outerwear like sweaters. At first, I was naively proud to wear the star and heartened that some Dutch in protest made their own versions of stars, labelled 'Aryan' or 'Catholic'. But after a few days of wearing my new badge, I started to notice how people without the star looked at me in the street – some with pity, others with real disdain and, perhaps most crushing, indifference. Then I felt the weight of this piece of cloth. 'They are trying to make us into pariahs!' I overheard my father hiss.

* * *

Mama was pregnant again. Her belly had just begun to show around the time we acquired our yellow stars. Two years previously, when she was pregnant with Gabi, the house was abuzz in happy anticipation, but this time it felt different. I was excited to get another sibling but I couldn't help but notice that Mama was becoming paler and her eyes, which usually flashed with intelligence and dry wit, seemed to have lost their lustre and were ringed with dark circles.

'I need to lie down,' she told me one day when my grandmother was there, handing me Gabi and retreating to her room. Gabi immediately wriggled out of my arms – at one and a half, she already always knew what she wanted. My grandmother saw me looking with concern at my mother.

'You have to understand, dear,' she began, and listed all that made life extra exhausting for my mother. Being pregnant makes you tired, she explained, but it's extra tiring when you are already caring for one baby, managing the inept but sweet Irma and trying to eke out a living with Papa, together working on translations into the night, and keeping the household going with all the rationing, food shortages and general stress – and then waking up and doing it all over again. No wonder she was tired, said my grandmother.

I was put on 'Gabi duty' more and more. It was hard to find time to do my homework in the shuffle of all that was going on at home. I at least had a tutor for geometry, on warning from my teacher that I might fail if I didn't get a better grasp of the subject soon; angles, theorems and proofs left me feeling dizzy and I couldn't imagine how I was ever going to wrap my brain around them.

Grandmother was right: food was becoming increasingly scarce, and that did add a lot of pressure to my mother. The reason was that the large occupying army of German soldiers demanded a lot of food. And it wasn't just its soldiers Germany was feeding but its people back in Germany. Vast quantities of Dutch cheese and other produce was shipped to the 'Fatherland' in long columns of freight trains. I saw large banners on the train cars reading, 'Gift of Gratitude from the Dutch People', which of course was not true – the Dutch resented their stockpiles being plundered, but that sign never ended up on any train. And it wasn't just about shortages – getting to the shop to buy food was getting harder too, as Jews could now only shop from 2 to 4pm and at assigned stores. But by that time, shelves were often running empty, so supplies were scarce.

Sometimes it felt as if there was not much more they could take away from us, without evicting us from our homes or sending us to prison. But then another rule was issued to chip away at our smallest remaining freedoms. Soon Jews were not even allowed outside after sunset. That meant my father could not go to pray the *Maariv* evening services at the synagogue any more, a huge loss for him. And no more guests for Shabbat dinners or going to anyone else's house for meals or get-togethers in the evenings. We were also barred from using the trains. Jews were told to deposit their money in specific banks under German control, which limited how much could be withdrawn. Dutch employers could fire a Jew for any reason.

By June 1942, Jews had to turn in their bicycles. This was an enormous blow to many as, with the exception of my family, in Holland everyone seemed to get around by cycling. If that wasn't bad enough, we couldn't even use the tram, the other main mode of transportation. This left us no option but to trudge everywhere by foot, no matter how far. It was about a 30-minute walk to school.

Pariahs. I turned over that word of my father's around and around in my mind, feeling its weight on my tongue. None of it made sense to me. Time was blurring and I missed being able to go the park, to spend all afternoon on a hot day at the pool. I missed feeling like we used to. But school was a refuge and so was playing with Gabi (though not feeding her, because she was still so fussy that it felt like punishment) and being with my friends. We were scared and uncertain about the future and frustrated and resentful of the restrictions placed on us in the present, but we were still 12- and 13-year-old kids who chattered incessantly, walking arm in arm, laughing at the silliest things that seemed hilarious in the moment but were forgotten five minutes later.

Now the weather was warmer, we scrambled up the steep stair-case to second-floor rooms at either Anne's or my apartment so we could climb out of the window to sit out on the roof, which was scattered with gravel. With the seashore and the pool forbidden to us, sometimes we put on bathing suits and soaked in the sun. Most of what was below us – in the neighbourhood that was once our play-ground, and further afield across the city – was prohibited to us, but still we laughed and joked and felt smug and even a little glamorous so high up above everyone else, as we lounged and struck poses on beach chairs. We knew our parents, wanting to protect us, weren't telling us everything that was going on – even mine, who had always been quite open and honest with me. But we still craved fun, and novelty, and excitement, even as the walls closed in around us.

One morning in early June, I was standing on the street whis-tling our usual whistle under the window of Anne's apartment. Anne was running a bit late and I was anxious to get started on our walk. I whistled again, more urgently this time, but mid-whistle I stopped and smiled, as I saw Anne flying out of the door. She pressed an envelope into my hands with my name on it.

'What's this?' I asked, as we started walking quickly towards school. She smiled and watched me open it. An invitation to her thirteenth birthday party on Sunday, just two days after her actual birthday on 12 June.

'Jacque and I typed them on my dad's typewriter – aren't they great?' she gushed. On the invitation there was also a cinema-style ticket with my seat number. 'Father's renting a film projector again so we can watch Rin Tin Tin!'

'I can't wait to come,' I told Anne.

Anne and Margot always had the nicest birthday parties. Mr and Mrs Frank would go all out overseeing games and serving Mrs Frank's delicious, freshly baked cakes and cookies. Like most of the world, I loved Rin Tin Tin films, even though I was terrified of dogs in real life and would cross the street to avoid one, even if they looked harmless. But Rin Tin Tin, the most famous dog in the world (a German shepherd who conveniently lived in faraway Hollywood), was a hero, friend, fighter and companion wrapped into one.

Everyone likes their birthday but Anne was one of those people who really loved it; she would tell anyone who would listen when it was coming up. So everyone seemed to know about it and our entire class of 30 boys and girls was invited to the party, along with old friends like Sanne and a new one, a 16-year-old boy named Hello (short for Helmut) that Anne liked and who she had been spending time with. Anne told me that Margot had a couple of friends coming too. Of course, all the guests would be Jewish because of the new laws barring non-Jews from Jewish homes and I thought about how it was the first time our non-Jewish friends from Montessori school or the neighbourhood wouldn't be at one of Anne's birthday parties.

On the Friday morning of Anne's birthday, I did our usual whistle under her apartment and waited for her to come down. 'Happy birthday!' I shouted as soon as I saw a beaming Anne rushing down her front stoop.

'I was so excited I woke up at six,' she told me, and then rattled off a list of gifts that had been waiting for her on the dining room table. There were books and a new pair of shoes, and most prized of all was the red, cream and beige checkered notebook with a pretty metal clasp she had pointed out to her father at Blankevoort, our local bookshop. She told me she was going to use it as the diary she'd always wanted. I wondered if she'd show me any of what she might write, but knew better than to ask. At school that day, Anne passed around cookies for the happy occasion and the whole class formed a circle around her and wished her a very happy birthday.

Sunday, the day of the party, was an unusually warm day. I arrived to see the Franks' living room had been transformed into a cinema. I spotted the projector in a back corner and noticed the rows of chairs lined up as if it were the real thing. I looked at Anne and, as usual, admired how confident and carefree she seemed. Her face was aglow and she fluttered like a butterfly between guests. Her hair looked especially pretty. Anne spent a long time brushing it every night and tried to coax it into curls (without much success) using pins and curlers. Margot poured lemonade from a large pitcher and we all clamoured for a slice of Mrs Frank's strawberry and cream cake, one of my favourites.

Among some of our new friends from school who came were Betty Bloemendaal, who was sweet and clever and had the highest grades in our class; Jopie de Beer, who Anne thought was a bit of a flirt and Eefje de Jong, one of the youngest girls in our class and also one of Anne's favourites. Among the boys were Jacques Kocernoot, a funny boy who sat right behind us in school and Werner Joseph, who fled here from Poland. He seemed sweet even though he was awfully quiet. And Appie Riem, who was one of the only other Orthodox kids in the class. It was such fun being outside of the classroom and chatting, sipping lemonade and joking around with one another, about to watch a film together – a rare treat.

It was to be the last party where we were all together. One of the last happy, carefree times for us as children on the cusp of our teenage years. Or at least, it was for me.

* * *

As the school year of 1942 came to a close, all we could talk about was who was going to pass and get promoted to the eighth grade and who might get held back. I felt nauseous just thinking about it. 'You'll be fine,' said my mother, the former teacher, trying to cheer me up. 'You've worked really hard.' I had and I liked studying and the new level of structure at the Jewish Lyceum. But I kept thinking about how Anne and I had both been admitted provisionally and my geometry skills were still shaky at best.

The day we got our results rolled around and I found out I had failed my geometry exam. I was devastated at the idea of being held back – and all because of stupid maths – but then some good news arrived: I was going to be promoted after all! And so were all my friends. I'd have to retake the geometry exam in the autumn but at least I wasn't going to be left behind.

I wished we could go to the seaside. I missed the smell of the sea and Gabi was the perfect age for building – and smashing – sand-castles with. Would we ever be able to take her to the beach, show her the sea? Anne and I could each hold a hand and play our one-two-three swing game, skimming her feet over the waves. But the reality was that money was only getting tighter in our house, and so even if Jews had still been allowed to take the train we probably couldn't have afforded to go on holiday anyway. Like last summer, we'd get by with ping-pong tournaments and ice-cream cones at Oase and … a lot more time at home, I thought.

On 5 July, a Sunday, word quickly began to spread around the neighbourhood that policemen had been knocking on the doors of certain families, brandishing call-up notices with the names of teenagers living there, as young as 15, demanding they report for work camps in Germany. Those called up were told to report to Amsterdam's central train station at a particular time – 2am! That seemed crazy to me. Why in the middle of the night? I wondered. I had always assumed the Germans would just take men away to the camps; I never imagined teenagers would have to go too – both boys and girls, no less. Everyone was in total shock. I was told those who were served the notice were given a list of what to bring: two woollen blankets, two sheets, food for three days and a suitcase or backpack. In that bag they were permitted only a few designated items. They were told they would go first to a medical inspection and then on to somewhere in either Germany or Czechoslovakia to work. Perhaps for the first time, I was glad I didn't have an older sister. It was terrible for the families whose teenagers had received their papers. No one knew what to do.

* * *

It was the start of school holidays and, predictably, pouring with rain when Jacque came over. My grandmother was there and playing with Gabi in the living room, which meant we could talk.

'I have to talk to you about Anne,' I said, flopping on my bed. Jacque joined me there and let out an exhalation. Anne and I had been going through one of our phases of not getting along so well. I would have rather not blabbed about it all, but I felt like I couldn't hold it in either. What we had fallen out about I now have no idea. Had I been oversensitive to her teasing about Alfred? Or treating me like I was younger than her? No doubt it was something insignificant, but in our little world, shrunk small by the restrictions placed on us, and at that age, our friendships felt vitally important. Any perceived slight could sting like something terrible had happened – until it was all over and forgotten about, sometimes hours later.

Jacque was quiet as she listened to me describe her hurt feelings. She nodded sympathetically. 'I've noticed she can be hard on you,' she said. 'You are not imagining things. I'd feel upset too. But you know Anne. I mean, you might know her best still. Those moods of hers always pass.'

I listened to her intently, feeling better after confiding to Jacque. I appreciated her low-key manner and common sense. I usually shared everything with my mother, something Anne saw as suspect, and probably even juvenile, especially since she didn't do that with her own mother. They had a very different sort of relationship and were often at loggerheads. But lately Mama didn't seem to have as much time – or patience – to soothe my anxieties over what I feared she saw as my fairly trivial adolescent dramas. There was so much taking up her attention and so much to worry about. But I was going to be 14 in November, so perhaps it was time I stopped relying on my mother so much. And maybe I was also being too sensitive. I knew Anne and I would always be good friends. I was looking forward to spending time together over the holidays.

A week after our conversation in my room, on Monday 6 July, the sun finally came out. The intermittent rain had kept me home but now I paused on the pavement and tilted my head back for a moment to soak in the sunshine. My mother was going to make strawberry jam this morning and she had sent me to ask to borrow Mrs Frank's scale.

When I got to Anne's door, I rang the bell but there was no answer. 'Where could they be?' I wondered. I buzzed again.

Buzz.

Buzzz.

Buzzzzzz.

The door finally opened and I was startled to see Mr Goldschmidt, the boarder. In all my years visiting, never did anyone but one of the Franks ever answer the door. He looked a bit startled and unhappy to see me.

'What do you want?' he grumbled.

'I'm here to borrow a scale from Mrs Frank. And, umm, is Anne home? I wanted to see if she could play,' I stammered.

'The Franks are not here,' he said. 'Don't you know that the Frank family went to Switzerland?'

Switzerland?

They seem to have left in a hurry, he added.

I don't remember how the conversation ended. I was so bewildered. I walked down the stairs, holding on to the cool metal of the railing to steady myself. My mind just couldn't make sense of this information. Why did Anne never mention they were going to Switzerland? I knew her grandmother lived there, also her favourite cousin, Buddy. He was four years older than us and he and Anne were both obsessed with ice skating.

The Franks are gone? But how can that be? How did Anne not let me know? Does anyone else know?

I rushed home to my parents. Mama and Papa seemed as shocked as I was. Our parents were close but it seemed the Franks had kept their planned flight secret from everyone, even them. Mr Frank's optimism had always been so reassuring. I could hear him saying, 'The Allies will turn the tide soon.' His hope was infectious, I clung to it. But if he, the eternal optimist, had decided it was time to seek safety in neutral Switzerland, despite the risky border crossing, and they had gone without telling anyone, what did that mean?

But as confused and shocked as I was, I soon concluded that I was happy for Anne. I imagined her reunited with her grandmother, going for walks in meadows under the shadow of the Alps and, come winter, she'd be sitting in a warm kitchen, snowflakes falling outside, while together they sipped big mugs of hot chocolate. I wished we hadn't had our little falling out before she went but we were like sisters, and I had to believe that it didn't matter, that she knew we would always be the best of friends really.

The first thing I did was tell Jacque. 'What? How can that be? We had a long talk on the phone just yesterday and she didn't say anything,' she said in a voice that sounded like a wail.

We decided to go over to Anne's place together. It seemed impossible that she was gone. It was like we needed proof she actually wasn't there. We also wondered if she'd left us anything, perhaps some kind of clue about her family's plans or maybe even a farewell letter.

As we walked to Anne's apartment, Jacque and I tried to reassure one another. 'The war will be over soon enough and we'll see Anne then,' said Jacque.

I agreed, making sure I sounded confident. 'I mean, how long can the war actually go on for? Aren't the Allies approaching? Now that America is in the war, the Germans will definitely lose,' I said, repeating words I'd so often heard Mr Frank say. They now felt like a prayer.

Standing in front of the Franks' door, I felt my heart thumping hard. I rang the bell again. Mr Goldschmidt, the tall, bespectacled boarder, let us in. I walked through the rooms gingerly, light pouring through the big front windows, just as it did just three weeks ago on the day of Anne's birthday party. What I saw stunned me. It was as if everything was suspended in that exact rushed moment of the Frank family's departure. The dining room table was still covered in breakfast dishes. The beds were unmade. It felt wrong to be there without them, like we were sneaking in. It occurred to me that I'd never been in their home without them there.

Meow, we heard, which made us jump in the otherwise eerie stillness of the rooms. It was Anne's beloved Moortje, her cat. We knew she would never willingly part with her; she doted on Moortje like a baby.

'What's going to happen to Moorjte?' I asked Mr Goldschmidt, the panic rising inside me. It felt terribly wrong that Anne would leave Moortje. He reassured us there were arrangements to leave her with a neighbour.

We walked through Anne and Margot's bedroom. A distilled light fell on a small Persian maroon-coloured rug that partially covered the teal floor. We noticed the Monopoly board and other games we played all the time were still on the shelf, including one called 'Variété', a recent birthday gift. Also left behind were a pair of new shoes Anne loved. Why wouldn't she have taken them? It felt somehow wrong just to leave all these things that were so important to Anne sitting there by themselves.

'Jacque, should we take some of Anne's things? You know, for safekeeping, to save them for Anne? Should we?' I asked.

Jacque shook her head no. She reminded me that for everything relating to Jews there seemed to be a prohibition. And indeed here too the Germans had declared that the removal of the items of a home left by its occupants as forbidden. We wondered if Anne's new diary was here. She had told us she'd written out a list of our classmates with notes on what she thought of each of us. So, being 13-year-old girls, we thought that if she had left it behind, did that mean we could read it? But of course we didn't find it. Not on her wooden writing desk by the window, not on any shelf or under her bed. I feel my heart pounding loudly again as I looked at her and Margot's room one more wistful time, saying a silent goodbye and prayer for safe travels.

As we descended the staircase to the front door, I felt my feet on each step, the opposite of my usual rush down them. I thought about Anne walking down these stairs just the day before and out of our neighbourhood, out of Amsterdam, out of the only world we knew. Vanished. Just like that. And now she was perhaps already close to Switzerland – her grandmother and cousins waiting. Godspeed Anne, I heard myself say. I closed the Franks' door behind me. I didn't know anyone else who had done anything like this. It was so daring. Most Jews had given up hope for getting out of the Netherlands by now. All pathways seemed closed to us. By late summer, there were whispers of people going into hiding but the Franks' sudden departure for Switzerland wasn't questioned.

My parents heard that Margot, aged 16, was among those who had got a call-up notice to report for transport to one of the work camps. I shuddered. No one knew who would be safe, who might be called up next. It was another layer of psychological control exerted by the Germans on top of the now almost endless list of restrictions for us to navigate. In our family, we felt a measure of relief when we found out that because my father and grandfather were on the German Jewish subcommittee of the Jewish Council we would be exempt from the deportations. Furthermore, the families of pregnant women were exempt, and my mother was seven months pregnant by then. An extra layer of protection. And surely even once the baby was born they wouldn't make us? But all around us, our friends, our neighbours, our community were in a state of unbearable tension as we waited to see who would be summoned next.

Alfred appeared at my doorstep. 'I've come to say goodbye,' he said. He was 15. He had received his call-up notice when Margot had received hers.

I didn't know what to say. I stood there stunned. We spoke about how some other young people who were called up thought maybe it would not be so bad. Perhaps it would be a bit of an adventure, with campfires and socialising at the end of a work day. Some girls even said they were bringing lipstick and hair curlers. No one thought they'd be gone too long, maybe just a few weeks. The war had to end soon.

I looked at Alfred. He was about the same height as me. Not particularly muscular. I wondered how much hard labour he could handle. His freckles made him look extra boyish, even younger than he was. He shifted from foot to foot, speaking quickly, almost breathlessly. I could feel his panic. We promised to write each other.

'You'll wait for me – until after the war?' he asked.

I nodded mutely.

Starting around midnight on 15 July, nine days after Anne left, the shadowy figures of teenaged boys and girls, most of them German Jews, backpacks on their backs, bundles of blankets in hand, could be seen from the windows on Merwedeplein and across our neighbourhood walking alone across squares, streets and bridges, making their way towards the train station. Their parents, banished from the streets because of the curfew, were not allowed to escort them.

We did not know then that those walking towards the Amsterdam Central train station in the middle of the night marked the beginning of the mass deportation of Jews from the Netherlands to their deaths.

I never saw Alfred again.

Chapter 7

The Noose

We kept the front door locked and the windows closed that summer. Dread and fear lingered inside so it always felt good to snatch an opportunity to get some fresh air. Almost every day, I took Gabi by the hand and walked downstairs to the garden under Mrs Goudsmit's apartment. Her son, Sjors (George), a little boy with blond curls, was about the same age as Gabi and they loved playing together in the sandpit, building and destroying sandcastles. My father looked cautiously out of the window while we were downstairs to make sure there was no danger. Mrs Goudsmit was a Christian woman from Germany whose husband was Jewish, a kind woman whom my parents spoke to often. A brave woman, I learned later she had A brave woman, I learned later she had hidden Jews in the cellar of the building during round-ups.

Every day, or so it seemed, we were now hearing of more people getting call-up notices for work camps in Germany. When a man of 40 or younger received a call-up, his family was deported with him. Most of the 4,000 who received papers by mid-July decided to obey the orders, figuring that if they played along with the German rules they were safer than if they were caught disobeying them. This was central to the German tactics to ensure our obedience. They made it very clear that punishment would be severe, and so the naturally law-abiding went along with the Germans' orders. But even so, the Franks were not the only family to have vanished.

Going into hiding was an expensive proposition, not just a dangerous one. And for families with children, it usually meant going into hiding separately from one another – an impossible dilemma. To even consider it, you had to be lucky enough to have someone who could hide you but you also needed enough money to cover the expense of being fed. In my family, we had neither the connections with non-Jewish Dutch who could help us, nor the necessary financial reserves. Despite the risks, some did not show up after receiving their summons to Hollandsche Schouwburg, a beautiful neoclassical theatre now acting as a deportation centre. When the police went looking for them at their homes, some jumped out of windows, sometimes into canals. The desperation to escape was everywhere.

A disproportionate number of those being called up seemed to be from the German refugee community. This enraged my father and grandfather and other German Jewish leaders and was in part what had led to the creation of the German-Jewish subcommittee of the Jewish Council, so that they could represent their own interests better. The council was usually updated in advance about deportation call-ups and could pass that information on to the community. Papa and my grandfather attended meetings regularly. They even had a special stamp in their ID papers that permitted them to be on the streets after curfew in order to go to them. The long walks to the meetings were hard on my grandfather but he insisted on going.

The Germans' plans were made purposefully opaque and they masterfully played out a 'divide-and-conquer' strategy, using the divisions within the Jewish community, specifically between the Dutch-born Jews and the Jewish refugees from Germany and other countries. There was never any declaration that all Jews in the Netherlands would be deported, so there was a sense that some might be safer than others – for example, Dutch Jews over foreign Jews. Membership or association of some kind with the Jewish Council offered a measure of protection for family members too. Everyone was desperate to have a stamp on their identification card, indicating they were exempt from deportation, so council members worked to employ as many Jews as possible so they could be included under this umbrella of supposed protection.

Mr Ledermann did occasional legal work and translations for the Jewish Council, so for now, the Ledermann family was also safe. Barbara Ledermann was among the only one of her friends who did not get a call-up notice when Margot Frank did. Mr Ledermann, urbane and astute, a model of German correctness and orderliness similar to my father and grandfather, believed that following instructions was key to remaining unharmed. Dark rumours circulated about what really happened in the German work camps but Mr Ledermann and many others, my father and grandfather included, found it impossible to believe them.

One night, the doorbell rang at the Ledermann apartment, just around the corner from us, at around 1am, waking the whole family.

'We were scared to death,' Sanne told me.

They did not dare answer. It was a short, rather civilised ring. And then nothing for a long time, followed by a rap on the door. Eventually, Sanne's father went to check what it was and discovered a letter addressed to him. It turned out to not be anything too important, but what a fright! Just hearing about it from Sanne I thought my heart might burst out of my chest. We lived in a state of constant tension, never knowing what a knock at the door or a letter might bring. We were so worried it could only mean arrest and deportation, we could not think of anything else.

Sanne and I talked about how hard it would be to go back to school and study again. So many of our older friends, or our friends' older siblings, wouldn't be there. On the one hand, I missed the routine of school, our wonderful teachers and my friends there. But how could we focus on learning geography, German or wretched geometry when all this was going on around us … ?

We heard of more arrests and round-ups, more people disappearing, going into hiding. When a Jewish home was empty for either one of those reasons, the German authorities would come and take the family's possessions away and ship them all – couches, side tables, lamps, beds, bedding – to Germany, to the cities there that had been bombed by the Allies. There were rumours that the goods arrived with an attached note that read '*Liebesgaben*', German for 'gifts of love'.

One evening, from our front window, I saw an older couple, neighbours named Mr and Mrs Strauss, being hauled away by the police. They were thrown into the back of a police truck with no more care than if they were a pair of old, broken-down chairs. Horrified, I hurried to tell my parents. It wasn't just teenagers and men any more – we were hearing stories of all sorts of people being taken after night fell. Mothers were waking their young children from deep sleeps, wrapping them in the blankets from their warm beds and carrying them into the darkness and the unknown. The elderly, the sick – no one seemed spared; all dragged into the streets and to waiting trucks and vans.

*   *   *

The halls and classrooms of the Jewish Lyceum felt different now. The buzz of newness had faded, although the camaraderie was still there, as was a sense of discipline and academic excellence. We stood up when a teacher entered the room and gave them our full respect. My father teased me after hearing me shout out in my sleep one night, 'The teacher says … !'

That first day of school when I came in to see Anne's seat was empty, I felt as if a knife had grazed my heart. Several other seats were also empty, including that of the very sweet and quiet Betty Bloemendaal, who I had last seen at Anne's birthday party. I heard she had been deported with her family. Every day it seemed there were more students missing. We never knew if an absent student that day meant they were simply sick or if yet another family had been deported or if that friend had gone into hiding. I felt it was hard to keep up morale when I never knew what awaited us when we got to our classroom.

Teachers were also disappearing. One day, our history teacher did not show up. We were told he was sick and that in his place Mr Presser would teach us. Mr Presser was known as an impressive academic, a poet and historian, an example of the high calibre of teachers at our school. Like many of his colleagues, he had been fired from a prestigious Amsterdam school – in his case the Vossius Gymnasium – because of the anti-Jewish laws.

We stood when Mr Presser walked into our classroom, a man in his early forties with dark wavy hair, a square jaw and round glasses. He looked at us with serious, sombre eyes and dove directly into his lecture.

'We are going to talk about the Renaissance,' he announced. He asked if any of us could explain the significance of that era. History was my favourite subject but I was always too shy to raise my hand in class unless I absolutely knew the answer, so I just looked down at my desk. He said historians tried to make sense of our complicated past by breaking into periods. We look back at the Renaissance as a time of transition, from the medieval period to the beginnings of the modern world we know today.

'One of the most famous Renaissance writers was Dante,' he told us, describing the celebrated poet and historian of Florence in the 1200s. He began to tell us the story of the love of Dante's life – the beautiful Beatrice.

'She was his passion, his inspiration, his mythically beloved,' he said.

We did not get to hear about romance much in history lessons, or really any lessons, so we leaned in to hear every word.

But then his monologue stopped abruptly. His shoulders began to shake and he collapsed onto the chair behind the teacher's desk, sobbing uncontrollably. I looked around at my classmates. All of us were stunned and silent. Most of us were looking down at our desks. It felt impolite to look at Mr Presser. None of us had ever seen a teacher cry.

He then stood up and quickly walked out of the classroom. A few minutes passed and the principal entered.

'Sit down, students, sit down,' he told us. He then explained that just that very morning, Mr Presser had received the terrible news that his wife, a woman named Debora Presser-Appel, had been arrested by the Germans. We found out later she had been arrested on a train after being caught without her yellow star and carrying fake identification papers. The rumour was she had been on the way to a hiding place. Mr Presser did not return to school after that. I never forgot the image of a teacher crying.

My friends and I exchanged stories of what we were seeing. Jacque, who lived on normally quiet Lekstraat just down the block from our synagogue, said that after hearing screaming below her bedroom window, she looked outside to see a young woman being shoved into the back of a military truck while a young man was trying to stop her from being taken away. He was pushed back into the street and left to watch as the truck drove off with the woman, a look of horrified shock on his face.

On Yom Kippur, the Day of Atonement, the holiest day of the Jewish year, I fasted and prayed at synagogue for most of the day. At synagogue, we read prayers that spoke of God's incredible compassion and ability to forgive. We are at the same time trying to reach that capacity within ourselves, my father explained. Can we forgive the Germans for making our lives so hard? I wondered. For all the people they have taken away, made to board trains in the middle of the night? For Alfred? For forcing Anne and her family to leave? And for keeping my parents up late at night wondering what on earth they should do? I thought to ask him but decided not to. I knew he would only get upset. My father, so clever and wise, had always seemed to have so many answers. But at 13, nearly 14, I realised that he probably did not have an answer for this one.

* * *

'The baby is coming soon, Mama,' I said, patting my mother's ever-rounding belly. I'd noticed that in the last few weeks, her usually elegant strides had slowed down and turned into more of a waddle as it became harder for her to walk.

'I know. Are you excited?' she said, lowering herself into a chair.

'Yes! I can't wait to meet him or her. To hold them, give them baths, push them in the pram in the neighbourhood. And Gabi can help too. She loves to sing, so she can help sing the baby to sleep,' I said. 'I think it's great that the baby is coming just around the happiest day in the Hebrew calendar.' My little brother or sister was due at the end of October, around Simchat Torah, the Jewish holiday marking the end of reading the Torah for the year. It was so much fun; I loved it. Men would carry the Torah scrolls through the synagogue while we danced around them, singing and gobbling up the apples and chocolates the adults passed around.

Gabi came in and, with difficulty, owing to Mama's bump, climbed onto her lap.

'Play with me,' Gabi demanded, pulling on Mama's dress. Although I could see from Mama's puffy eyes that she was tired, she told me to bring over Gabi's wooden blocks and together they began stacking them on the table. Mama patiently counted out, 'One, two, three blocks. How many blocks are in our tower now?'

Though she was only two, Gabi was already extremely verbal. She spoke in full sentences and seemed to immediately understand what you told her. She was also quite mischievous. Just the other day, Mama, knowing my love of chocolate, had put a couple of pieces on a table in the bedroom I shared with Gabi as a treat for me. But left alone for her afternoon nap, Gabi somehow reached over her crib walls to grab the chocolate for herself. When my mother came in to wake her, she found her wide awake, sitting up in her crib with her face and her blanket streaked with milk chocolate. 'Hannah, come here,' Mama called me. We both looked at Gabi. We looked at each other. And then we both burst out laughing.

Towards the end of October, close to my mother's due date, I overheard my father tell my grandmother that he was concerned. Mama was not feeling well. The doctor had been coming to check on her and he reassured my parents that the baby was doing just fine and that he expected a smooth delivery.

The next day, however, my father's face was drawn and tense when he occasionally emerged from my parents' bedroom. 'You are in charge of Gigi,' he told me, looking past me, not at me, before he vanished inside the bedroom again. My mother was in labour. Just as for Gabi's birth, she'd decided to give birth at home, mistrusting the treatment she might receive as a Jewish woman at a hospital in a country under German occupation. She also feared that, with all the deportations, even hospital patients might be swept up in a round-up. Dr Neufeld, a Jewish doctor, and a midwife, a kind redhead named Julia Goodman, who was half Jewish, were tending to her. They had helped to deliver Gabi too.

I warmed up some soup for Gabi and tried to focus on getting her to finish it. But inside, my mind was thinking a thousand thoughts. 'Mama will be fine,' I repeated to myself. I heard a low wail from behind the bedroom door and the murmuring of low-pitched voices. It was hard to hear, but I think Dr Neufeld was saying, 'Mrs Goslar, we are with you. You are strong.'

I walked over to the living room and looked out of the window. It was getting dark. When my father prayed from home, wrapped in his prayer shawl, he faced east, towards Jerusalem. I started to pray too. Not any specific prayers, but prayers from the heart.

My grandparents were in the apartment too. A few hours later, after I had put Gabi to bed, they told me go to bed too. But it was too hard to go to sleep, waiting for the baby to come, so I stayed in the living room.

At some point, the voices got sharper and louder. *She must be getting closer, the baby is really on its way now*, I thought. Then more muffled voices. And then nothing. No voices, no shouting, no baby cries. It felt like the nothing went on for a long time. The door to my parents' bedroom opened slowly. It was Dr Neufeld but he didn't say anything. He just went to the kitchen and poured a glass of water.

Then my father came out and looked towards me and then my grandparents. The expression on his face was one I had never seen before. It was drained of all colour and his blue-grey eyes were wet with tears. I was scared to see him like this. What was happening? His words came slowly, as if he was trying to understand them himself as he said them. The baby was breech, that's why the birth was so hard, he told us. That meant he never turned downwards, like babies are supposed to do. The baby, it's a boy. But he did not make it. He's stillborn.

His words trailed off.

My grandmother quickly asked: 'And Ruth?'

My father said she was weak but resting.

I didn't know what the word 'stillborn' meant. My grandmother quietly explained. After a while, I was allowed to go into the room and be with Mama. Her long dark hair hung loose on her shoulders. She lay in her bed, the same bed I ran to during thunderstorms and on the morning the Germans invaded. The same bed she had got up from earlier today and, as she always did, walked to the kitchen and brewed her pot of strong morning coffee. An eiderdown quilt was tucked close to her. She seemed to be in a deep sleep. I stroked her hair and squeezed her hand, but there was no squeeze back. At the foot of the bed my father wept.

As usual, family updates from Amsterdam went via Uncle Hans in Basel. The news travelled quickly from our home and Uncle Hans cabled his worried oldest sister in Leeds, England: 'Ruthchen very hard delivery boy stillborn parents very anxious.'

Mama laid mostly still for hours. Sometimes she seemed to be stirring; her head would move, her mouth sounding a low murmuring moan. Dr Neufeld kept checking her pulse and occasionally offered sobering assessments: 'Her situation is not stable,' he said.

I looked at Mama. Skin pale, eyes closed. I felt a heaviness in my bones. I wondered what hurt more, giving birth to an upside-down baby or finding out her little boy was dead. Was that why it was so hard for her to wake up? But still, I did not realise how serious the situation was.

At some point, I left her bedroom and checked on Gabi. The rest was a bit of a blur but I heard my parents' bedroom door open and my father's footsteps. 'Mama is gone,' he said. He did not have to say more. I couldn't take it in but I understood. I went back to her room and stayed there with her until she was taken away.

Everyone was crying. Papa, my grandparents, Irma. Gabi looked at us, eyes wide and confused. 'Where's Mama?'

Soon, the house filled with people for the shiva, the traditional seven days of Jewish mourning. Gabi walked up to guests, asking: 'Where is my mama?' She kept asking and asking. We tried, through tears, to explain to her in words she might understand. The little girl who had always seemed to understand everything you told her, since she was tiny. Eventually she stopped asking.

A letter from grandfather was posted immediately. On its arrival, another telegram was cabled from Basel to Leeds: 'Poor Rutchen died, 27 October heart weakness'.

The next day following the end of the shiva, my mother was buried at Muiderberg cemetery, about ten miles outside of Amsterdam.

I don't remember why, but I was not permitted to go. Was I deemed too young? Did my father or my grandfather think it would be too painful for me to bear? I don't know. Instead I stayed at home in the company of a few of my classmates.

The eulogy was given at the graveside by a family friend and fellow refugee from Germany, a scholar named Dr Albert Lewkowitz. He started with words from Isiah, 'Cry out' – words that resonated hard in my chest. He spoke of my mother's kindness: 'The warm tenderness, the subtle agility of your mind, the beauty and grace that radiated from you and made your house warm and beautiful.' He went on: 'Not only the most devoted and tender mother to your children, she was also a friend and playmate, who, with a carefree spirit, was a child with her children and listened in loving reverence to the blossoming of her children's souls.'

* * *

In the days and weeks that followed, I tried to digest that I had lost my mother and the baby brother she was trying so hard to bring into the world. Outside, the sky was grey and flat, a vision of nothing-ness. I felt numb. There was no joy, not even the smallest ounce of it. I wondered if it would always be that way.

Amsterdam was transitioning into winter. Short days where the sun vanishes by 4pm. Nothing blooming, the tree branches bare. The glorious gift of long summer days, ice-cream cones with Anne and our friends, felt like an impossible, faraway dream. I moved slowly, as if through layers of mud. But there was Gabi to take care of, that was my focus. Papa seemed to be short on patience for me or her.

My grandparents helped us to move us through the routines of the day. But things were only growing more difficult now. Shopping was limited to two hours a day, there was no tram, we were not allowed to own phones any longer nor were we permitted to use the phones of non-Jews in their homes or their businesses. The shortages were getting worse too: less coal, less butter and other staples.

It felt strange to have no address to send a letter to Anne, to let her know what happened. She and Margot would be shocked and heartbroken to hear my mother was gone, that there was no new baby to bathe, coddle and push on Merwedeplein in a pram, like we did with Gabi. So would Mr and Mrs Frank too. Her parents were like honorary extra sets of parents in our makeshift, transplanted tribe of Wandering Jews. Our mothers baked and savoured the same kind of sweet yeast cakes and jam-filled doughnuts, dressed us as young girls in similar hand-knitted cable sweaters and well-tailored dresses, shared the same nostalgia for a homeland in Germany that no longer could be home.

My mother was my confidante, my cheerer-on, she who knew me best. She had loved me and spoiled me in the small ways she could. I would have done almost anything for one more Wednesday afternoon crossing Dam Square to reach De Bijenkorf, our hands gliding over the silks and satins of dresses made in Paris, sipping our cups of warm hot cocoa for me, coffee for her. I missed her devotion to me, the intimacy we built over those years when I was the only child, fortunate in my devoted, doting parents. Where was I in this world that kept getting darker if she was not there to help me find my way? I'd sometimes creep into the bedroom she had shared with my father and open her wardrobe to hold her dresses to my face, eyes closed, imagining I could still feel her here with me. On my fourteenth birthday, one week after she died, I thought of the word 'motherless' and realised that's what I'd be for the rest of my life.

People I knew – meaning the best but breaking my heart – said that I was 'quite the little mother' for Gabi. But I didn't want to be her mother. I wanted our mother back.

Papa told me that the lessons Mama had taught me through the way she lived her life were now part of me too, woven into my heart and there to tap, even if I did not understand that now.

*   *   *

Another new word had entered my vocabulary. *Razzia*. The name for Nazi round-ups of Jews that seemed to be happening more and more. One of our layers of 'protection' had been my mother's pregnancy; the other was that my father and grandfather were members of the subcommittee of the Jewish Council. But who knew how long that would last, what weight that really carried. Uncertainty was our one constant. It drove the adults in our lives into terrible moods. They were completely on edge. Sanne's mother, Mrs Ledermann, described Mr Ledermann as 'unapproachable' and that's how I felt about my own father too, who was both grieving my mother and feeling increasingly trapped. There was of course little my mother could have done for us were we to be caught up in a razzia, but her loss left me feeling even more exposed and in danger. She was gone just when we needed her protection and reassurance most.

The doorbell rang one afternoon. It was some German Nazi officers, wearing long green coats and high boots – the Grüne Polizei, 'Green Police' (so-named because of the colour of their uniforms and to differentiate them from the 'Black Police', who were Dutch). They had come to ask if any Jews lived there. I thought I might faint from fright. My father took a deep breath and opened the door, saying little as they told us to gather our belongings and go. All my Jewish friends had packed an 'in-case' suitcase. After my mother died, Mrs Ledermann had come over and helped me pack one, making sure I had what I needed, including sanitary pads, something my father wouldn't have thought of, and helped me also pack for Gabi. With the Green Police waiting, my hands trembled as I tucked in a few last things – an extra sweater for Gabi, my hairbrush. My grandparents, father, Gabi, Irma and I walked down the stairs, out of our building, and were hurried onto a truck. It started driving towards the centre of the city. Rivierenbuurt and its quiet, manicured streets disappeared behind us. This was it. It was our turn.

Through the window, I peered out at the city I loved. The squares that would once have been thick with crowds were hollowed out, with just smatterings of people. With so many shortages, there was less and less to shop for. Cafés once brimming with customers were largely empty. The barges on the canals that I used to love to watch floating by seemed dark and cheerless. We approached the Jewish quarter and I saw the central street, formerly named for Jonas Daniel Meijer, the first Jewish lawyer in the Netherlands who had helped win legal emancipation for Dutch Jews, now given the German name Houtmarkt. The Germans had changed all streets considered to have Jewish names. Our destination was the Hollandsche Schouwburg, the former Dutch theatre-turned-deportation location for Jews from Amsterdam and other Dutch cities. When we arrived, I saw swarms of Wehrmacht soldiers armed with rifles.

'Line up here,' a soldier told us. 'Have your papers ready for examination.'

I looked at my father, grandfather and grandmother. Their bearing was upright and tall, as if to say, without words, that no one was going to steal their dignity, even amid the extreme stress and mayhem of the moment. I winced at the sound of babies crying, the physical pressure of people jostling in line, the sight of so many suitcases, rucksacks and bedrolls, and the anxiety etched in the faces of those sitting next to them.

'Hold my hand, Gabi, don't let go,' I told her urgently. Her tiny shoes made a pitter-patter sound on the pavement. I also held Papa's hand so tightly I thought he might get annoyed and shake it off, but he didn't. He just gripped my hand even more firmly. My grandfather's arm was looped through my grandmother's. They stood close behind us, together with Irma, whose dark brown eyes were clearly trying to take everything in. I felt bad that my mother was not there to console her and explain things to her as she used to try so hard to do. Poor Irma had trouble following instructions and explanations at home, let alone here, where there was shouting, soldiers and fear.

I watched as a poker-faced German officer slowly thumbed through our papers. He examined the writing and photos on each identity card. He lingered over the stamp that our family members had thanks to our Jewish Council affiliation, onto which we had put so much hope that it would exempt us from whatever fate awaited those forced to board the trains. Irma, however, was not a relative; she had no such marking in her identification papers. So when we were told we were free to return home, a soldier put his hand on Irma's shoulder.

'She will be staying here,' he said.

'No, no!' she began to cry out, her eyes darting between my father, my grandparents and me as if to say 'Help!' I could feel her panic. My father exchanged some words in German with the overseeing officer, imploring him to release Irma, but he could not be budged. The relief that had washed over me moments before was replaced with a sick-to-the stomach feeling, knowing we were going to have to leave Irma behind, with the soldiers and their rifles, and the others being loaded onto beige-coloured trucks. They were headed first to Westerbork, a detention camp about three hours north of Amsterdam, on the Dutch–German border. We understood from there they would be sent onwards to work camps in the east.

I gave Irma a quick hug just before she was swallowed into the crowd of Jews, who, unlike us, were not fortunate enough to be returning home. We still did not know exactly what happened at the labour camps but we knew it was not a place anyone would want to go.

'When will these razzias end?' I asked my father when we got home.

'No one knows,' he answered.

* * *

It was around this time that Barbara Ledermann, Sanne's big sister, went underground. At 16, she had met a young Jewish man named Manfred who was a member of the Dutch underground. He told her the labour camps were death camps. She did not believe him at first but he told her stories of young men who had escaped and told other underground members what they had witnessed.

Mr Ledermann feared it was more dangerous to be caught in hiding than to be deported. And he could not imagine defying orders. 'I am a lawyer and I've never broken the law and won't break the law now,' Mr Ledermann insisted. Headstrong Barbara repeated the warnings she'd heard from Manfred, argued that these were not lawful laws, that these were not the genteel Germans her father remembered from his Berlin days but Nazis whose work camps were not for labour, but for death. Manfred told Barbara that if she was called for a round-up, 'You are not to go. Everyone who goes and gets into their hands will be killed. They are all going to die.'

These shocking claims did not change Mr Ledermann's mind – maybe it was just too much to believe. Even after Manfred had fake identity cards made for the entire family at considerable cost and risk, Mr Ledermann refused to hear of going underground, even though Mrs Ledermann was supportive of the idea. It was Mrs Ledermann who gave 300 gulden to Barbara to purchase fake papers.

When we returned to school in January, Jacque was another face missing from class. But her story was different. For weeks, her Catholic-born mother had been frantically trying to find a way to reclassify her as a non-Jew. Mrs van Maarsen was a dressmaker and she was French. This made her a rather rarefied figure for Jacque's friends; we saw her as extra glamorous and worldly. Jacque told me how her mother had dressed in one of her finest pre-war tailored outfits, make-up perfect, and presented herself at the Euterpe Street headquarters for the SS, also known as Nazi Intelligence.

She told the officer she met that her Jewish husband had classified her two daughters as Jews against her wishes. 'Now they are in danger,' she told him. She was told to return with proof of her four grandparents' Christianity and Jacque and her sister's Jewish status would be annulled. It must have been incredibly difficult collecting these documents during wartime and I don't know how she managed it, but she was eventually able to get the damning large letter 'J' stamp in her daughters' identity papers removed.

The office which approved the status change was overseen by Dr Hans Calmeyer. It oversaw all claims that one or more of a person's parents or grandparents were not Jewish. This downgrading soon became a matter of life and death because only 'full Jews' were ordered to work camps in the east. It could be said that Dr Hans Calmeyer tried to help in his own way by bending certain rules and turning a blind eye to others. Sometimes there are people like this in the world. He managed to save about 2,000 Jewish lives this way.

So, now no longer considered a Jewish girl, Jacque enrolled at the Girls' Lyceum, the prestigious public school Margot Frank had attended before Jewish students were barred. Margot had missed her friends from there so much, she sometimes could be found waiting for them after school next to the bike racks during that one and only year she spent at the Jewish Lyceum.

We still stayed in touch, even though Jacque was in the new school. Though what she told me I found hard to believe: her new schoolmates did not talk about what was happening to the city's Jews – not the anti-Jewish measures, not the deportations. It was as if we were living in two entirely different worlds. And it was strange to think that with a stroke of a bureaucrat's pen, Jacqueline could take part in all that was forbidden to Ilse and me and our other friends. She could ride a bike again, use a phone in her house, travel by tram and train, not be singled out as inferior with the big mustard-coloured star. I found her transition to 'the other side' mind-bending. Her uncle and first cousins were deported, but she no longer had to worry that she might be. It was like she inhabited a parallel world. But she was still tied to ours. Months later, she went to our classmate and friend's Nanette Blitz's apartment to visit – against the rules – only to discover she and her parents and brother had been deported. A neighbour saw her ringing the doorbell to no response. 'All taken away,' he said twice, no emotion in his voice.

Also in January, as Jacque was given back her freedom and safety, Ilse Wagner, her mother and grandmother were arrested. We did not have a chance to say goodbye. It felt terrible when Ilse was gone – my warm, sensible friend and steady companion at synagogue and youth group. I no longer had any of my close group of friends at school. Soon, my family and those of a few of my remaining friends would be among the last Jews still living in our own homes in Amsterdam.

I asked my father what we were going to do. He said I had to keep up my hope. We were among the fortunate ones, he said. But then one day he asked if I'd agree to go into hiding. It would mean, he cautioned, splitting up – myself, Gabi, my father and grandparents all going underground to separate hiding spots. After losing Mama, I couldn't bear the thought of being parted from them. 'We have to stay together,' I begged my father. He let out a long exhalation and just looked at me intensely for what felt like a long time. He said he agreed.

I saw my grandfather writing to ever-resourceful Uncle Hans daily. I knew Uncle Hans was following every possible lead to help get us out of Holland. What I didn't know then was that my father had briefly entertained the possibility of making a daring escape a few months earlier. His younger cousin Joachim Simon, known as 'Shushu', was a Zionist activist who had also fled to Amsterdam from Berlin. With his wife, Adina, he had been part of a dangerous and brave plan to find a way to smuggle fellow activists and other Jews out of the Netherlands. Together, they had crossed the border into Belgium in the autumn of 1942. There, they researched and planned a route through Belgium and France, and eventually across the border to safety in either Switzerland or Spain. They made it to Switzerland, where Adina stayed, while Shushu returned to the Netherlands to help others escape. He approached my father about smuggling us all out, but my father decided against it. My mother was heavily pregnant then and Gabi was only two, so it would have been almost impossible to make such a physically demanding journey.

Shushu's plans to rescue others came to an end when he was caught with forged identity papers and wads of cash crossing into the Netherlands from Belgium and arrested on Christmas Day 1942. Somehow, he was able to get a message out to his friends that read, 'I was caught. Tell Adina gently.' Two days later, he was found dead in his cell, in what appeared to be suicide. It was considered his final act in protecting his friends, as he must have known he'd be tortured in a bid by the Germans to get information on them.

The news of Shushu's daring and his death left me both inspired and devastated. I remembered him as my kind, intelligent older cousin with round wire-framed glasses and thick, dark hair who would occasionally come over for Shabbat dinner. How could someone so young, clever and brave now be dead? And I felt terribly for his wife Adina – safe, but now alone, a young widow in Switzerland. They had trekked through snow-covered mountain passes together, pushed each other through hunger, blistered feet and fear. I shuddered thinking of Shushu's end.

Early spring 1943, thankfully, brought some good news at last.

'Hans writes that the head of the Geneva Office of the Jewish Agency for Palestine says that the whole family has been included on a list submitted to the British Mandatory government in Palestine for approval,' grandfather said, reading from Hans' letter as we gathered around him in our living room.

There's more, he said, continuing to read. 'Hans has also confirmed that grandmother and I can now obtain Honduran passports, now that the Goslar family [my father, Gabi and I] have passports from Paraguay.'

We had just learned that Uncle Hans had recently bought us the Paraguayan passports and were delighted to hear that Honduran ones would be approved for my grandparents. We were not sure of the practical significance of these passports beyond that they served as another layer of possible protection. They wouldn't allow us to travel to British Mandate Palestine or even emigrate to South America. What we did know was that Jews who held passports from such neutral countries might be exempt from deportation. We were so relieved we almost broke out into a dance around the dining room table. I learned later that these passports were procured thanks to a small band of Polish diplomats and Jewish activists working together in Switzerland. The passports came to be referred to as the 'Lados passports', blank passports purchased at a cost of some 500 francs each (about 3,500 euros in today's currency).

'If you are going to be a citizen of Paraguay, you have to be able to answer some basic questions about the country,' my father told me. So I dutifully studied some of its geography and memorised some facts, including that the capital was called Asunción.

More hopeful news followed. By May, we knew that our entire family had been put on a list for what were called Palestine Certificates. This meant we were eligible to go to Palestine in exchange for German prisoners of war being held by the British.

If only we could be exchanged – and soon!

Chapter 8

Deportation

At dawn on Sunday, 20 June 1943 just two streets away from ours, at the Ledermann's home at Noorder Amstellaan 37, the day's first light was falling on the family piano in the living room. The apartment was quiet; everyone was fast asleep. They had stayed up late the night before as there was great excitement in the house: Barbara, Sanne's older sister, who had been living underground for months, surprised them with a visit. It was a rash and dangerous thing to do – her boyfriend Manfred had warned her against it. But Barbara felt deeply homesick. She had missed them all so much. There were tears and joy at this bittersweet reunion. The terrible fights Barbara and her parents had had about the risks of her using a false ID card and going underground were set aside in the overwhelming relief at being together again. All the tension and recriminations melted away during the reunion and the family went to sleep happy, deeply grateful to again be four under the same roof.

Then, at 6am, their sleep was broken. Tap, tap, tap. It was the sound of knocking at the door. They opened it to a woman from the underground who went by the name Cassandra. I wonder if anyone made the connection in their shock and grogginess that in Greek mythology Cassandra was the princess who spoke of prophecies no one believed …

'I just heard. This whole area is closed off,' she informed them. 'All the Jews are going to be picked up. This is not a little razzia. This is … everybody.'

Outside, it was still quiet. Just the sound of birds chirping, the faint sounds of neighbours waking up; some would have been getting up to go to church. Inside, panic filled the room.

What none of us knew at this point, apart from those in the Ledermann home, was that overnight, while the city slept, German and Dutch police offices had been sealing off parts of Amsterdam – all the way from Ringvaart in the east to Linnaeusstraat in the west. German tanks blocked roads and armed soldiers and police stood guard on every bridge, forming a miliary ring around the neighbourhoods that comprised the bulk of where Jews still lived in the city, including our own. No one was permitted to cross in or out. There would be no escape. Amsterdam, a city of rivers and canals crossed by bridges, was an easy place to close down.

Assisting the Germans to make their plans and pinpoint the location of their victims was a map called 'Verspreiding van de Joden Over de Gemeente' meaning 'Distribution of Jews across the Municipality', created two years earlier by city workers at the command of their German overseers. Each black dot represented ten Jewish people living in the city. Our neighbourhood appeared as a black sea of smashed-together circles.

This razzia was a top-secret Nazi plan. Unlike the others, no advanced word leaked out so it caught us all by surprise – except 'Cassandra', who learned of it only at the last minute. The Jews no longer had phones or radios in the house, part of the German's deliberate strategy to cut us off from the rest of the city and country – and the world. News came mostly in hushed whispers or rumours if it came at all. This time there had been no reports, no tip-offs, no updating of the Jewish Council.

In our apartment, we were startled by the sudden blaring of loudspeakers echoing up and down the street and throughout the neighbourhood: 'Jews, Prepare for today's departure. You are to assemble at Daniel Willinkplein.' The chilling words ricocheted off the cobblestone streets and brick walls and reverberated in my body. My grandparents hurried over to us and my father made the call that we did not have to go down to Daniel Willinkplein.

'We will be OK. We have *speres*,' he said, referring to the vaunted exemption stamps. 'There's no need for us to go. If the Green Police see our papers they will let us go, just like at the previous round-up at the theatre. We stay.'

I was nervous but trusted my father was right. I helped make breakfast with my grandmother and tried, as usual, to convince Gabi to finish her toast. At 10am, however, it was our turn. The dreaded pounding on the door, a German officer instructing us to open it.

'Papa? Papa?' I asked, feeling sick to my stomach. 'Are you going to answer?'

My father fixed his eyes on the door and slowly walked towards it, repeating his reassurances that everything would be cleared up. We had a *spere*. I had started to see those paper privileges – the stamps and our new passports – as magic amulets helping us ward off the Nazi menace surrounding us. Surely they would be enough?

The Green Policeman was unmoved by our *spere*. He told my father in German that all Jews were to report to the square: 'You have 20 minutes to pack your things.' Twenty kilos at most, he added.

I quickly bundled together the blankets we had ready for this eventuality and grabbed the suitcase packed months earlier with the help of Mrs Ledermann, as well as Sanne and Ilse. Ilse. It hurt thinking of her. Where was she now? I wondered. It had now been six months since she was deported in an earlier razzia with her mother and grandmother. Every day, I hoped a letter from her would arrive, but nothing came. I wondered what she'd tell me to pack now after having been sent to a work camp herself. We knew so little about what awaited us. Just the rumours …

It was hard to understand that this time it might really be happening. After all the fear and uncertainty. After the disappearance of my friends and neighbours. After Mama. I don't now even remember if I brought food, like a loaf of bread, some cheese. My mother was the practical one. She would have been taking packets of dried fruit from the cupboard, tucking whatever she could find that might prove useful into bags and pockets. My father, as she used to tease him, sometimes floated just above the ground, instead of walking on it. He was less good at taking care of practical matters. I plonked Gabi on my bed while I gathered our things. Her eyes were wide with confusion as she watched my father and I rush around. I gave her a quick, tight hug and told her if she stopped asking questions I'd give her a cookie. 'Hurry, Hanneli,' Papa said, from the other room.

A wave of sadness hit me as I fastened the buckles of my suitcase. Would we be back in an hour or were we really were being sent away this time? I looked around my room and did a quick survey – my bed, my desk, my various collections of Hollywood stars and royal family cards.

'Hanneli!' Papa said again, louder.

'Bye, house,' I said quietly, as I walked out of my room and down the hall. 'Bye, house,' Gabi said, repeating my words. I tugged my suitcase out the front door with one hand and held onto Gabi's hand with the other.

On the landing, our neighbour and friend Mrs Goudsmit, the mother of Gabi's favourite playmate, who had a soft spot for motherless Gabi, rushed out to try to intercede on our behalf.

'What are you doing?' she asked the Green Policeman overseeing our expulsion. 'Can't I at least take the little girl? She's so young. Her mother recently died. Please let her stay with me, I will care for her.'

The policeman snarled, 'You, a Dutch Christian – you want a Jewish child? Aren't you ashamed?'

'No,' she replied. 'I'm a German Christian and I'm not ashamed.'

None of our other non-Jewish neighbours came out of their front doors to see how we were or ask why we were being taken away like criminals, though as we left our apartment building, we saw, above us, some neighbours peering out to get a better look at the unfolding spectacle, their freshly poured morning coffee next to them on their windowsills. I also caught sight of some people on rooftops with binoculars watching us Jews being taken away. I burned with humiliation but also felt numb with shock.

As our little family walked down our street, my eyes turned for a moment towards Merwedeplein 31. I thought of Anne's front door, closed and silent. Almost exactly a year ago, I had knocked and knocked, wondering why there was no answer. *Lucky Anne*, I thought again, as I had so many times since that day. *You are safe in Switzerland. But why did you never write to me?*

I hated seeing my dignified grandparents endure this. Walking distances was difficult for my grandfather, who used a cane. My

Hannah with her family. From left to right: Hannah's grandmother Therese Klee; Hannah; Hannah's uncle Hans Klee; Hannah's aunt Eugenie; Hannah's baby sister, Gabi, on the lap of her grandfather Hans Klee; Hannah's mother, Ruth, and Hannah's father, Hans Goslar (standing).

Hannah, aged three, with her father, Hans Goslar, in Berlin.

Hannah with her grandfather Alfred Klee, a lawyer and close associate of Theodor Herzl (the founder of modern Zionism).

Hannah beside her mother, Ruth, and her baby sister, Gabi, in Amsterdam.

Inscriptions in Dutch from Hannah to friends in an autograph book.

Hannah and her sister, Gabi, on the right, with neighbours.
The little boy is George Goudsmit. His mother, Maya Goudsmit,
told the Nazis she would keep Gabi if they came to deport the Goslar family.

Hannah and Anne play with friends in a sandbox in Amsterdam in 1937.
From left to right: Hannah, Anne Frank, Dolly Citroen, Hanna Toby, Barbara
Ledermann and Sanne Ledermann (standing). The Ledermanns were close friends of
the Frank family – Barbara survived the Holocaust by using false papers and living
underground, but her sister Sanne and their parents, Franz and Ilse, died at Auschwitz.

Hannah and Anne with friends in Amsterdam, *c.* 1935.
Sanne Ledermann is on the left, beside Hannah. Anne
and Margot Frank are fifth and sixth from the left.

Hannah and Margot Frank on the beach
at Zandvoort, the Netherlands, *c.* 1935.

Hannah pointing to a map of the Netherlands at the 6th Montessori school in Amsterdam *c.* 1936. The map was not labelled, so students would have to memorise names of cities and towns and identify them on the map.

Hannah and Anne Frank in their classroom at the 6th Montessori school in Amsterdam, 1938. Hannah is on the far left, seated towards the back, and Anne stands in a white pinafore to the left of their teacher.

Source: Anne Frank House, Amsterdam.

Anne Frank and Hannah playing at the Merwedeplein in Amsterdam in May 1940.

Hannah and Anne with friends in Amsterdam at Anne's tenth birthday party on 6 June 1939. From left to right: Lucie van Dijk, Anne Frank, Sanne Ledermann, Hannah, Juultje Ketellapper, Käthe Egyedi, Mary Bos, Ietje Swillens and Martha van den Berg.

grandmother had only recently recovered from a fall down our stairs that left her with three broken vertebrae. And yet there they were, struggling to carry their suitcases and bedrolls. I could no longer carry Gabi and the suitcase I was holding, so I put her down and encouraged her to walk as quickly as she could.

It only took a few minutes to reach Daniel Willinkplein, a grassy plaza lined with trees and bushes at the intersection of three streets: Amstellaan; our street, Zuider Amstellaan; and Noorder Amstellaan, where the Ledermanns lived. Above us loomed our local landmark, the 12-storey 'skyscraper' apartment building. I took in the strange sight: dozens of other people, some of whom we recognised, milling on the grass, waiting for whatever would happen next, drawn faces marked with dread and fear. There were young children and babies, some of them howling amid the confusion, their mothers and fathers trying to console them. I noticed a mother of four-year-old twins who lived on our street prop up her suitcases to block the sun, fashioning a makeshift sleeping space for the children as the waiting continued.

To distract myself, I watched the people in the square. Men in smart fedora hats, bags slung across black and navy tailored wool coats, the yellow stars sewn on them marking them as Jews, were conferring with one another. Most people were wearing or carrying winter coats or trench coats, despite the summer weather. We didn't know how long we'd be gone and we all knew how cold winters could be. I felt sweat trickling down by neck and removed my coat. Some people had tied rolled blankets with rope, others had them slung across their arms. There were girls in knee socks, loafers and pleated skirts, and women clutching leather purses. Older women like my grandmother found spots on benches where they could and rested their heads on their hands. There were clumps of belongings scattered across the grass, loaves of bread and bottles of milk lined up next to them. A girl with plaits was sitting on a bed roll; little boys in shorts and coats were carrying bags that surely weighed more than they did. Women with hats fashioned with bows, gold brooches fastened to the high necks of their silk dresses. I counted double-breasted tailored wool coats, young men in argyle sweaters. It was as if everyone wanted to look as presentable as possible to the Germans, to remind them we were people too.

Lines of men in dark jumpsuits with yellow stars on their chests came to 'assist' the Green and Black Police. 'Who are they?' I asked Papa.

'They are Jews who are already at Westerbork, the detention camp,' he said. 'It's where they send all the Dutch Jews before they go to work in the east.'

I thought to myself: *Is this what will happen for us now? Is there really no escape?*

Eventually, we were brought, under armed guard of the police, and with the Westerbork Jewish police, to the tram. It had been over a year since I was on a tram. Walking to school in the rain, I had dreamed about being allowed to go on one again. But now I was simply afraid. It felt chaotic, with children crying among so many men with rifles. Although we had been occupied for three years, I was not used to being close to so many guns. It was also bewildering to me that the Germans found us so dangerous that they needed to take us away at gunpoint.

Papa explained tersely, 'It's so we won't resist.'

I squeezed onto the tram, clutching Gabi's hand, and pressed next to my father and grandparents. We crossed the Amstel River and I looked at my transformed city: the boarded-up shops, the sealed-off houses where other Jews had lived. The disorientation and the fear I felt contrasted with the people I saw enjoying the perfect June day, kids playing under the blue sky, young couples strolling arm in arm across cobblestone squares.

About 30 minutes later, we disembarked at Muiderpoort train station in the east of Amsterdam. As we walked inside, I saw families heading out of the city for picnics or to pick cherries. It was so hard to reconcile their situation with ours. I thought back to earlier that day, the rushed goodbye to Mrs Goudsmit, and our home, the sunny living room, and my parents' bedroom where Mama's perfumes and creams remained, next to her closet where her dresses still hung. *Mama, where are you now?* I wanted to cry.

The platform vibrated with shouting and commotion. The Green and Black Police walked alongside us, keeping us in close reach.

'This is your train,' one of the policemen announced when we got to the end of a platform where wood-slatted train cars waited. 'But these are for animals!' someone in the crowd said.

Why are they putting us in trains for animals? I wondered.

'Is there anywhere to sit down?' I asked as we were bundled into one of the cars. I was clinging to Papa; Gabi was clinging to me. My grandparents were holding on to one another. Straw was scattered on the floor. Each family found a spot to sit tightly together. I heard a whistle blow and felt the hum of the engine and suddenly we lurched forward, dozens of us crammed together. It was so hot, I felt my clothes sticking to me. There were no windows, but I imagined the open sky and flat countryside that I loved so much rushing by, the lowland heathland, woods, meadows, lakes and small towns, as the sun beat down on our crowded train.

Eventually we reached Westerbork, the transit camp still on Dutch soil, 100 miles from Amsterdam. We had been among the last of the Jews still left in Amsterdam and now we had been coughed up into this boggy, windswept landscape in the northeast corner of the country, next to the German border. Our wave, a mix of working class and educated, well-dressed bourgeoise and intellectuals, about 2,000 people per train, had, until now, been the lucky ones; by dint of connections, wealth or good fortune we had all been exempt from earlier deportations. We knew that before us had come young people, like my boyfriend Alfred, and poor families from the Jewish quarter, who eked out livings and didn't have the resources to try to avoid deportation, as well as middle-class families, like my friend Ilse's, who did not have exemptions, and the elderly and the ill rounded up from hospitals, bodies already in decline, some blind, some disabled. After the three-hour sweltering journey, I felt relieved to be off the nauseating train and breathing fresh air. It was the time of year purple lupines were in bloom and I saw clusters in a field on the other side of the barbed wire, past rows of guard towers manned by soldiers with rifles.

I learned later that about 5,500 of us arrived that night and the next day, summer solstice, the longest day of the year. Coming off the train, some people were reunited with friends and family deported in previous razzias. It was strange that despite the apprehension, there could also be moments of delight, as friends and neighbours spotted one another, rushing into embraces and greetings. In the crush of meetings, we too had one: we found the Ledermanns.

But it was only Sanne and her parents. Barbara was not there. She had stayed behind. In those last frantic moments after they got the message from 'Cassandra', it was decided that Barbara would try to get away. Mrs Ledermann, who had never spoken against her husband's wishes before, said, 'Franz, *sie geht*' – Franz, she goes. 'She has to leave, you know that.'

Mr Ledermann looked at Barbara. 'Bless you,' he said. 'Go.'

Chapter 9

Westerbork

'Hanneli, they are saying you and Gabi will stay at the orphanage.' Papa made his voice as low and gentle as possible, something he did when trying to tell me difficult news.

'But I want to stay with you! Why can't we stay with you?'

The tears came, hot and strong. I suddenly felt four years old, not 14. I wanted to hurl my whole body on this sandy, marshy ground and have a proper tantrum. *Please, please don't split us up.*

My father was doing his best. 'Women and men stay in separate barracks here. Because you don't have a mother to stay with you in the women's barracks, you girls will go to the orphanage. But I know Mr Birnbaum, who runs it with his wife, from Berlin. He is a good man. He says that the food is better quality and you will have excellent care. But I won't be far away, and neither will Oma and Opa. Don't worry, my brave, sweet girl, we'll be able to see one another. Please Hanneli, please, don't cry. We can do this,' he urged.

Papa folded us both into a hug. Then Opa and Oma did the same. I looked at Gabi, now aged just over two and a half. *She should only know a world of comfort and love*, I thought, frightened but also seething. Not this place.

I could see the confusion in her searching eyes and remembered that I was the big sister. I had to look after us both. So I took a deep breath, tried to channel Mama's pragmatism, and told her: 'Don't worry, Gigi, I'm going to be with you. Like always. And we'll see everyone else tomorrow! It's time for us all to go to bed.' I hope she didn't notice that my voice was cracking.

All that long, miserable day, I had been trying so hard not to cry. Standing in the endless line to 'register' our family in this bleak, isolated place, I kept thinking: *we were free just this morning, this very same day.* But what were we now? Detainees? Prisoners? Criminals? Rows and rows of deportees, in the thousands – exhausted, in sweat-soaked clothes, stomachs rumbling – were waiting, powerless to do anything but stand there. All of us wondered what would happen next as we waited for our turn to submit our names and addresses at the tables manned by Jews who had been arrested and shipped to Westerbork before us. Above us, the deep blue sky held the last moments of light as we neared midnight.

'Welcome, Hanneli and Gabi,' said Otto Birnbaum warmly. He had come to meet Gabi and me to walk us over to the orphanage. He was not much taller than I was, with thick, dark hair and round glasses. He kept smiling the whole time we talked and I began to feel my stomach unclench. He seemed so nice.

He steered us towards a collection of five wooden barracks, similar to the other shabby wooden structures that lined the camp roads, explaining that four were dormitories and the other was the orphanage dining hall. We walked into the one in which we were to stay, number 35. I looked at the long rows of triple-decker bunk beds under a slanted wooden roof. The rough wooden floor creaked under my step. *So this is it*, I thought to myself. I just hoped we would not be not here for long and could soon go home or be exchanged.

Mr Birnbaum's wife, Hennie, took over, taking my hand in hers and giving Gabi a quick hug. Quietly, so as not to wake the dozens of children around us already sleeping, she said, 'It's going to be just fine. Tomorrow we will tell you more but it's been a very long day, so let's get you to bed.'

She showed us to an empty bunk and helped me pull the sheet I had brought from home over a thin burlap mattress filled with wood shavings and straw. I felt too tired and too sad to think much. Gabi curled up next to me and I pulled the pair of wool blankets we brought from home over us. It felt strange and a little scary to sleep in a room with so many others. I closed my eyes and told myself to sleep. Then I started to feel itching on my legs. First one, then another. Fleas, I instantly knew with dread. I scratched, I squirmed. *Mama, where are you? Mama, I miss you*, I thought, tears rolling down my cheeks.

The next morning, Mrs Birnbaum taught me how to neatly make our bed, as per regulations, the blanket smoothed and tucked in tightly. I tried to focus on her instructions but I felt deeply anxious. When were we going to see Papa and my grandparents? Gabi and I were not orphans. I resented that we had to be here. Who were these other children, I wondered, most of them younger than me? I felt so badly for them. Did none of them have parents?

Mrs Birnbaum explained to me they were children found in hiding by the Germans. Children and parents were often hidden in separate places, so there was a good chance their parents were safely still in hiding. Did they know their children had been betrayed and taken away? Did they have any way to communicate with them here? My heart ached hearing that this was who these children were.

So many thoughts swirled in my head as I clipped back Gabi's short, silky hair with her tiny barrette so it would stay out of her eyes. But there was no time to dwell further because we were being rushed to the dining-hall barrack for breakfast. Our first stop there was a woman in blue overalls, the standard work gear of Westerbork inmates. She gave Gabi and me one deep red-coloured enamel bowl and cup each.

'You cannot lose these. Do you understand me?' she asked, looking directly at me. 'You cannot lose them.'

That really struck me. What would happen if we lost them? A girl sitting on the bench at one of the long, crowded tables where we found a spot answered my question: 'If you lose them, you will have nothing to drink or eat with.'

Breakfast that first morning was milk and bread. Gabi and I gobbled up everything hungrily, even though we would have preferred some butter and jam to go on our bread. The only butter and jam at Westerbork, it turned out, came from care packages sent by friends or relatives.

My thoughts again turned to finding our family. 'We have to find where Papa is staying,' I told Gabi. She nodded and shouted out, 'Papa! Where's Papa?'

I was determined to find out how to see him so I started asking where the men's barracks were. When I found out they were close to the orphanage barrack which housed the communal toilets, I had an idea. Even kids my age had jobs at Westerbork so I decided to volunteer for a job no one else wanted: cleaning those toilets. They smelled absolutely awful and were used by 200 children, but

I figured this job could be a good way to see my father more easily. It was worth a try.

I was also assigned to help clean and care for the younger group of children, which included Gabi. If I could look after Gabi and find a way to see Papa then it might be OK. I would then just have to find Opa and Oma, and Papa would surely know where they were. I was told there were teachers at Westerbork who volunteered to teach classes during the days so we kids could keep up with our studies. When I heard this my spirits lifted. I really hoped to be back at school soon and did not want to fall behind.

Later in the day, more Jews arrived from Amsterdam to this sandy, mosquito- and flea-bitten outpost. I saw the trucks that rumbled in with them. There were fewer of them than those of us who arrived by train. Word travelled fast in Westerbork and we heard they were people who had tried to evade the razzia the day before by hiding, many of them in their own homes. But the police returned and conducted house-to-house searches. They even thrust bayonets through walls, into closets and into floorboards searching for people. I was so glad we had not tried to hide in our apartment. It was too awful to imagine.

I learned that Mr Birnbaum had first met my father in the Orthodox community in Berlin. A former school teacher, he and Mrs Birnbaum were parents to six young children, who they cared for alongside the children in the orphanage. I was so grateful for their kind, competent presence. Mr Birnbaum told me Westerbork had originally been established before the Occupation as a detention centre by the Dutch for Jewish refugees from Germany who had crossed into the Netherlands without permission after Kristallnacht. It was run by the Dutch, but the everyday workings were overseen by the German

Jews themselves. The Germans kept that system roughly in place when they took control of the camp in July 1942. The Birnbaums were one of the original German Jewish families detained there and they had taken on managing the orphanage. Now the detention camp was a crowded deportation camp – the point from which Dutch Jews were sent onwards to work camps in the east, usually Poland. Fearful of what these 'work camps' entailed, having heard all the rumours that had been spreading over the past few years, Westerbork's inmates were desperate to stay on Dutch soil. Many, like us, seemed to have deferments from deportation. Those who did not scrambled to somehow stay on. One way was by being declared an essential worker. There were also rumours that deferments could be bought.

As I went into the toilets that first day of work with a bucket and scrubbing brush, sick to my stomach from the stench and filth, I felt very sorry for myself. I started scrubbing and thought back to this time last summer. Mama was alive still. I had no idea what grief felt like or that my friends could just vanish. The school year was ending; Anne, Sanne, Ilse and Jacque and I were still in the Little Dipper Minus Two club; still living in our homes, playing ping pong and eating ice cream. The rivalries and squabbles felt very far away. But still the confidences shared and jokes and gossip traded felt so close. I could almost hear us giggling as we sat on the stairs of Anne's building facing Merwedeplein.

After about an hour, the smells I was trying to scrub away were too much to bear. I felt light-headed and stepped out for a break. I looked out towards the men's barracks and heard someone call out my name.

'Hanneli!' It was my father's voice!

'Papa!' I shouted, rushing towards him. He told me he was in Barrack 62, one of about 150 men there crammed in a single large room of 50 triple-deck bunk beds. It was noisy and crowded.

'But it's not so bad. I'm struck by how kind the other men are,' he told me. 'They really go out of their way to be courteous; it's like it's their way to make this wretched situation more bearable.'

My grandparents were doing well, he said, though they were in separate barracks too. 'But in the evenings, we will be able to visit one another,' he added.

Hearing this and seeing him felt like a massive weight had lifted. I had been more anxious than I even realised. He reassured me we would be protected from being sent east because of our Paraguayan passports and Palestine certificates.

'You'll see, we will be on one of those exchanges soon to Eretz Yisrael,' he said, using the words for the Land of Israel.

It was hard for me to imagine what Eretz Yisrael looked like. I had a gauzy image of this Biblical land of milk and honey. From the picture postcards we had at home, it was a place of orange groves, camels crossing sandy stretches of desert and young Jews harvesting grapes and figs. It was a place, my grandfather had told me, where we would not have to feel like refugees. This information and his confidence felt like a balm. Papa was one of the smartest people I knew; I trusted his every word. This was all only temporary. We'd either be all together again soon in Eretz Yisrael or maybe, I thought, if the Allies won quickly, back home on Zuider Amstellaan Street.

Papa also told me we were going to have to lean on the only people we knew on the outside who could mail us the supplies we would need while at Westerbork. We had Uncle Hans in Switzerland, although packages would take longer to arrive from Zurich than

Amsterdam, so Papa thought we should try Mrs Goudsmit, our lovely neighbour whose son Gabi spent hours playing with outside our building.

When I had a break a couple of days later, I sat down and wrote my first postcard to Mrs Goudsmit. It felt strange writing out her address on our own Zuider Amstellaan. In a weird way it already felt like it no longer existed. I felt so far from home. I began:

> *My little sister and I are well accommodated in the orphanage. I'm sure the little one will settle in well in a few days and will play nicely with the other little children. We hope that your dear husband and the adorable Schorschi* [our nickname for Sjors] *are very well. We think of him and you all the time and talk about Schorschi's sweet little tricks … My Papa's writing day is Sunday and he will write you a comprehensive letter then. We would be very grateful for a fine-tooth comb and a hairbrush for me and a bottle of shampoo for washing our hair.*

I paused and stared out in the distance, thinking about how to sign it. I added:

> *Best wishes to you three,*
> *From your grateful*
> *Hanneli*

I found myself getting used to the rhythm of the orphanage. It felt like a cheerful place, despite the situation. There were lots of well-known people at Westerbork – actors, musicians, professors, authors – and many of them, both the famous and less famous, would come by to help amuse and occupy the children. Clara Asscher-Pinkhof, one of my favourite children's authors, an Orthodox woman, would come regularly for storytime. I loved listening to her unspool tales about traditional Jewish life, just like the books she wrote for Jewish children that I adored and had on my shelf back home.

After those weeks and months of worrying when and if we might get deported, terrified of a knock on the door, now that we had actually been sent here – with my family nearby and so many friends and acquaintances too – I felt a sense of relief. I wanted it all to be over, of course, and my hands were chafed from cleaning toilets with harsh chemicals. But there were moments, especially when I was with Papa, Gabi and our grandparents in the evenings, when I could almost pretend things were normal.

In the early evening, I and the other older girls had our hands full with the young children. We fed them their soup, sometimes helping spoon it into their mouth when they fussed. I washed their clothes, including their cloth nappies. We'd also help bathe them. I loved hearing their infectious giggles when splashed with water, especially Gabi's. I wrapped her up with as much love as possible, giving her hugs, singing silly songs with her and the other little children, playing games of hide and seek. One of my favourite things was to take turns putting her and her new friends on my knee and bouncing them along to a classic German children's song most of us knew from home about a horseman's exceedingly dramatic long fall from his horse:

Hoppe hoppe Reiter

'Hop hop goes the rider,' I'd begin, bouncing them to squeals of laughter.

Wenn er fällt, dann schreit er

'When he falls he screams.'

More giggles ensued until we worked our way to the crescendo when the rider falls into the swamp and I'd tip the child forward with the words they were waiting for every time:

Macht der Reiter plumps!

'The rider makes a thump!'

'Again, again!' they demanded, their voices bouncing off the floorboards of the barracks.

Papa and I continued to write to Mrs Goudsmit for her help and to some other friends we were still in touch with, asking for supplies. She sent us some rhubarb and carrots, which were a relief from the monotony of the camp food. Papa thanked her for her kindness: 'Here, we particularly appreciate anything fresh, as well as anything that cleanses the throat, because we constantly have colds and sniffles.' He asked for a pair of simple enamel mugs with handles for himself and a small cooking pot for me because I could occasionally cook or warm a little something on the small orphanage stove. Papa also asked if she would be able to send 'a fairly deep enamel bowl', as, contrary to the advice I had received on my first morning, he had given his away, and only had a small plate.

Also among the people we were grateful for in our new situation were the Birnbaums. I saw them as real-life angels. At the orphanage they were always close by, helping, organising, tucking another child into bed. And behind the scenes, the couple were consumed by doing everything they could to protect their charges from the ever-looming threat of being deported east. I learned later they had different tactics, like commissioning forgeries of baptism certificates or sometimes even claiming a child was the illegitimate son or daughter of a German soldier. Like other 'old timers' of Westerbork, they had their own small wooden house. Because Mr Birnbaum and my father were friends from Berlin, they would sometimes invite us to their home for Shabbat dinner. I closed my eyes and sang along as Mrs Birnbaum blessed the Shabbat candles. 'Sha-bbat Sha-lom,' Mr Birnbaum's sing-song voice would ring out after the reciting of the ritual blessings.

'God will prevail and protect us in these days just as He has throughout time,' Mr Birnbaum said.

Papa and Opa chimed in, citing Biblical passages and commentaries about previous generations persevering through trials and hardship. Then, sitting around their snug table, singing *nigunim*, religious songs sung in groups, we'd enjoy Mrs Birnbaum's masterful ways of stretching out the limited food supplies.

'I love the vegetable soup,' I exclaimed, savouring its rich flavour.

'It's thanks to a powder she procures,' her husband said with a wink.

Mrs Birnbaum also transformed pieces of bread and small amounts of sugar into a type of cake. The first Shabbat dinner at their home I felt warm and contented. For a moment, it almost felt like being back home.

In the middle of the night, soon after we arrived in Westerbork, I awoke in the pitch-black darkness of the barracks to the sounds of whimpering and low moans. I scrunched down in my bunk and covered my head with my blanket, trying to ignore it, hoping it was just one of the children having a bad dream. But through my sleepy fog, I quickly realised that the sounds were coming from Gabi. I rushed down from my bunk to hers, just below.

'Shh, shh, Gigi,' I murmured. 'Go back to sleep, I'm here.'

But she wriggled away and started to cry. Her crying wouldn't stop no matter how much I tried to soothe her. I worried she was going to wake up the other children. It felt like hours till she finally dozed off a little bit while I lay at the foot of her bed.

By the time morning light started to creep across the wooden floor, she had started crying again. I could now see that she kept touching her ears, pulling at them. She screamed when I tried to get near her. Remembering Mama's procedure when I was sick, I touched her forehead. It felt like fire. *Oh no, she has a fever too*, I thought. I instantly rushed over to one of the other older girls just waking up nearby and asked her to fetch Mrs Birnbaum.

'Poor thing,' Mrs Birnbaum said, arriving minutes later and kneeling down next to Gabi's bunk. 'Let's get her to the infirmary.'

I hoisted Gabi's tiny frame out of the blankets and put her over my shoulder. With Mrs Birnbaum, I rushed her over to the hospital barracks, about a ten-minute walk away. Once there, I sat with Gabi while a nurse and doctor examined her. My father and grandparents were summoned and we were soon all gathered around her bed. She looked so wan and small; it seemed as if the bed might swallow her up. There was nothing much we could do. We just had to wait and pray that the fever would break soon.

Papa wrote to Mrs Goudsmit, reporting that Gigi had a 39-degree fever and was feeling quite miserable.

Today the little mouse was sent directly to the hospital, where we just visited her this evening. It seems to be bronchitis and we will have to wait and see how it develops. In any case, she is now being cared for properly, while the orphanage is not equipped for medical care at all. Hopefully, she will soon get back to normal. She is quite worn out and listless; no longer the little wild thing you know. When we say to her:

'When you get well again, you can play in the sand,' she says:
'At Schorschi's?'

Four days later, Gigi's fever hadn't broken. And now Oma was also in the hospital with a high fever and what appeared to be the flu. I felt desperate. How could they get well in a place like this?

The doctors and nurses were all fellow Jewish detainees. Soon, one of the doctors, a renowned ear, nose and throat specialist, diagnosed Gabi as having a serious ear infection. Her best hope for recovery, he told us, was an operation. Papa told me that Gabi would have to have an operation here in the hospital barracks.

'Here? But this isn't even a real hospital,' I protested. 'What if the operation does not go well?'

Papa tried to calm me down. 'Hanneli, I know it feels scary but the doctor is a specialist and this is what he says Gabi needs. Her infection is so acute, medicine alone cannot treat it. He told me ear infections among children here are common because of the wet, cool climate. The operation is something he's done many times before. He'll create a small incision inside her ears, in the eardrum, and that will allow the excess fluid to drain. Without this operation, things will be very dangerous for Gigi. It will take time, but our little girl will recover,' he said. 'You'll see.'

She seemed so fragile as the doctors and nurses took her behind a curtain for the surgery. I don't think the procedure can have taken long but it felt like forever till we were able to see her again. I was startled to see her head almost entirely swallowed up by a white bandage. It was wrapped around her ears and stretched all the way around her head. Pus still seeped through. But the doctors reassured us that was part of the healing process. Still, they cautioned us, she was quite ill. Recovery would take time.

Once awake, Gabi stared up at us with her large brown eyes. Her skin was pale; her fever was still raging. We pressed cool compresses on her forehead and sang her lullabies. All I wanted to do was hold her and make her feel better with kisses to her forehead.

We had heard of deaths of babies and young children who had ear infections and other ailments, like respiratory infections, at Westerbork. Lots of people got sick. For all of us at the camp, the constant struggle was to remain healthy. Sanne and her father were both also bedridden with different ailments at the time. We had no choice but to accept it as part of camp life, just like the blazingly hot sun, sandstorms or heavy rains.

Every day, Papa, Opa and I clustered by Gabi's bedside. Oma thankfully recovered from the flu and could soon join us. Gabi didn't want to eat, even though she desperately needed to regain her strength. We all took turns trying to coax her into drinking broth and eating porridge. It wasn't easy. She was given blood transfusions and improved slightly as time went on but full recovery seemed elusive. We tried to cheer her up as much as possible with storytelling, songs and little games. I'd look up from tickling her and catch my father's gaze, looking at us with wistfulness, and I knew, without him saying, he was thinking of Mama.

*   *   *

Nicknames for things abounded at Westerbork. The *Joodse Ordedienst* were the Jewish police of Westerbork, 'the ODs', who went, probably often at gunpoint, to assist the Germans with deportations. They were loathed by us in the camp for doing their dirty work and dubbed 'the Jewish SS'. An open grassy knoll where people gathered in their free time was called, with heavy irony, the beaches of

Westerbork. And the main road, either sand-clogged or more often a muddy thoroughfare because of the near-constant rains and storming in that part of the country, was dubbed the *Boulevard des Misères*, the Boulevard of Misery. It cut through the centre of Westerbork and on Tuesday mornings at 7am it took on the spectre of the Valley of Death. That was when the ODs would go barrack to barrack, collecting people whose names had been called out the night before in the men's and women's quarters, usually by one of the Jewish leaders within the camp, for the next transport east. Those lists were compiled by the SS and reviewed by the camp's Jewish Council. Mondays felt like agony as rumours flew around about whose names would appear on the dreaded list.

As I was in the orphanage, I did not hear the names being called. I had to wait for someone to tell me. Sanne and other friends described the screams that would follow and panic-stricken mothers falling to their knees and wailing. Children cried; the faces of teenaged boys and men were frozen in horror at hearing their names. Those who were spared would sometimes burst into tears themselves, the tension was so thick; others broke out in spontaneous dance, knowing that for one more week at least they had been spared.

On Monday mornings, we saw and heard the trains arrive, a long line of wooden cattle cars, lurking there like a predator in wait. My father constantly reassured me that we would be OK because of our protected status as potential exchange prisoners, and my grandfather was among those on the camp's Jewish Council, but my heart still pounded all day long on Mondays.

Then, on Tuesday mornings, I watched as the ODs lined the Boulevard des Misères, trying to block those who approached for a closer look or perhaps to say goodbye to a loved one. I noticed it was almost always the same configuration, the ODs marching people in rows of three. Each prisoner had a bag for bread slung over one shoulder and a rolled-up blanket on the other. I studied their faces while my heart silently broke for them. There were the stoic ones, facing ahead or looking down. Other faces looked like crumpled rags, lips trembling, tears falling between sobs. I found it especially hard to see the older people staggering under the weight of their bags as they trod the bumpy ground and tried to avoid stepping into the puddles.

Once at the train, those being sent east were counted. The Green Police, the Nazi German police, had to make sure the number of those boarding the battered cattle cars was the same as the number on the lists. When someone tried to back off or resist in any way they were pushed, kicked or beaten by one of the Green Police or even the ODs. Then they were all forced onto the train, the men and women together with children, the old, the weak, the infirm, the disabled. How cruel, how wrong. How were these young children, the babies, the elderly, those in wheelchairs going to be able to work at a labour camp? I heard that just before they boarded, they were forced to give up whatever valuables they might still have – a silver watch given to them by a beloved grandfather, or cash, maybe jewellery. Everything taken from them, I thought. I was supposed to be scrubbing toilets those Tuesday mornings, like every morning, but, like the others who came, I felt drawn to the train tracks, to witness, to say a silent goodbye.

After the final checks, the hoisting of people and rucksacks and bedrolls onto the hay-scattered train car floors, the doors were slid shut – and then bolted – by one of the Green Police. At about 11am, the train whistle blew, its shriek a stand-in for our own horror. The damp, bone-chilling winds swept over us but the real chill was from within. A feeling of emptiness hung in the air. Those trains swallowed up 1,000 people whole each Tuesday.

'We all live by the week here; it starts Tuesday morning and ends Tuesday morning: the minute the train pulls out,' wrote Jacques Presser after the war in his fictional account of Westerbork in a book called *The Night of the Girondists*. He was the history teacher who fled my classroom the morning his wife had been arrested.

When I first arrived, I was shocked by the role of the ODs on these heart-crushing Tuesday mornings. I asked Papa what he thought.

'The Germans have put us Jews in impossible situations, choices no human should ever be forced to make,' he said. 'It is not for us to judge.'

In the orphanage, we all knew the story of a boy named Fred Speigel. A few months before I arrived with my family, he was put on one of those Tuesday-morning trains. In the thick of the crowd and noise he panicked. 'I don't want to go onto this train,' he howled. When his cousin Alfred heard him, he too started screaming. An SS guard heard the commotion and asked a Dutch policeman what was going on. The policeman told him, 'The children are afraid and don't want to go on the train.' The SS officer gave a command to remove them from the train and the OD who, minutes before, had been shoving the screaming pair onto the train plucked the two boys off it.

It was the only story I heard of anyone being rescued from the train. But every week I held out hope that I'd hear more like it.

Mondays and Tuesdays were crushing in their brutality, but in the time between the deportations, the feeling of resilience among the people in Westerbork was palpable. My grandfather gave lectures to the youth about Zionism and his memories of working shoulder-to-shoulder with Theodor Herzl. A powerful orator, he'd regale them with stories of the early days launching the Zionist movement and paint enticing images of life in Eretz Yisrael, the Land of Israel. He would describe a place where young Jewish men and women worked the land by day and danced around campfires by night as they worked to build a utopian society, one that would be a safe haven for Jews from around the world.

Some nights there were soccer games. The 'synagogue', a large tent, was full of worshippers on Friday nights and Saturday mornings for Sabbath services, which I attended with my father and grandparents. A well-known cantor led them, along with Rosh Hashanah and Yom Kippur services. There were concerts and sometimes cabaret shows, featuring some of the biggest names in German and Dutch cabaret. The Jewish actors and singers rehearsed intensely and put on splashy, colourful shows with specially bought costumes under bright lights. They hoped their participation would save them from deportation, but they too were eventually put on trains. The SS would sit in the front rows and Jewish inmates further back.

Westerbork seemed to be full of people I knew from Amsterdam; about half of my class was there. Sanne's grandmother, a cheerful woman whom we all liked, had already been there for a few weeks by the time we arrived. Mrs Ledermann was assigned to work in the barrack with pregnant women, new mothers and their babies. She liked the work and told us she found it fulfilling, despite being hard. She had to wash the floors, do all the laundry, help bathe the babies and calm down the pregnant women, who were of course terrified to give birth in Westerbork, so far from their own homes or a real hospital.

Sanne's father, Mr Ledermann, was stuck sorting legumes eight hours a day. When he was not working, he decided to take on a new course of study: Hebrew.

Barbara, who was living in Amsterdam with her false papers, sent the family lots of packages using cover names. Even so, it must have been risky for her to mail packages to Westerbork at all. She sent wonderful things, like sweets and cakes, breads, fruit, fresh beans and fruit, but also supplies we needed, like bandages for infected mosquito bites or new shoes for Sanne, who was in the midst of a growth spurt and, a couple months into arriving at Westerbork, had already outgrown hers. We were delighted when a knitted dress arrived for Gabi from Barbara. She wore it all the time, even though she was still at the hospital barracks, and everyone loved it.

We learned over time what to ask for from our people on the 'outside': rye bread or Swedish bread, because it was less likely to go mouldy, tea strainers, honey cakes, honey, jam, warm clothes – we already needed more warm clothes and it was only the beginning of autumn – and even fuel tablets for cooking on an open fire. Mrs Goudsmit continued to be a reliable sender of both the necessary and the delightful. She sent a gift package of biscuits and other goodies for Gabi's birthday in October, and I was thrilled when she sent me a biography of Florence Nightingale, which I read and reread many times, as it was the only book I had.

It felt wonderful when we got letters. Sanne and I would re-read the letters we received – hers from Barbara and mine from Mrs Goudsmit – over and over. We were starved for word from the outside world and no small detail was too mundane for us to hear. Sanne, who was a very affectionate friend and sister, wrote Barbara letters constantly, sending her kisses in her send-offs 'enough to last you for the next two weeks'.

For those around us, we only had the gift of our company, which was thoroughly appreciated. On 10 October, Sanne turned 14. A few of us girlfriends came together to celebrate over ersatz coffee in our enamel mugs and a cake that Barbara had sent by mail. We looked at one another and burst into a fit of giggles when her father told her the one gift he had for her was a kiss.

Chapter 10

Limbo

By November, the biting, damp winds blowing across the scrubby marshlands of Westerbork had intensified and the nights were especially cold. My hands felt like ice when I scrubbed the toilets. I'd look down at them and was stunned to see how red and raw they were. Sometimes I would still retch from the stench. But I didn't complain. I was grateful for the assignment as long as it continued to mean more time to talk to Papa, which, for now, it did. I always felt so much better in his presence.

'Hanneli, my sweet,' he'd say. Like many of my friends' parents, he was not overly demonstrative in his affection. There were not many hugs or flowery verbal declarations of what I meant to him. But I always felt his love. It was strong, solid. After my mother died, he relied on me to help him with Gabi, which I know he appreciated. I think in those months, something shifted. We had always been close but now we were fellow survivors of the sudden and tragic loss of Mama. And we were trying to find our way through her gaping absence in a time of great uncertainty and fear. We didn't speak of it out loud, but I felt our partnership; I relied on him, but he relied on me too. And we both very much leaned on the support and love we had for and from Oma and Opa.

Despite this, I knew Papa was worried about my grandfather, and so was I. Opa's heart had been bothering him in recent weeks. He had what he called 'heart spasms' that were keeping him in bed sometimes for half the day. This was totally unlike the active Opa I knew. He thrived in the company of others and was a devoted friend to many. He was 67 but, aside from needing a cane for longer walks, I always saw him as quite fit.

As difficult as it was for Papa and me to adjust to living behind barbed wire in this strange state of limbo, with the incongruous mix of cabarets and concerts, physical labour, the terror of living between Tuesdays, raising our voices to God in prayer as a community, the lack of privacy and barracks that smelled like sweat and mould, I started thinking how it must be even harder for Oma and Opa. Most of their lives had been so entirely different from this upside-down reality. Opa had litigated high-profile cases in courts all over Germany; they'd had a rich social circle in Berlin and enjoyed the status of being pillars of the community. The abrupt, unplanned move to Amsterdam was hard on them both but the indignity of being deported by gunpoint and herded into cattle cars to be deposited in this forgotten outpost must have been particularly disorienting – and heartbreaking – for them.

'One day the Germans will return to their senses, they have to,' Oma would repeat daily when we were sitting around Gabi's bedside in the hospital. It had been months now and her ears had still not healed. It was Oma's mantra and Opa always nodded in agreement, still the picture of a gentleman lawyer in his tailored suit, even if he had to dust off the sand and dirt. Though I started to notice how he'd sometimes look away, a pained expression on his face. I know he felt betrayed by the Germany he knew. I don't think he was waiting for the Germans to come around any longer.

I was feeling the frustration of time passing. When we arrived, it was June. I had really hoped that somehow this would all be over by now and we'd be back at school for the new academic year. Sanne and I fretted together about how far behind we'd be once we finally returned to our studies. We both took classes with teachers in small groups of about eight to ten children our age a few times a week. They were good teachers and I enjoyed learning, but it was not school.

I came to adore the children at the orphanage but I had a favourite: a slight girl with long dark hair named Sarah Eva. She was seven years old and there with her brother. I imagined her parents putting their children in hiding in a farmhouse in the Dutch countryside, thinking they'd be safer this way, living far from neighbours who could have been tipped off by their cries or the sound of their laughter and turned them in. I assumed their parents were still safely underground because they had not come through Westerbork. I liked to imagine Sarah Eva and her brother reuniting with them when this madness ended. Until then, I thought, I'll help watch out for them, especially Sarah Eva, who slept in my bunk. In the mornings, I'd plait her dark brown hair. I tucked her in every night with a kiss. During the day, when I was in the orphanage, she'd follow me around and tug on my skirt. It was our game because she knew that when she did, I'd turn around and try to catch her. 'Hanneli, here I am!' she'd giggle and dash behind a bunk. I loved the sound of her laugh. It was pure and clear, like bells ringing. Watching her play reminded me of Anne and I at her age, chasing our hoops in Merwedeplein Square, free and unburdened. It also took away some of the pang of missing Gabi while she was being cared for by the nurses.

10 November was a Wednesday. We were still trying to shake off the crushing sadness following the departure of another train the previous day. To distract myself, I initiated a game of hide and seek with Sarah Eva and a few other children. We hadn't been playing long when I saw Mrs Birnbaum striding purposefully towards me. I noticed the change in her body language – this wasn't her usual cheerful, bouncy gait.

'Hanneli, I need to talk to you,' she said. My heart froze. Was it Gabi? Was Gabi OK? 'Your grandfather,' she told me. 'He had heart pains. He's at the hospital barracks.'

I ran all the way there. I found Oma and Papa already by his bed. Oma was holding his hand. There was no colour in his face. Doctors were trying to resuscitate him but he appeared to be unconscious. Realising that I, a child, was there watching, a nurse whisked me out. She led me to a chair on the other side of the barracks. A few minutes later, Papa found me. As soon as I saw his downcast eyes, his defeated, slow steps towards me, I knew the news was not good. I burst into tears.

'He loved you so much, Hanneli,' Papa said, putting his arm around me. 'His heart was weak, the stress too great.'

Later, standing with Oma, who found it hard to even speak, I was in shock. I could not help but note how our small family was shrinking. Just a year ago, we were six. Now it was just the four of us. And Gabi was still in hospital.

The group of young Zionists whom Opa had given lectures to and befriended were so saddened by his death that they insisted they escort his bier to the crematorium. From there, his ashes were sent to the Jewish cemetery where my mother had been buried just 13 months earlier. A memorial service for him was quickly arranged at Barrack 84, where he had spent the final months of his life. I stood between Oma and Papa as his fellow barrack-dwellers and friends, including prominent rabbis and intellectuals, paid tribute to him. Among them was Dr Albert Lewkowitz, who had eulogised my mother a year before. Several prayers were sung, most hauntingly *El Malei Rachamim* ('God is full of compassion'), a Jewish prayer for the dead traditionally sung at funerals. Mendel Rokach, the former cantor of Rotterdam, a man in his late thirties with greying hair and a goatee, chanted the prayer in his rich, full voice. His singing reverberated against the bunk beds and wooden floors, filling this unlikely space with a sense of holiness. I squeezed Oma's hand. In place of Opa's own son, Uncle Hans, far away in Switzerland, my father stepped in to recite the Kaddish, the mourner's prayer. It gave us some peace knowing Opa's ashes had been sent to Amsterdam, to be put in the cemetery where my mother was buried.

Oma wrote to Edith, the good-hearted Czech refugee dentist Uncle Hans had become engaged to recently, asking her to relay the shocking news to their son that his father had died: 'I ask you in your usual loving and tactical manner to prepare him for the terrible news that I must report to you.'

Receiving the news, Uncle Hans then relayed it to Aunt Eugenie in Leeds by telegram: 'Our good Alli died after short heartcramp 10 November afternoon, poor Theschen wrote.' (Alli was a family nickname for my grandfather, Alfred. Theschen being a family nickname for Oma.)

Eugenie and her husband cabled back: 'Our thoughts go out to Westerbork only comfort if any possible Alli no longer suffering no deportation embrace poor lonely Theschen children Hans.'

Two days after his memorial service, while we were still trying to digest that Opa was gone, another dreaded Monday arrived. The camp had become extremely crowded and we heard that 2,500 Jews were supposed to be deported the following day – over twice as many as were usually sent. But of the approximately 25,000 people at the camp at this time, most had some kind of exemption. Albert Konrad Gemmeker, the SS Commander of Westerbork, who had a reputation for at least appearing humane (by the standards of a concentration camp), felt the pressure to meet his deportee quota. So he made the decision to cancel all but two of the approximately 40 so-called Palestine lists – registers of people like us who had Palestine certificates and thereby were eligible to be exchanged for German prisoners of war held by the British.

My father, knowing I'd be worried about our situation, came to find me. He assured me that our family was on one of the two Palestine lists that had not been cancelled. Our protected status remained intact.

'But what about the Ledermanns?' I asked. They were on a list too.

'I just don't know,' he said, looking smaller and sadder than I'd ever seen him.

I gave my father a quick hug and then rushed off.

It seemed we would be safe for now but there was other terrible news to come. Mr Birnbaum had gone to great lengths to spare the orphanage children, successfully advocating to have them listed on those Palestine exchange lists. It had worked so far but now Gemmeker would not be moved; the orphans would go. Birnbaum's frantic pleas, citing the children's young ages – some being sent east were just toddlers – were rejected.

Word travelled back to the orphanage barracks that most of the orphans would be put on the train the following morning. I could hardly comprehend the news. We had become one big family in my time there. I felt dizzy; I worried I might even throw up. I steadied myself by leaning on one of the bunks. How could they take away these innocent children? What had they done to anyone? What meaningful work could they even do at a labour camp? I thought about their poor, brave mothers and fathers who made the ultimate sacrifice of handing them to other people to watch over them in hiding. What an excruciating decision and selfless act that was. I could only imagine the agony of those partings and every moment they had endured apart since. I had to find Sarah Eva. Luckily, she seemed oblivious to the news swirling around Westerbork and was playing a game of cards with a friend. I watched them for a while, preferring not to intrude on this moment of innocence. I pushed away tears that had started spilling down my cheeks. Then I saw Mrs Birnbaum approaching me. I could tell she too was trying not to cry.

In a flat but calm voice, she said, 'Hanneli, we need your help to start making packages with sandwiches and sweaters for the children to take with them.'

'Of course,' I said. I took a deep breath and turned to follow her. We wanted to at least be able to help keep the children warm and fed on their journey. I was grateful to have something practical to do.

My next assignment, together with a few others, was packing up each child. I felt like I was in a trance, sitting on the floor folding shirts, pants, dresses, tiny socks and the occasional lace hair ribbon into rucksacks. The children knew they were going on a trip the next morning by train; some were fearful and asked questions. Some hung on my back as I packed their bags and played with my hair. One or two of the little ones tried to plop themselves into my lap. The Birnbaums had created such a stable, warm atmosphere. Now they'd be heading into the unknown. I tried to focus on my immediate mission.

'Don't think. Just keep packing,' I told myself.

Later that night, a steady rain fell. After dinner together in the dining-hall barracks, Mr and Mrs Birnbaum asked all 200 of the children of the orphanage to stand up and come together. They introduced Rabbi Vorst, who had come to bless them before tomorrow's journey. I watched as the 200 children gathered as a mass in front of the rabbi, a man of about 40 with a beard. For a moment, it reminded me of times the rabbi at our synagogue in Amsterdam would call the children up to the pulpit to sing one of the closing prayers together. I scanned their faces – a little girl with red hair and freckles holding the hand of one of the bigger girls, a boy with dimples who was known as one of the best soccer players in the orphanage. I searched for Sarah Eva. I couldn't find her, she was so small, until she spotted me and smiled and gave me a little wave.

Rabbi Vorst asked if everyone was ready for a very special blessing.

'This is a blessing of comfort, of peace, of feeling connected to God,' he told the children. 'Come closer, come closer.'

He unfurled his prayer shawl made of spun wool, lined with black stripes, and stretched it out as wide as possible, holding it over the heads of the children gathered underneath. I noticed his voice cracked as he blessed them, reciting in Hebrew:

May God bless you and keep you.
May God shine light on you and be gracious to you.
May God turn towards you and grant you peace.

I felt shivers go up my spine.

The next morning, at 7am, several ODs in dark wool cloaks appeared at the orphanage to take the children to the waiting train. They seemed ghoulish and menacing, doing the Germans' dirty work. Accompanying the children were teachers who had bravely volunteered to go on the train with them, so they would not be alone. I and the few other children not being deported, including the Birnbaums, walked as far as we were allowed to go with the children down the Boulevard des Misères. It was a cold morning and the path was thick with mud from the previous night's rain. I hoisted one of the toddlers into my arms and carried his bag. I could hear singing ahead of us as we joined the river of people trudging forward towards the train. Some were singing patriotic Dutch songs, others the *Shema*, the Hebrew prayer known by most Jews.

Would God hear our prayer? I walked as if in a trance, barely noticing the people standing outside their barracks lining the track, taking their last look at this march of unlucky ones.

An SS officer with a rifle jolted me out of my stupor as we approached the platform, shouting, 'From this point, only those boarding the trains can pass.'

I gently handed the little boy I was carrying and his bag to one of the teachers going on the transport. Sarah Eva was next to me, her dark plaits hanging down from under a wool hat. I leaned down to give her a kiss on her forehead, just as I had every night when I tucked her in.

'May God watch over you, sweet girl,' I whispered.

I kept my eyes locked on her as she walked ahead until she was swallowed up in the crush of people being loaded onto the trains. Our journey from Amsterdam had been hot and uncomfortable, but it was only a few hours. Getting to Poland could take days, I thought. I stood there for a while, my feet anchored in the icy mud. But at some point, more guards came and pushed me back.

Many friends and acquaintances were also swept up in that transport. I found out later that Sanne and her parents were among them. We did not even get a chance to say goodbye. I wonder what we would have even said. Sanne was always so bright and cheerful. I thought about her sweet nature, the beautiful words she put together in her poems. I could barely comprehend it. What if she had stayed with Barbara and also gone underground?

Her mother was able to write a farewell postcard to Barbara and other relatives. Like all those being sent east, they were encouraged to write to loved ones by the SS commanders of the camp. Much later, I was able to read the words that Mrs Ledermann wrote on a postcard that rainy Tuesday morning, 16 November 1943:

> *My loved ones, we are together ... on our first journey in a long time ...*
>
> *Don't be sorrowful for us, we have good hopes and it would only hurt us if you were sad. We want to see each other again ...*
>
> *My Barbel child, take care. Your last parcels still delicious. We've got porridge with us. Also Dad's bathrobe, the wool and everything you sent to Granny.*
>
> *Friendly people here. All still without certificates. We're going. Bye Darlings.*
>
> *All the love, all the best. Bye.*

I entered the barracks of the orphanage, now silent and emptied of its children. In the distance, I heard the shrill cry of the train whistle. I collapsed onto my bunk. Apart from the day we lost Mama, this was the saddest day of my life. I felt more alone than ever. My heart ached. My whole body ached as I rocked myself back and forth in the crushing silence. It had never been a quiet place. Even at night, someone was always stirring, shifting in their bunk, coughing or whimpering in their sleep for the mothers and fathers they missed. I felt the absence of wide-eyed, sweet Sarah Eva and the other children. How could absence feel so present? I felt the loss of Sanne and her family and imagined them trying to find a place to sit on the train without being trodden on. I was confounded by the power of a name on a typed list that could determine who stayed on Dutch soil and who was forced to undertake that dreaded journey.

If the Ledermanns were on that train, so might my family and I have been – we could have been among those hoisted onto one of those airless cattle cars, hurtling into the unknown. We were all so different but to the Germans we were all the same, no matter whether we were Orthodox, secular, baptised, Zionist, socialist, Dutch, stateless former German citizens, potato sellers, diamond merchants, doctors, teachers, soccer players, architects, shopkeepers, elderly, children, toddlers, newborns. To Hitler and his supporters, we were the enemy. The Jewish enemy. I could not understand why this was happening – what had we Jews done? Why were we being punished? As far as I could tell, our only sin was being Jewish.

No one could say what exactly happened at these work camps but we knew it was nothing good. When I tried to imagine what kind of 'work' people might do there in that bleak, faraway place, my only reference point was what I saw at Westerbork, where people were assigned to work details doing everything from operating machinery and sewing to making brooms, toiling in the kitchen and harvesting potatoes. Perhaps, I thought and hoped, it was just more of the same there. But to what end? I knew Hitler railed against the Jews, called us vermin and had declared 'war' on us, but what was the point of all this misery? How would sending whole families to labour camps accomplish anything?

It was becoming bitterly cold here, and with winter approaching I could only imagine how frigid it might be in Poland. Even here I felt like I could never get warm enough but further east there was ice and snow for months. How would they handle that bitter weather? I hoped Sanne and Sarah Eva, and Ilse and Alfred and our friends who had been there for so long already, had found a way to stay warm enough. I hoped they were keeping healthy. Just thinking of them I began to shiver. I was grateful that at least Anne was snug and safe in Switzerland.

*　*　*

The weeks passed. Time was on a terrible loop. I watched more and more Tuesday trains leave. Every time it felt excruciating. Bearing witness is its own form of torture.

I was still spending hours, together with my father, trying to coax Gabi into eating a bit of broth, some mashed potatoes. Anything we could get her to swallow. Her ears were still infected. I reread the biography of Florence Nightingale that Mrs Goudsmit had sent me over and over and I soon knew its pages by heart. I thought about all the effort and expertise and care it took to help someone ill. The care I read about in the book and witnessed at the hospital was impossible to reconcile with the scenes I saw each week of people trudging down the Boulevard des Misères.

There wasn't much we could do but we tried to keep ourselves healthy. Diseases like tuberculosis, measles, diphtheria, yellow fever, whooping cough and scarlet fever were common at Westerbork. It was hard to avoid lice. Illness was a constant fear, even if being in quarantine was one way some managed to delay being transported. I also heard of suicide attempts that usually took place on Monday nights by desperate people whose names were on the transport list. I knew of the psychiatric ward in Barrack 3 where those who attempted suicide but did not succeed were sent to recover.

Soon the orphanage was filling up again with new children. There were new boys and girls to welcome and help care for, which I did. But I could not forget Sarah Eva and the other children, and their absence loomed large.

Young adults at the camp, in their late teens and twenties, were part of youth groups who tried to look out for us children, all of us hungry for structure and distraction. They set up a children's choir, soccer games and other sports events, lessons about everything from Bible stories and upcoming holidays to famous writers. They reminded us we were not the subhumans the Germans made us out to be; we had a rich heritage to celebrate and explore. They did all this even though their own ranks were constantly being depleted by deportations.

Ahead of the holiday of Hanukkah in December, the youth counsellors made small presents for the younger children and gathered us together to tell us the Hanukkah story. The Syrian Greeks were led by a king named Antiochus IV, they explained to their young and eager audience. He liked to call himself Epiphanes, which means 'Divinity-Made-Manifest'. Some of the Jews of the time called him 'the madman'. He was determined to destroy Judaism as part of his overall plan to enforce Greek culture. He outlawed observing the Sabbath, religious study, obeying Jewish dietary laws and circumcision. Jews who resisted were killed. Syrian troops put up statues of their gods in Jerusalem and broke down the doors of the temple with axes; they poured pig's blood over the holy texts and set them on fire. The miracle of Hanukkah, when one day's worth of oil in the temple in Jerusalem lasted eight days and eight nights, helped our people rededicate the holy temple in Jerusalem after it was desecrated. It's a key part of the story of our ancestors, they told us, whose small and mighty band of soldiers called the Maccabees managed to beat the Syrian Greeks in battle against all odds. Hanukkah means 'dedication' in Hebrew.

'Do you know how we remind ourselves to rededicate ourselves to our community and to our own strength?' one of the counsellors asked.

'By lighting the menorah!' some of the younger children shouted out in reply.

'And what do we say?'

'A great miracle happened there!' the children shouted back, repeating what they had learned.

On the seventh night of Hanukkah, a party was held. A song was written for the occasion by Clara Asscher-Pinkhof, the children's author I loved so much, and sung by Susanne, the 13-year-old daughter of Hans Kreig, a well-respected composer who directed the children's choir and taught music and singing at Westerbork. He was known for carrying his guitar around and singing to help boost morale. A Schiller play was also adapted and put on for us. That night, all of us children gathered close to the menorah, some of us in hats and coats with the yellow Jewish star visible, as a young man named Leo Blumensohn, one of the counsellors, lit the candles, one by one.

Like the other children, I was mesmerised by the fire, the light in the darkness, both in its physical sense and as a spiritual message. It was also the first time I could remember marking Hanukkah outside of our apartment in Amsterdam. At home, we'd put the menorah in the front bay window, so others could see its glow. Just like at home, together we said the prayers after the menorah was lit: 'We kindle these sacred lights in remembrance of Thy wonders, miracles and salvations.'

All this talk of miracles made us yearn for our own.

* * *

The next month, January, Papa told me he had good news: 'We are being sent to Bergen-Belsen soon, in Germany. It's an "ideal camp", with good conditions.'

'An ideal camp?' I asked. 'What does that mean?'

Papa said he and others had been told by officials at Westerbork that we would be treated well and have good housing and food. This was not being 'sent east' to a labour camp, this was a good place to wait out whatever time we had left before being exchanged. 'They are going to transport us on proper trains, real trains, don't worry,' he said, trying to reassure me. 'It's a camp for prisoners of war, where we will be held until we are exchanged for British prisoners of war.'

We had now been in Westerbork for seven months. Even though I was ready to put Westerbork behind me, I was very apprehensive to leave Holland. I'd seen people go to great lengths to try to avoid the Tuesday deportations. But Papa's audible relief and excitement was reassuring. We had a direction. We were going to an 'ideal camp'.

Gabi was still in the hospital, but Papa was hopeful she'd recover in better conditions.

It was Monday, 14 February 1944 when I heard our names called. Hans Goslar, Hannah Elisabeth Goslar, Rachel Gabrielle Ida Goslar, Therese Klee. Even though I had been waiting for it, I felt sick to my stomach when the Jewish camp policeman said our names, reading from the list of those who would be sent east in the morning. Despite my father's reassurances, I was still terrified. That beast of the Tuesday-morning train would be waiting for us this time.

Chapter 11

Bergen-Belsen

I awoke before dawn, too anxious to sleep. Today it was our turn to walk down the Boulevard des Misères, the frigid wind in my face, my hand holding the burgundy-coloured suitcase, one of my last material vestiges of home. I thought about how I would soon be crossing through the high barbed-wire fences that encircled us, past the towers and searchlights, across the moat filled with water. Westerbork had been our 'home', if you could call it that, for eight months, and I felt a pang of not exactly nostalgia but longing for the camaraderie and the relative security I had found there, our feet still in Holland, not in the unfathomable 'east'. But we had no choice. All I could do was hope we were going to a well-kept place where we'd have food and could stay healthy, before being exchanged.

When my father picked Gabi up from the hospital barracks, I looked in dismay at the pus-stained bandages wrapped around her ears. The nurses had done their best to keep them clean, though all medical supplies were scarce. They gave off a faint, sickly smell. The walk through the camp felt long. But once we reached the train, we were quickly plunged into the scenes of commotion I had previously witnessed only from afar. Police and Jewish police shouting and herding us, parents holding crying children, people balancing bedrolls and suitcases. We climbed onto one of the third-class rail cars (that they were not cattle cars was seen as a good sign) and I saw the rows of hard wooden seats, the window shades pulled low to block our view. It was almost as cold inside the train as it was outside and I nuzzled close to Gabi, grateful for her warmth. I don't remember much talking between us or others on the train. Though it was crammed with people, the carriage was blanketed by anxious silence.

Each one of us on that train was on our way to what we understood to be a 'privileged exchange camp' because we had the right papers, whether we were on the Palestine list or had South American passports, or other foreign passports or a connection to a foreign country, like the so-called 'Diamond Group' – diamond industry workers and their families. Among us were also those who had some kind of mixed Jewish and non-Jewish heritage. Gabi and I were listed on my father's Paraguayan passport; at the bottom of the document were three photos, one of each of us. Our Palestine certificate was an International Red Cross document from Geneva and certified: 'Mr Hans Goslar and his family have been registered on the veteran Zionist list for immigration into Palestine and exchange.' These flimsy pieces of bureaucracy had delayed our deportation from Amsterdam and helped us remain longer at Westerbork than many others. They now seemed to be granting us passage to somewhere it was claimed we would be treated well. But when would they give us back our freedom?

Patrolling the train were SS guards who we were not accustomed to seeing at Westerbork. They looked fearsome to me, with their young but hardened faces. One of them shouted out, 'If anyone throws anything out of the window, I'll shoot you.' I could hear my heart pounding. I looked at my father, who tried to silently reassure

Oma, Gabi and me with his eyes until the soldier moved on to a different part of carriage. After he left, Papa explained he was trying to scare people out of throwing notes from the train, hoping a kind Dutch or German person might find their pleas for help along the train tracks or send word on to loved ones, evading the censorship of our mail from Westerbork.

My hopes were shaken again when the Germans confiscated the jam and sausages packed for us by the Jewish-run administration in Westerbork, leaving us only the bread — and not that much of it at that. In the end, we subsisted on a few slices of bread each on the journey, which took three days, the train lurching and stopping at various points, including two overnight stops.

'I'm thirsty,' Gabi cried out early on, but there was hardly any water available. Soon we were all thirsty.

'Papa, how privileged is Bergen-Belsen going to be if even on the way there they don't give us enough food or water?' I asked my father. He tried to reassure me. 'It will be fine; the Germans need us to be in good health for exchanges. They have to answer to other countries about us.'

I thought about this as I snuck a glance of the view passing by. Snow fell as we rolled past fields and forests, the train slowly cutting across northwest Germany. The rank smell from the pus seeping into Gabi's bandages made me feel woozy. I was too cold and agitated to sleep.

* * *

I was exhausted by the time the train pulled up to the station for Bergen-Belsen at around noon, three days after we set out on our journey. We were only 40 miles north of Hanover, where my father was born. Descending onto the platform, I saw SS guards with bayoneted guns screaming at those of us not moving quickly enough. With them were German shepherds who barked and snarled. I had always been terrified of dogs, and I clung to my father's arm and held Gabi close. Oma was always right next to us.

The train station was just a platform in the middle of nowhere, not a station at the camp. The camp was five miles away and it would take the able-bodied teenagers and adults carrying their belongings at least two hours to arrive there by foot. Because Gabi was small and ill, I was put on a truck with her, along with mothers with their young children. I could hear the SS guards yelling at those who began their trek but were not walking quickly enough for their taste. They hurled curses and called them weak.

'We'll see you there,' Papa said, trying to sound cheerful as we parted ways amid the shouting and chaos. I imagined him and Oma disappearing behind us as we bumped along a dirt road through a rural village. How would I find them at the camp? There were so many people.

'Hanneli, where are we going?' Gabi asked me for what felt like the hundredth time. I had been telling her we were going somewhere good: a good, new place where we would be together and have comfortable beds and warm soup. I believed in Papa's hope and she believed in mine.

The first thing I saw as we approached the camp were grey buildings surrounded by spruce trees and large front lawns. Maybe that's where we will be housed, I thought hopefully. But then I saw a sign that said it was for the SS Totenkopf regiment. That meant the 'Regiment of the Skull'. So that was where the SS stayed. We came to a red-and-white barrier manned by SS guards armed with machine guns, their signature skull and crossbones insignia on their right collar. Once through the barrier, we climbed out of the truck under cloudy, grey skies. The first thing I noticed is that we were surrounded by rings of barbed-wire fences. Everywhere I looked there were guard towers with searchlights. I could not imagine how one could ever escape. Beyond the barbed wire, I could see towering green fir trees. Beyond the trees were snow-covered fields. The natural world appeared so tranquil, it felt sullied by the bleak horizon of massive wooden barracks.

We're in Germany now, I thought, feeling the sharp pain of what it might feel like to be forgotten by the rest of the world, far now from the seeming safety of Holland.

A group of us women and children were marched to a large, cold shower room with a cement floor.

'Undress here,' an SS guard told us. He and some other guards remained standing there, making it clear they were going to watch us remove our clothes. I hesitated but another woman nudged me along. 'Just do it. Pretend they are not here.'

But I could not pretend, I felt their eyes staring at us. While I was desperate to wash off the journey, I thought I might melt away from shame and embarrassment. I focused on Gabi, instructing her to try to keep her head out of the direct line of the shower because I was worried about her soaking her bandages.

I was relieved the water that day was warm. But soon I was shivering again, in a much colder, damp room. All we had to cover ourselves up with was a small towel as we stood in line for the doctor who checked our heads for lice.

We were then taken to what was called the Sternlager Camp, Star Camp, named after the yellow stars we wore as Jewish prisoners.

This was the touted privileged 'exchange' camp, one of several within the larger camp complex. Bergen-Belsen was cobbled together over time but was divided into three main sections by the time we arrived. There was a prisoner of war camp, where thousands of captured enemy soldiers were held, many of them Soviet; a 'residence camp' that contained various subcamps for 'exchange Jews', including ours; then a smaller 'prisoners' camp', designated for non-Jewish prisoners from across Europe.

The Germans considered us 'Schutzjuden', or 'protected Jews', and kept us away from the other prisoners as, with our passports from other countries, we were candidates for potential exchange for German servicemen captured by the Allies. Compounds throughout the camp each had their own population, from political prisoners to Jewish Poles, criminal prisoners to Russian prisoners of war. Our compound was divided into three sections: one for men, one for women who stayed with the children and the third for the hospital camp. There was a main thoroughfare through the middle of the compound linking the different areas that was nicknamed 'High Street'. Star Camp contained about 3,000 people spread across 18 barracks. I asked when I'd see my father and grandmother and was told Gabi and I were being placed in a women's barrack, but that I'd be able to see them later.

Despite being supposedly 'valuable' to the Germans, it was increasingly clear to me that we were not going to be treated that way. Walking into the bunkhouse I shook from the cold; it was almost as freezing inside as it was outside. I hated being cold and here it was markedly colder than it had been at Westerbork. I was once again grateful for the wool coats Mrs Ledermann had insisted I pack for both of us. The barracks smelled like a mix of disinfectant and cabbage. Most of the space was crammed with rows of triple-decker bunk beds, similar to the ones we slept in at Westerbork. The distance between the bunks was so narrow I had to slide in sideways. In all, about 170 women and children were housed here. In the front, there was a long table and chairs for mealtimes. There was one oven. I tried to warm myself and Gabi next to it but there were other women crowding round it as well and we kept getting pushed to the side.

I found a pair of adjacent lower-level bunks for the two of us. The straw-stuffed mattresses were dirty and thinner than in Westerbork, I thought, as I sat down on what would be my new, flat, hard bed. The air lay thick and heavy. I saw a rat scamper across the floor. I'd soon find out disease-carrying fleas were rampant here.

'Where's Papa? Where's Oma?' Gabi asked as I tucked her in.

'I'm sure we'll see them tomorrow.'

We were both beyond exhausted at this point, functioning on only a few hours of sleep since we left Westerbork. I think I passed out as soon as I put my head down; my entire body ached for sleep. But when I awoke at dawn, the first light of morning visible on the barrack's scuffed wooden floor, I was sweating, despite the cold. At first, I was confused. *How can I be so hot when I can practically see my breath?* I thought to myself. I sat up and immediately felt like I needed to throw up. Just then, I felt my body lurch forward and I leaned out of bed and was sick. I was seized with fear: how could I be ill?

An older woman who I recognised from our neighbourhood in Amsterdam approached me. She said, 'I know you can't see it yourself, we have no mirror here, but child, your skin is yellow. You must have jaundice.'

'Jaundice?' I asked. 'What do I do?'

'The Germans are terrified of disease. And when you have jaundice it means you might be carrying something contagious. You will have to quarantine,' she said.

'I can't be sick, I have to take care of my sister,' I burst out. I barely knew where we were in this bone-chilling dank new prison that so far did not look even one little bit 'ideal'. I didn't know where Papa and Oma were or how to find them. I felt sweat trickling down my neck from nerves and my fever. My nausea was constant. I wished we were anywhere but here. I looked down at Gabi, those enormous bandages swaddling her ears. I didn't even know how to change them. *What do I do with Gabi?*

Our former neighbour soon returned with a woman who she said was her niece. The first thing I noticed was how tall she was and that she must be very Orthodox by the way her hair was covered in a kerchief tied behind her neck.

'I'm Mrs Abrahams, I'll take care of your sister. Don't worry, she'll be fine with me. My youngest child, a little girl named Lily, is just her age, so they can play together. I have six older children, including a daughter your age.' She put her cool hand against my burning forehead. 'But you have to go to the hospital barracks.'

At first, I could hardly understand her words – was she really offering to take on this still-recovering tiny girl? I protested it was too much to ask. But she told me she had heard of the good works my father had done for so many people and she'd be honoured to do the same for our family now. 'I'll take good care of Gabi,' she told me. 'Your job is to get better. Now go.'

I'd never before felt such relief and gratitude.

* * *

The hospital camp, including the quarantine barracks, made up five blocks. We were separated from the rest of the camp by barbed wire. Our doctors and nurses were fellow Jewish prisoners. They cared for the patients with great dedication and thoughtfulness, even though they usually did not have the medicine or tools to provide too much help. I was placed in a cold and draughty stone barrack that had once been a horse stable. I slept in a top bunk where, during the first couple of weeks, I still felt miserable but gradually my fever receded, as did my nausea and headaches. To pass the time, I listened to the rain falling and tried to ignore the penetrating cold as I again read and reread the Florence Nightingale biography Mrs Goudsmit had sent me. We had enough to eat – we were told we received more than those in the regular barracks. But it was pretty tasteless and limited to ersatz coffee (with no milk or sugar) in the morning and evenings and our main meal at noon – soup with pieces of swede and a slice of bread. Twice a week, we'd also get some margarine or jam for our bread.

Papa and Oma quickly found out I was in quarantine and after a while they were allowed to start visiting me. Mrs Abrahams also visited. I delighted in her stories of how well Gabi was doing. Her ears were improving, the pus was diminishing and she and Lily were fast playmates and friends. Years later, a doctor would tell me the relatively drier climate of Bergen-Belsen would have helped heal her ears.

I heard planes flying overhead as I walked with still weak and slightly trembling legs back to the barracks a month after I left them. I wondered what was going on in the world outside of this place. If only we could receive letters or read newspapers. I wondered if they were British bombers on their way to Berlin or some other city to attack. It felt disorienting to be this cut off but at least I'd be with Gabi again. I couldn't wait to see her. She had not been allowed to visit me as I recovered and I had missed her and worried about her so much, despite the positive updates from my family and Mrs Abrahams.

'Hanneli!' she shouted, spotting me as I entered the barracks. She was one of the youngest and smallest children living in the barracks but her voice could carry and I heard her right away. We ran towards one another and she covered me in kisses and hugs.

Mrs Abrahams came to greet me and walked me over to the area of the barracks where she and her sister, Mrs Emanuel, had set up a makeshift home for themselves and their children, including a bunk for Gabi. I was sad when I realised there was no empty bunk for me, but Mrs Abrahams asked the woman in an adjacent bunk to leave it so I could sleep there. Relieved, I set down my rucksack and started unpacking my things. My suitcase was still there, with our belongings. Because of our potential exchange value to our captors, we were afforded privileges not received by other Bergen-Belsen inmates, such as being allowed to keep our belongings and wear our own clothes, and our hair was not shorn. I was shocked when I first saw prisoners from other parts of Bergen-Belsen with shaved heads and coarse grey-blue striped prison uniforms.

Mrs Abrahams introduced me to her five daughters, including Lily, Gabi's playmate, and her eldest daughter, Helena, who was also 15, like me.

'Join us and we will live like a family here, together,' she said.

I felt a warm feeling rise inside of me. I again marvelled at my luck meeting someone as fundamentally good as Mrs Abrahams. I thought about the Jewish story Papa had told me – the tale of the *lamedvovniks.* These were thought to be 36 righteous people, basically human saints, who existed in the world, undetected by others because of their humbleness, but within whom the fate of the world resided. I wondered if Mrs Abrahams might be one of them. She felt like a miracle.

My education in daily life outside of the hospital barracks of Bergen-Belsen started right away. The floor that was ice-cold on socked feet, the blue-grey horsehair blankets we were made to use instead of the soft, familiar ones we brought from home – even that small pleasure was taken from us in the name of the German craving for uniformity. Lights stayed on from 5am till 9pm.

That first morning, I took Gabi outside to the latrines where we suffered the indignity of sitting on holes cut in long planks of wood. I tried not to retch from the stench. I said a silent prayer of gratitude that Gabi was potty-trained back in Amsterdam. At first, I was worried she'd fall down the hole into the putrid abyss below, but she had already learned well how to sit on the edge safely. Back in the barracks, I splashed cold water on my face and Gabi's, drank a bitter cup of ersatz coffee and then returned to my bunk, where Mrs Abrahams taught me how to perform my most essential mission of the early morning: making my bed as per regulations. This meant putting my and Gabi's nightclothes away into my suitcase, flopping it and my rucksack onto my thin mattress and covering them with a blanket, smoothing the edges and top down till the blanket appeared as smooth and straight as possible. The challenge was to flatten or rather disguise any lumps. Only once our beds were made to this rigorous vision of perfection – and approved by an SS officer – could roll call begin. Mrs Abrahams told me that if a bed was not made to his liking, the SS officer would sometimes throw the bedding and baggage onto the floor.

Roll call began every morning at 6am. It was called *Appellplatz* in German or 'appell' for short, a word I learned for the first time there. This was the main – and most dreaded – daily regime.

'Hurry, Hanneli, we can't be late,' Mrs Abrahams told me as she hustled me to make it on time. 'Anyone who is late can be punished.'

'*Raus! Raus!*' (Get out!) shouted a guard who burst through the door just as we hurried outside.

I followed Mrs Abrahams' lead and lined up in a row to be counted together with our other barrack members. These counts were taking place across the camp, each in front of open areas next to the barracks. We had to stand to attention in lines of five in a row. That meant standing straight and looking forward. Little Gabi stood next to me, now a veteran after doing it for the past month without me. What would my mother have thought seeing her, standing to attention like a child soldier? Or rather, a child prisoner.

A frigid light drizzle began to fall, turning into heavier rain. Gabi did not cry or whimper; she had apparently learned not to. The cold was bone-chilling and set my teeth chattering. I watched as the SS officers strode by us on horseback or sometimes on foot. I was both intrigued and intimidated by their uniform: black boots, hats with a visor, long wool coats. Some had whips or clubs in their hands, which they sometimes used on those they deemed 'guilty' of anything from poor posture to stained or dirty clothing.

'Eighty, eighty-one, eighty-two …' I heard my fellow prisoners count off. When it came to my turn, I heard myself shout in a loud, clear voice, in German, 'Eighty-nine'. And, motioning to Gabi, I gave her number that morning: 'Ninety'. Of course, no one asked for our names. To them we were just numbers, not human beings.

Every morning was the same. In rain, snow, hail or high winds, we stood there until the numbers added up to what our overlords thought they should. If they did not, we'd start the count again. The whole ordeal could be wrapped up in about an hour and a half or stretch on for as long as eight hours. Punishment for a count not adding up might be taking away our food provisions for the day or beatings. If you had to go to the bathroom, you went in your pants.

We were supposed to be absolutely quiet during the roll call but sometimes when the guards were doing the count on the other side of the yard, women would whisper to one another, exchanging 'news'. Of course, we had no way of knowing if it was actual news or just rumours, or some kind of conflation of the two. I was delighted to find out there was even a nickname for this kind of information: the IPA, which stood for the Israelite Press Association.

The idea of the appells was ostensibly to make sure everyone was accounted for, but even Gabi could see it was more about intimidating and humiliating us. But we had no choice other than to endure the misery until the count was hailed as 'correct'. It was known that some of the SS men and women made mistakes with the count to prolong our suffering. For the young children, the elderly and the ill, these headcounts were especially cruel.

I don't know who contemplated running away when that could – probably would – mean being shot. Where could anyone run away to, even if they somehow slipped past those soaring barbed wire-topped gates and machine guns? Where would I go and how could I possibly risk Gabi's life if I tried to run away with her? I could only imagine a German farmer's face seeing two raggedy girls with matted hair and a yellow star sewn on the coats we had visibly outgrown.

Once the appell was finally finished, the adults and teenagers my age and over set off to begin our 11-hour days. At first, I had a job making bags from sheets of cellophane. For hours, I stood in a workshop with other women. Our task was to twist cellophane into braids that were fashioned into bags. We worked without a break till the early afternoon when a couple of women would bring in a vat of boiling soup with the usual swede floating on top and a few precious potatoes at the bottom if we were lucky. We always tried to make sure the server scooped the soup for us from the bottom. After a few weeks, because I was only 15 and had a younger sister to care for, I was exempted from working and instead spent my days in and around the barracks caring for Gabi and helping watch over other young children about her age.

There were a range of different jobs. The ones that dealt with camp management, including work in the kitchens, although strenuous, were most desired because they meant having occasional access to more food. The so-called 'labour commandos' were the most physically gruelling: tasks included road building, hauling coal and the 'Stubenkommando', which meant digging up and removing trees from the frozen ground. It was dangerous work with casualties. Beatings were common but it seemed those working in construction, which included a disproportionate number of elderly and weak, received them more than anyone. SS guards supervised all workers, always armed with sticks and bats. I heard of some people who were beaten so badly they were severely injured and left near death. There was also a group of workers that had to clean the homes of SS officers. This was considered a choice job as there was a lot of food there one could try to take, but if you dared to and got caught, you could be killed.

My father had a difficult job. He was part of what was called 'the shoe commando'. He worked at a factory where used German military boots were piled high. These boots had seen active service and were often caked and hardened with mud, dirt and even blood. He told me how he and the others had to take the shoes apart and then patch together the good bits of leather that were still usable to recycle them into new pairs of boots. They were each given unrealistically high quotas for the number of boots they had to fashion, making the work, he said, extremely stressful. Thick layers of dust and dirt filled the air from the work, coating the men's lungs. My father started returning to the barracks in the evening with a hacking cough. I was grateful we were briefly able to visit one another, and Oma too, in the evenings, but I grew worried as I saw him looking visibly paler and weak.

'Don't worry, Hanneli,' he would say. 'I'll rest and feel better. This is all temporary. We just have to get through this time until we can be exchanged.'

It was almost spring; the days were beginning to warm up. There was an earthy scent in the air and with it we felt more hopeful. Everyone thought we'd be exchanged by summertime.

Papa was becoming well known in his barrack for gathering boys for lessons about Jewish thought and Torah stories, especially on Shabbat and the holidays. He tried to bring them to a spiritual place, far from the realities of our day to day. As conditions in the camp began to worsen, with even less food, more hunger and widespread illnesses, he'd sit perched on his top bunk, three bunks high, and give his talks from there. On Shabbat, they were often about the power and holiness that came from rest when one observed Shabbat. One teenage boy, just a little older than me, told me, 'Your father helps lift us up from our despair.'

In Judaism, we learn that there's hope for redemption and seeing God's light, no matter how bleak the hour seems. Papa found a way, even as his own health began to fray, to be that light.

*   *   *

The majority of the almost 4,000 people in Sternlager Camp had, like us, been deported here from the Netherlands. But there was a small group of Greek Jews too, and they had been put in leadership roles. In the men's barracks, Papa reconnected with a German Jewish man named Zvi Koretz he had known in Berlin. Although not Greek himself, he had served as the chief rabbi of the port city of Thessaloniki in northern Greece, which had the largest Jewish population in the country. The city had so many Jews, the port shut down on Shabbat. The Germans had occupied the city since April 1941.

Rabbi Koretz looked out for my father, making him his deputy and putting him in charge of the barrack for the elderly and disabled men. Papa moved into this barrack, which had a key benefit: not having to stand for the daily appells. This was especially fortunate as Papa seemed to be slowing down more lately.

Children under three received two cups of milk a week in addition to our food rations. Gabi was now three and a half so she didn't get any. But she was weak and getting weaker. Rabbi Koretz's wife Gita, who I knew as Rebbetzin Koretz, was in charge of distributing the milk and she insisted on giving Gabi the milk allotment as well. She had heard from her husband about Papa and his good works. I really believe that the milk made a life-and-death difference for Gabi.

She seemed to get stronger as a result. The way I saw it, two miracles happened to us at Bergen-Belsen: meeting Mrs Abrahams, our very own human saint, and the milk I believe saved Gabi's health.

I didn't have the words to describe it, but we were all engaged in a fight for survival. It wasn't a struggle just for physical survival, but one for the survival of the soul, too – to remain human in these terrible, inhumane conditions. I saw this happen in different ways, for example, in lectures on Jewish thought and religion that my father gave or in the drawings and even paintings people made and hid under their mattresses, and in the poems and journals they still wrote. Souls were also nourished in discussions held about art and music. Then there were the teachers who taught lessons to the children. One of Gabi's favourite activities was an 'art class' led by one of the mothers in the barracks. She gave each child a stick and showed them how to draw butterflies and flowers in the dirt. I didn't think about school so much any more but I was reminded when I heard inmates swapping lessons in French, English or physics with one another.

Rations were being further reduced and we were always hungry. The women in my barracks would conjure up detailed plans for multi-course dinner parties, recounting recipes from memory for their favourite soups, sauces and seven-layer chocolate cakes. I did not know a thing about cooking but I listened closely to these reveries. My own food fantasy was quite simple: buttered toast and a soft-boiled egg. I imagined eating it for breakfast in bed, luxuriating on a warm, soft mattress, snug under clean sheets and cosy blankets. And then a nice hot bath, alone.

The German guards, always imaginative when it came to opportunities for further cruelty, developed a habit of making a batch of delicious-smelling goulash for themselves, knowing how the smells would torment us. I heard that sometimes they would open the door and let Jews beg for it and then, after giving it to them, set a German shepherd guard dog on them. When I heard stories like this I could feel myself shaking with fury and disgust. I was desperate to go home.

It was also terrible to bear the insults hurled at us, especially by the female SS supervisors known as the Aufseherinnen, and the Ukrainian criminal prisoners at Bergen-Belsen. They would scream 'dirty Jew' or 'filthy swine' and the like. The Ukrainian kapos seemed to especially relish the job of holding power over us, a people they were told were 'lesser' than them.

But the aspects of camp life I perhaps detested the most were the latrines and having to shower under the watch of the SS guards. Both were humiliating experiences that made me feel exposed and ashamed, just as they were intended to. I never got used to it. Men and women used the same latrines – just rows of long wooden planks with holes cut out of them. There was no privacy, no screens. The smell was overwhelming – a mix of disinfectant and bodily waste. I tried to hold my breath but the rank smell made me want to vomit. I felt sad that Gabi had no memory of sitting in the quiet coolness of our tiled, clean bathroom at home. We were provided with no toilet paper of any kind. We were not permitted out of the barracks after 9pm and that included being barred from using the outdoor latrines. So in the barracks I had a pot for us to use in case we had bathroom needs during the night. I did not menstruate while at Bergen-Belsen, probably because I was malnourished, but the women who did were allotted no sanitary materials. Sometimes, they would use cut-up strips of rags they secured on their work details for that purpose. But that was considered 'illegal' by our dehumanising guards and I remember a story of SS guards ordering women to fish out those rags from the bottom of the latrines.

We were desperate to stay clean, for our own dignity and to protect ourselves from lice, fleas and other vermin. The only warm water we had was from the watery ersatz coffee made of chicory or acorns, so once a week we'd wash our hair using it. Our shower time was continually reduced. We could only clean our clothes with cold water. My fingers would turn blue submerged in the icy water, scrubbing Gabi's clothes and mine.

But despite everything, I was aware that things could have been worse for us. Prisoners in the different camps could not mix or communicate. It was forbidden for us to speak to one another, a transaction punishable by death. But I could see them across the barbed wire and, even from a distance, it was clear their conditions were even worse than ours. During their appells, the sick, weak and elderly were not allowed to stay indoors if they felt unwell, as ours could. Instead, these unfortunate women were counted as they lay on the dirt.

* * *

The rain continued to fall and any walk outside felt like wading through a sea of mud. But I was still grateful for the warming temperatures, as well as the rumbling of American planes flying overhead, often quite low. They must have known they were flying over a concentration camp, since they got so close. At first, it was jarring hearing the thunderous noise the bombers made – it reminded me of the day the Germans invaded the Netherlands. But of course, they represented our hope. On Easter Sunday 1944, a sunny day, we heard planes come closer than they ever had before and they strafed the camp with gunfire. I lay down on the ground as I saw others do. I heard that in some parts of the camp, SS guards and Jews found cover laying side by side in the same gutter. Then, towards the end of April, our hopes were raised when air-raid sirens started going off regularly. People talked about what this might mean and the 'Israelite Press Association' was alive with rumour and hearsay. The conventional wisdom was that it signalled the British were making progress in their attacks on Germany.

One evening in May when Gabi and I were visiting with Papa and Oma, I got a fright. I had not seen Papa for a few days and, in a rush, it hit me just how much his health had deteriorated. He was constantly short of breath and had a hacking cough. He blamed it on the stuffy air clogged with clouds of dust and dirt he breathed all day in the shoe commando hall. He, like the others, had to scramble to disassemble their daily quota of 40 pairs of boots each day.

'When I breathe, cough or even sneeze, my chest hurts,' he told us. 'I also have pain that seems to worsen when I move any part of my upper body, especially my shoulders and back.'

Oma urged him to see a doctor at the hospital barracks. But he was worried that would make it harder to see us if he was to be kept there. Which, I thought, looking at him, he surely would. But by the end of the month, he had no choice. He had been diagnosed with pleurisy. He explained to me that this meant that the thin layers of tissue that separated his lungs from his chest wall had become inflamed. That's what was causing the chest pain.

I was very scared and worried about him all the time now, but despite his initial fears I was actually able to visit him in the hospital barrack almost every day. There was even some privacy during our visits as he could pull a curtain around his bed and sit and talk. He looked so small, practically swallowed up by his pyjamas as he lay in bed. He loved seeing Gabi; he loved her spirit. She liked to sing, clearly musical like Mama. She'd sing us little songs and sometimes describe whatever she was doing or thinking in song, instead of speaking.

'Seeing and sitting with you is my best medicine,' he told us.

But weeks passed and he was still not released.

Papa told me to keep up hope that we would all soon enough be exchanged. We were also encouraged by the IPA news that filtered through, although we were never sure what was real and what was rumour. By the end of June, there was talk of the Allies landing on the beaches of northwest France. Maybe the war would be coming to an end soon after all? In the meantime, our strange limbo continued – a mix of boredom, hard labour, picking lice and nits out of one another's hair and the collars of our clothes, and squatting on the latrine through spells of diarrhoea as your next-door latrine neighbour endured the same.

In July, we heard the good news of an upcoming exchange of those with Palestine certificates to go to Eretz Yisrael, our imagined land of milk and honey that appeared to be our safe haven. Would our family be on the list?

We finally heard – my grandmother was on that list, but the three of us we were not. We presumed it was because my father was in the hospital, deemed not fit to travel perhaps, and so we had been knocked off it. It was good and bad news, painful in so many ways. We had longed for this moment and here it was, so close at hand, but we would not be going as a family. It felt like a blow to remain in this banishment even as we watched others prepare for freedom. The contrast was so great – trapped behind this barbed wire or sailing towards the Land of Israel.

'Oma, we are so excited for you!' I told her. And I was, though I was also scared to be there without her. I did not see her much but when I did she felt like a touch of comfort, representing home and Mama and love. She had been living in the bunks for elderly women but had to move to a quarantine bunk in preparation for the transfer, so we would not see her again before her departure.

'I'll be waiting for you in Eretz Yisrael, ready to welcome you when you arrive,' she said. 'Imagine that, keep that picture in your mind.' Gabi and I gave her long hugs. She kissed our foreheads goodbye. We thought that was it – all we could do was pray that we would all be reunited in Jerusalem.

But two weeks later, we were stunned when Oma was removed from quarantine and put back on our side of the camp. She had approached an SS officer – a brave thing to do because speaking directly to the SS was strictly forbidden and she could have been punished. She told him of her ailing son-in-law in the hospital camp and that she had two granddaughters she felt she could not leave behind alone. She asked to be removed from the exchange list.

'But Oma,' I wailed, 'you were almost free!'

She looked at me and smiled. 'This was the right thing to do. Now I'm nearby again, close to you and Gigi.'

* * *

By the end of summer, conditions were getting even worse. A constant stream of new arrivals meant the barracks were more crowded than ever. Since the beginning of the summer of 1944, Jews had started arriving in ever-larger numbers by train or by foot from other camps in Poland. We saw them clad in black and white stripes and the occasional blanket, heads shaved, weak and rail thin. I had to look away because they looked so awful. Word started circulating that the Germans were sending them here because the Russian army was approaching and they were intent on pushing as many of them as possible away from the chance of liberation.

'Liberation'. This was a new word that I rolled slowly on my tongue. It stuck in my head, even though it felt like an illicit dream to even consider.

The fence between the men and women's camp came down as some of the barracks were needed for the new arrivals. The 'exchange Jews' were packed into a smaller number of barracks, forced to sleep two people to a bunk. Luckily, I could just move in with Gabi. We slept every night head to head.

A small group of Jews from Benghazi, Libya, was put into our barracks. They only spoke Italian and Arabic so it was difficult to communicate with them. They had no warm clothes for the colder weather that seemed to be too rapidly upon us as summer ended. I felt so badly for them in their thin clothes. I'd watch one of them, a young, very religious man, a teacher who lived in a men's barracks nearby, gather a group of the boys together, sitting cross-legged together in a circle outside while he taught them Hebrew.

I listened in on their lessons. *'Einayim'* means eyes. *'Reglayim'* means 'legs'.

Kommandant Kramer, the recently appointed SS officer in charge of Bergen-Belsen, whose previous post, we'd heard, was at a camp called Auschwitz, declared that anyone found without permission on 'High Street', the central street in our camp, was to be shot. We had a nickname for him, on account of his penchant for beating and torturing people imprisoned at Bergen-Belsen, including, I'd heard, setting dogs on them. We called him 'the Beast of Belsen'.

The Germans were always looking for ways to further torment us, including using the Jewish holidays against us. They succeeded again on Yom Kippur, which fell at the end of September that year. It is the holiest day of the year for us; even non-observant Jews tended to revere Yom Kippur. It is the culmination of ten days of repentance in which Jews ask God for his forgiveness for their sins. One is supposed to exist like an angel, with no need to eat or to bathe. The focus is on the life of the spirit, in order to be fully open to prayer and holiness. Observant Jews do not bathe on Yom Kippur and so of course, on this day, the German guards herded us into the showers.

I and the others in my barracks were extremely angry they made us shower on this day of all days, even though we were otherwise desperate to get clean. I removed my clothes and stepped into the shower room with Gabi next to me. As usual, I felt the humiliation of being watched by SS guards but with an added level of disgust and anger because it was Yom Kippur.

Soon, the first of the frosts arrived. We soldiered through the increasingly Arctic chill of interminable appells. Around us, more people were falling sick. There was less food all the time. Bread rations were reduced to a four-centimetre cube of bread, cut with string and parcelled out while we waited in long lines. My stomach growled so often it had become background noise for me. Gabi learned to stop asking for more food because there was no more food to receive. On 12 November 1944, I turned 16. Nothing was done to mark the day for me, aside perhaps from an extra piece of bread. On Christmas Day, a few small pieces of meat could be found floating on our watery soup. No one asked what kind of meat it was. Being kosher no longer mattered; getting any extra amount of protein was more important. But I remember the young Libyan teacher refused the meat. He was that devout.

My daily visits to Papa continued. I was worried that he seemed to be getting worse, not better. Gabi, Oma and I would talk at these visits, while he mostly listened and nodded. He did not know this but I saved up my bread rations to buy about a dozen penicillin pills from a man who had brought them in from Westerbork. The doctors gave them to him. I hoped it might cure him but he still coughed, was occasionally feverish and remained weak.

'The war will be ending soon,' I told him, repeating the IPA reports I had heard. 'You will get better and we will be free.'

Chapter 12

Anne

There was no slowing of the stream of new arrivals as we descended into another freezing winter. It seemed like tens of thousands had come to Bergen-Belsen in recent weeks. Some came by train but others, we understood, had suffered forced marches. The Germans evacuated the concentration camps where they were being held and made them march west, away from Allied forces. Some would be forced to work as slave labour in factories. I had no idea how someone could have endured walking through sleet and through snowdrifts in those threadbare clothes. No shelter, little to eat. They were accompanied by armed guards. We heard through the IPA that the guards shot them if they stumbled and fell – or if they tried to flee. How many had set out but not arrived?

Among the arrivals were women and girls, crammed into tents in the camp just next to ours. We could see them through the barbed-wire fences. Like the others, they came from the east, from a camp called Auschwitz. The women in our camp referred to them as the *Zeltfrauen*, the 'tent women'. During a storm with high winds and heavy rain, a few of the tents were blown away. The women inside them were stranded outside, soaked to the bone by the rain and cold. I felt terrible for them. I again thought about how grateful

I was for the minimal conditions we did have. The Red Cross had just sent Sternlager Camp inmates small boxes of food. We each received a book-sized box containing rusk bread and dried fruit. Their dispersal in our barrack was cause for minor celebration – the provisions a lifeline from another world where people, we thought to ourselves, must have known something of our plight. It was encouraging to feel less invisible but we wondered why we had only one box of provisions each? Certainly the Red Cross would have sent more, so why were we not receiving more? We thought the Germans were probably keeping them.

It was hard to stay grateful for the little we had. Where once there were six large washing sheds, by winter there were just two for all of the men, women and children of the Sternlager Camp. Imagine – 12 taps for almost 4,000 people. Our camp now also included a few hundred Jews from Albania and Yugoslavia in addition to the Dutch, Greeks and Libyans. The latrines were crowded and overused, so some people stopped using them. I'd wake up in the morning and see – and smell – piles of excrement and want to retch.

The days started to feel more and more unbearable and not just because of the squalor. Our daily life was filled with injustices that were hard to witness: a mother punished and given only bread and water for three days for trying to cook some soft food for her baby on a little burner, an inmate bleeding after a guard unleashed his German shepherd on him for not working quickly enough. One especially cruel and strange punishment was meted out to an old man working in the shoe commando who had dozed off over a boot he was dissembling. He was made to stand unmoving under a leaking roof where drops of water splashed on the same spot of his neck. The evil at Bergen-Belsen was arbitrary and awful. My only hope was to make myself as small and invisible as possible, hoping no SS officer would have cause to notice me, and that way Gabi and I could stay safe.

We now also had to make do without any Jewish camp leadership as the group was disbanded by the end of 1944. They had been charged with helping to keep order, and they listened to our anxieties and woes and did all they could to make our lives easier.

With so many ill or too weak to work and the number of dead rising all the time, most of the work commandos came to an end. I'm sure the SS wondered what to do with us. We spent most of our time in barracks now. The most grievously ill people around me stared out from their bunk beds blankly, seemingly beyond caring any more whether they lived or died. It was chilling, the look of apathy from people I had known to be vital even weeks before.

It was February 1945. A whole year had passed since we left Westerbork and Dutch soil, and it was coming up to two since we were deported from Amsterdam. I could never have dreamed the war would have gone on this long or that I would ever be living in such conditions. Amsterdam felt like another planet, though one I visited often in my daydreams, wishing I was back there with Anne, Sanne, Ilse and our other friends. I tried to keep Gabi entertained with stories about our lives back in Amsterdam. I described the bedroom we shared and how Mama would play blocks with her and take us out on walks to the park. I wanted her to remember who Mama was and how much she loved her. Gabi said she still remembered Sjors and all their fun times in the sandbox. I told her after we were free, we'd play in the biggest sandbox we could find and that after that we'd go to the sea and play in the waves.

* * *

One day, I noticed that the fence dividing us from the tent camp was stuffed with straw. I was puzzled but someone told me it was so we would not be able to see one another. But we were all hungry for information and people risked going to the fences, defying the direct order not to communicate with those in other camps, out of a mix of solidarity and curiosity. New transports were arriving all the time who sometimes had fresh information.

'There are Dutch women among the new transports,' a woman announced in our barracks one day in February. 'I heard Dutch being spoken.'

This sent us all into a flutter. We all wanted to know if there were relatives or friends on the other side of the fence – people we last saw back in Westerbork or our hometowns. Women from our camp started approaching the straw-filled fence, calling out in Dutch and exchanging quick bits of information. Soon, a woman who had known my family back in Amsterdam came to find me. I would never, ever have dreamt what she told me. Anne Frank was among the Dutch women and girls on the other side of the fence.

'Anne is here?' I asked her, repeating her words but not remotely comprehending them in that moment. 'Anne is just a few metres away? Here? Here in Bergen-Belsen?'

My mind tried to process this information. It felt impossible. Anne was in Switzerland, safe, warm, living in a heated home, going to school, doubtlessly breaking some boy's heart, and enjoying life with her family, grandmother and cousins. Anne had been spared this torment. This is what I had believed to be true since the day I came to her home and found it empty, except for her beloved Moortje and the frazzled tenant on that impossibly faraway warm July day in 1942. It was now February 1945. How in the world would

Anne have wound up here? And if she was part of the transport arrivals that meant she had been in a concentration camp in Poland. None of it made sense to me.

But if Anne really was only metres from me, then how could I not set out to find her, even if I could get punished for trying? There was so much to ask her about and so much to tell. I was so excited I might see her that my heart beat harder in my chest. Then I immediately felt my shock morph into something else entirely – a deep, mournful sadness. My friend, my lively, clever Anne. If she was here, she was not free. It had been such a balm thinking she was in Switzerland. She was really the only friend I did not have to worry about, besides Jacque in Amsterdam. Everyone else I knew who was Jewish – friends, relatives, teachers, neighbours – I thought about and worried for their fate.

I had to try to see her. I ordinarily never took risks. My safety and Gabi's was the most important thing. But how could I not? So I decided I'd slip out of my barracks before the 9pm curfew that night. Mrs Abrahams and my other friends in the barracks were appalled.

'It's too dangerous,' Mrs Abrahams warned.

'You could be shot,' said someone else.

'What about Gabi?' said another. 'What if something happens to you out there?'

I told them about Anne, her spark and sense of wonder and fun and how we grew up together in Amsterdam, our lives and our families' lives intertwined. I explained I thought she and her family had escaped to Switzerland, leaving this mystery of how she became one of the new transports here.

'I'll be careful. Don't worry,' I said, even though I knew I was convincing no one. 'Anne is like my sister too. I have to go to her.'

Before I left, I tucked Gabi into the narrow bunk we shared and sang into her ear the prayer I said to her every night: the *Shema*. I prayed that night for her but also for my own safety. I spoke to her about Anne, reminded her how Anne and her sister Margot loved her and treated her like their own doll when she was a baby.

'We'd push you in the pram and fight over who could hold you,' I told her. She laughed. I loved Gabi's laugh, like the sound of tiny bells.

I rubbed her back for a few minutes, till she was beginning to doze off. I took one last look at her and took a deep breath. I pulled on my coat as I pushed through the words and warnings of Mrs Abrahams and the others. I opened the door into a frigid, windy night. My cheeks stung from the rain that had just begun to fall. I pulled my worn wool coat closer to me. Its sleeves rose above my bony wrists. In the almost two years since I folded it into my suitcase, I'd grown taller even as my weight continued to drop. I'm sure I looked as emaciated as everyone else in the barracks.

The mud-clogged path was slippery and I focused on not falling. As I carefully made my way closer to the fence, I was still trying to digest that I might soon be seeing Anne. I remained flooded with disbelief; it was hard to let go my gauzy images of Anne in Switzerland, so far from the disease and death I saw here.

I was well aware of the watchtowers manned by SS guards with machine guns and that they also patrolled, German shepherds on leads, on both sides of the fence. Fences surrounded us and divided us. I had not forgotten that the punishment for talking to prisoners on the other side of these fences could be death. I was shivering from the cold and from fear. But I was also thinking about Anne and my feet kept walking me onwards for the five minutes it took to get there.

I could smell the fresh straw stuffed into the fence and, as I approached, I steadied myself, running my hands across it. *There is no time to waste,* I told myself.

'Hello? Hello?' I called out in a soft voice. 'Is there anyone there?'

A voice answered back, also in Dutch.

'Yes?'

It sounded familiar.

'My name is Auguste van Pels,' I heard the woman say.

Mrs van Pels! She and her husband and son Peter would sometimes visit the Frank family. They lived on our street and I knew her husband worked with Mr Frank.

'It's Hannah. Hannah Goslar here,' I told her.

Right away she replied, 'You must want to speak to Anne. I'll bring her. Margot is here too. But she's too sick to come.'

I was thrilled I'd found someone to bring Anne to me so quickly. But Margot ... Margot was here too? And she was sick? I glanced around nervously, crouching as the lights from the guard towers swept the camp. My heart was thumping so loudly I was almost surprised I could hear the small, quiet voice that called out: 'Hanneli? Hanneli, is that actually you?'

'Yes, yes, Anne, it's me!' I answered.

We both instantly broke into tears, the same cold rain falling on us on opposite sides of this cursed fence. We didn't have much time, so through tears I managed to ask: 'How is it that you are here? Why aren't you with your grandmother in Switzerland?'

She told me they never went to Switzerland. That story was all a ruse. I noticed her voice was fainter, weaker. It was not the boisterous, confident chirp I knew. Anne quickly explained where they had been. 'We were in hiding in my father's office, upstairs in rooms behind a secret door. We were there for over two years. Two years I never stepped outside,' she said, her words now rushing out. My mind flashed back to our Sunday afternoons on Prinsengracht 263, playing on the phones and splashing passers-by on the pavement below with water. In hiding, she told me, they had been safe from the Nazis, from deportation and the camps. But in August someone betrayed them, a terrible shock. They were arrested and sent first to Westerbork then to Auschwitz.

'They took my hair,' she said, her voice still full of disbelief. I felt the sting of her indignation. Her silky dark hair. She was forever brushing it, experimenting with curlers; it was her favourite feature. And she was freezing, she told me, dressed only in rags. I shuddered thinking of her totally exposed to the freezing wind and rain blowing around us. Margot was sick with typhus, too ill to move from bed, she reported. She told me the terrible news that her parents were dead. Surely gassed to death, she said.

More words that made no sense to me. Gassed? What did that mean? I had seen people die from starvation and illness at Bergen-Belsen, and we knew that trying to escape – or potentially even talking to one another like this – could lead to one being shot, but gassed to death? I had heard rumours of killing at the other camps from those imprisoned with me, but organised gassing of people?

It was too much to comprehend. Anne's voice belonged to a world away from here, to our own Merwedeplein Square where we spent our afternoons lost in the world of play and our own imaginations, where we never went hungry and slept in warm beds, tucked in by loving parents. But in that voice I knew so well, she was saying that people at Auschwitz were gassed to death, including her own parents. How could that be possible?

That's what happened, she insisted. Especially for anyone over 50, like her father. She had seen the curls of crematorium smoke. That's what happened to people's loved ones. I was stunned, even though I too had seen things I never could have imagined back in Amsterdam. People beaten and kicked at random, whipped and hit with the butts of guns. Horrible cruelties. And, more recently, more and more death. Bodies were beginning to pile up. The first time I saw stacks of bodies I looked away and I had not looked again since.

There was so much more I wanted to ask but I knew it was dangerous to linger. A guard could spot us at any time. Instead, we continued to share our news of the dead and the living in rushed whispers. My voice cracked when I told her my mother had died in childbirth. She only knew my newborn brother had died; she had not been told about my mother. I told her Papa was extremely ill but I didn't have time to tell her how scared I was for him. I told her that my grandfather had died of a heart attack when we were still at Westerbork.

'But Gabi is fine. And my grandmother is here too,' I said.

'I have no one,' she said, words that landed like a knife.

We were both sobbing now. Two terrified girls under a rain-soaked night sky, separated by this barrier of straw and barbed wire. How had it come to this?

'I'm absolutely starving. Do you have food? Can you bring me some?' Anne asked.

'Yes, I'll try,' I said, wondering as the words came out how I possibly would.

'I'll come back, in just two more nights. Wait for me,' I instructed her.

She said she would. We said a rushed, sad goodbye. I looked around, carefully scanning the periphery of the fence for guards before I headed back towards the barracks. I felt like my entire body was buzzing from the rush of meeting Anne again. But my heart was aching too. She was such a broken figure, a shadow of the Anne I knew.

'Hanneli, thank heavens you are back,' Mrs Abrahams said, rushing towards me as I slipped back inside the barracks.

'It's Anne, it's really Anne,' I told her and a small group of women who gathered to hear more. 'But she's freezing with nothing but ragged prison garb to wear, and more ravenous than any of us here in the Sternlager Camp.'

I told them more about Anne, how she was the most dynamic, confident person I knew. My friends in the barracks giggled when I explained how my mother would tease: 'God knows all, but Anne knows better.' But now she was so diminished, so entirely changed, I explained. I noticed how they looked at me – with such empathy and sorrow in their eyes. I imagined they may have been thinking of their own best friends lost in the mix of this terrible war, wondering where they might be.

I needed to return to the fence, to Anne, with some food, I explained. But how would I possibly be able to get her anything?

'Don't worry, we'll make sure you can bring her something,' one woman said. And then others volunteered to help as well. They had so little themselves and didn't even know Anne. I was overwhelmed by their kindness. Over the next couple of days, they came by my bunk with their offerings. The women pitched in with some of what they had saved from our small Red Cross parcels. Here, a loaf of bread was divided into four-centimetre pieces, shared between several families and had to last for two days. But still these women gave what they could. Sometimes that meant a sock or a glove.

The next day, I set out to visit Papa in the hospital barracks. I just had to tell him I'd found Anne – he would be stunned to hear she and Margot were here. Also, I had to ask him if he'd heard anything about the gas chambers that Anna said existed in Auschwitz. He kept telling Gabi and me to keep our hope, that we would be exchanged after all, to be patient, to hold on, to wait – did he know the Germans were not only passively letting Jews die as they were here in Bergen-Belsen but actively murdering us? I thought about his innate pessimism. And yet it was Mr Frank, ever the optimist, who, it turned out, had planned for the worst and plotted out a place to hide.

As I walked towards the hospital camp, I smelled something sour like boiling glue. It was coming from what I had been told was the crematorium just outside of Bergen-Belsen, where the bodies of those who had collapsed and died from hunger, disease, exhaustion or all three were taken to be incinerated. Seeing Anne reminded me that I was a 16-year-old girl. I should be in school learning my favourite subjects like history and geography and laughing with Anne and my other girlfriends at some silly thing one of us had said. But instead, here I was walking through a concentration camp to see my ailing father to ask him if Jews really were being gassed to death.

He was the colour of a grey sky when I found him, lying shrunken in bed. He seemed to be getting progressively frailer, drifting in and out of sleep. Most of the time his blue-grey eyes were open and I felt like he was looking at me and really seeing me and understanding. But other times he seemed absent, checked out. Today his eyes were closed, which was disappointing. But I still drew the curtains around his bed closed and sat down next to him. In one breathless gulp everything poured out of me – about meeting Anne, how the

Franks did not go to Switzerland after all, how they hid together with the van Pels family and a dentist friend in an attic behind Mr Frank's office until they were betrayed and sent east to a camp called Auschwitz. I told him how terribly broken Anne seemed, so unlike the Anne I remembered. I took a deep breath and squeezed his hand to ask: 'Is it true? Do Jews there get sent into shower rooms where they are gassed?' His eyes were open at this point and he seemed to be listening, but no response emerged. He would not speak, could not speak? His breathing was heavy. I cursed the exhausting, senseless work with the shoe commando that had stolen my father's health away.

'Oh Papa, stay strong,' I told him, using words he would tell me. 'You and I and Gabi and Oma will be exchanged soon. We just have to be patient. Right?'

*   *   *

I told the women in the barracks that, according to Anne, gas was used in Auschwitz to kill people. Some of them had heard the same. But none of us believed it. We thought those who had arrived from Auschwitz must have been driven mad from the terrible marches and train journeys here. They had eaten so little, were left to freeze and starve or be shot if they did not move quickly enough. They must be so far gone if they could believe and spread such a story. Even the Germans, as psychotic as they were in their seeming delight in making us suffer, even they would not do that.

By the afternoon of the next day, when I'd planned to meet with Anne again, I'd collected a mix of dried fruit, pieces of rusk bread and a couple of corners of crackers pooled together from people's valued but meagre Red Cross boxes. I stuffed the precious collection along with the glove inside the sock. Packaged all together like this it was about the size of a small ball.

I repeated my routine of tucking in Gabi in our bunk and then bundling myself into my coat. I pulled my hat as low as possible over my ears – it was another cold night out there but at least it was not raining. Again, I walked carefully and slowly, looking out for guards. At the fence, I called out to Anne by name. I also whistled our old childhood whistle, the opening bars of the Dutch national anthem. I heard footsteps.

'Hanneli, I'm here,' she answered.

This time there was no risking a conversation.

'I have food for you,' I told her. 'Watch for it, I'm going to throw it to you now.'

'OK, ready,' she replied.

I hurled it high into the sky, watching it soar over the barbed wire. I felt a surge of adrenalin.

But then came terrible screams. It was Anne crying out from the other side. I heard a brief argument and footsteps of someone running away.

'Anne, what happened? What's going on?'

'A woman has caught it and won't give it to me,' Anne screamed. She was sobbing.

'Anne, I'm going to come back again. I'll see what else I can find,' I said. Her cries were so loud I could tell she was convulsing with tears. I felt panicky and just wanted to do something, anything to console her. 'I promise. I'll come back with more food. It will be OK.'

But how would I be able to collect food again? As I walked back to my barracks, I felt my anxiety rise. How was I going to pull this off? Every day it felt like there was less to eat as the number of prisoners grew; the whole camp structure seemed to be breaking down. We were down to just about one bowl of thin soup a day, along with the four centimetres of bread every other day. The soup now came at erratic times. Sometimes it would be delivered at 8am, sometimes at 7pm.

'How did it go?' I was asked as soon as I stepped foot back in the barracks. 'Did Anne like our package?'

I thought I might burst into tears like Anne. I described what happened, how distraught Anne had been when the food was snatched away from her. Everyone was so dismayed. I was stunned when they said they would all help again. And about two days later, I had a couple of pieces of rusk bread and some more dried fruit, all tucked into a pair of stockings ready to deliver. When I returned to the fence, I felt focused and determined to get the package to her.

'Anne, Anne …' I called. 'Hello? Anne?'

To my relief she heard me and came quickly.

'I have a new package for you. Say hello again so I can hear exactly where you are,' I instructed.

'Hello, hello,' she called.

'OK, get ready to catch it and I'll throw it over.'

'Ready,' I heard from the other side of the fence.

I've never been athletic and I was weaker and hungrier than I had ever been, but I summoned all my strength and, based on her voice, visualised where she was standing. I threw the package over the fence in her direction, watching as it sailed over the straw and barbed wire.

I heard it land with a thunk on the cold ground.

'Got it!' she called, her voice sounding more like her old self.

I exhaled.

'I should go,' I said, knowing any time spent at the fence was risky. 'But Anne, I'll come back again soon.' I crept back in the clear and cold night towards the barrack, my heart pounding the whole way. What a relief, what an absolute thrill it was to know she had the food. She'd got it! I looked skywards and saw glittering stars. I thought of our Little Dipper Minus Two club and smiled.

Gabi was already sleeping deeply when I returned. I carefully lowered myself into our bunk. I marvelled that she was able to sleep amid so much noise. The barracks were so crowded now with hundreds more people and their voices echoed off the rafters. It was quite a din. The long wooden tables for gathering and eating had long been cleared out to make room for new bunks – and with them only more misery.

There were so many ill women. Some moaned from their filthy beds, others screamed from what must have been horrible pain from arms and legs swollen from various edemas. Some languished, unable to stir from their bunks, exhausted from diarrhoea. I heard the crematorium was not big enough for the number of corpses it had to burn. Sometimes, a woman in our barracks would die in the evening and her body was left there until the next morning. There was one little girl, her body scratched dry from lice, who went to get soup one evening to bring to her ill mother. But when she came back to the bed, her mother had died.

Disease was rampant, not only because we were starving but because it had become so hard to stay clean. Very little water was available. We had running water only once a day at this point but still I made sure to find a way to keep scrubbing Gabi and myself every day. I also picked any lice or nits off her hair and clothes and tried to do the same for myself. At night, head to head, we sang the *Shema* together. Gabi was developing a sweet little soprano voice. The Hebrew words I had sung every night with Mama felt like a salve.

*　*　*

After roll call one morning, an SS officer stood at the threshold of the barrack door, shouting out names. The list included mine and Gabi's. It took me a moment to understand that this meant we were on the list to be exchanged for German prisoners held by the Allies. But when?

Tomorrow! Tomorrow? The officer said we had to report immediately to the camp infirmary to be examined by a doctor to confirm if we were indeed healthy enough to be exchanged. I could barely contain my delight and surprise. Papa was right! We would be exchanged after all! I could not stop smiling. But I felt self-conscious too; so many of our friends were staying behind, though they – Mrs Abrahams and Mrs Emanuel among them – were now surrounding us with words of congratulations. And now I knew Anne was here, and Margot. They were starving and sick and I couldn't do anything about it. Relief and pain swirled in my heart.

I held Gabi's hand as we walked with Oma to the hospital camp to be examined by a tall, broad-shouldered SS doctor. It went quite quickly and the three of us then gathered next to Papa's bed, with the doctor. I noticed Papa's skin was even greyer in pallor than it had been the day before and, frustratingly, his eyes were closed. He did not even respond to his name. But his breathing was steady. None of the usual coughing or spluttering. That gave me hope. I fixed my gaze on the doctor's hands checking Papa's heart with a stethoscope. It was obvious, even to me, that there was no way he was healthy enough to be approved to travel for an exchange. When the SS doctor looked up at me I dared not ask him with words, which were forbidden. Instead, I pleaded with my eyes, praying he understood what I was silently begging: 'Let my father come with us.'

He looked back at me, directly into my eyes, telling me through his expression that he understood exactly what was at stake. The air around us went still and silent. 'Hans Goslar, approved,' he announced and ticked off his name from the list on his clipboard.

An SS doctor, an officer, had shown us a moment of humanity, a moment of grace. I couldn't believe it. I silently recited *Al Ha'Nissim*, a Hebrew prayer for miracles.

That night, the kind Jewish nurse and doctor that tended Papa changed him from his pyjamas into his tailored grey suit, in preparation for the train ride scheduled for early the following morning.

The next day, 25 February, Oma, Gabi and I arrived at the hospital with our packed bags but Papa's bed was empty. 'Where is Papa? Where is Papa?' chirped Gabi.

Hearing Gabi, the doctor came in to inform us in a gentle, low voice that Papa had died in the night.

'But we are finally going – we are being exchanged. Finally exchanged. Finally, finally, finally. We are going to Eretz Yisrael, the Land of Israel, just like he always wanted,' I desperately told the poor doctor, who had tears in her eyes. I felt too shocked to move. The doctor's words hung in the air, frozen and impossible. At the same time, I could feel Papa was gone.

'*Meine lieben Mädchen*,' said Oma, my dear girls. She wrapped Gabi and me in an embrace, her own arms bone thin. Oma tried to explain the situation to Gabi, who was baffled by our tears and struggling to follow what was going on. But she seemed to understand

Papa was gone and cried with us. Our heads bowed together as we walked back out into the icy morning air. I was consoled by just one thought: he died thinking he and his daughters and Oma were going to be free, were going to be exchanged and allowed passage to Eretz Yisrael. His longtime dream – it was going to come true. I ached that he would not be a part of its reality.

We tried to cover our mouths against the stench of bodies that were accumulating on the sides of the icy and snowy pathways, collected by prisoners pushing wheelbarrows. I averted my eyes. I had seen how arms and legs stuck out of those wheelbarrows and I did not want to catch sight of Papa's dead body by accident. I knew instinctively to protect myself from that nightmarish image.

Our sad trio trudged, rucksacks and suitcases in hand, towards the administrative building to report for the exchange. When we arrived, we saw a long line had formed outside the building of others on the list. We found the end and waited. Gabi complained her hands were cold. My hands and feet felt like blocks of ice. We stamped our feet and clapped our hands to try to get some warmth going and we waited. We stood for almost four hours in those Arctic temperatures. The numbing cold was at least a distraction from my shock and grief at losing Papa.

All of a sudden, an SS officer emerged from inside. We immediately turned towards him, awaiting good news. Instead he, like the doctor that morning, uttered words that seemed unfathomable.

'The exchange is off, cancelled,' he announced.

No reason was given.

'Now go back to your barracks,' he snarled.

In a stupor, we somehow gathered ourselves and made it back to our barracks: Oma to hers, Gabi and I to ours. I felt sick to my stomach as I pushed open the barrack door to see a place and people I had just said goodbye to a few hours earlier. Returning felt worse than enduring the last year here. I saw our bed had been taken by another woman. Mrs Abrahams, seeing our faces, intuited our sense of defeat and grief. I heard myself telling her words I somehow manage to form but was only beginning to absorb: 'My father is dead, and the exchange has been cancelled.'

She whispered something to the woman who had already moved her stuff into our bunk and she left it. Gabi and I fell into the bunk and closed our eyes.

In the camps, there was no time nor place to mourn our dead, to sit the traditional Jewish seven days of shiva. But at least, with the exception of the torture of the daily appells, I could stay inside on our bunk, doing my own version of a shiva. We had now stopped even talking about the possibility of liberation. Instead, we talked about hoping we'd get more food, hoping we'd last another day. For me, there was no time to contemplate not surviving. As always, I had to keep Gabi alive.

A few days after Papa died, I decided to return to the fence, to again look for Anne. I wanted to talk to her, to tell her about Papa, to commiserate together. I approached the fence but I could see through new gaps in the straw that the tents on the other side had been cleared out. Anne, Margot, Mrs van Pels, everyone was gone. Vanished. It was if they were never there.

Chapter 13

The Lost Train

Often when people in our barracks died, they left behind glimpses of who they once were. I watched a yellow silk monogrammed handkerchief flutter down from the bunk of a young woman as her possessions were being cleared after she died in the night. She had once been known for her beauty. I remember there was a book of equations under the pillow of a woman who had been a physicist. Sometimes the reminder was a person: a sister, a little son or daughter or best friend left behind in the land of the still-living, if you could call this living.

The naked forms of the dead from our camp were bundled into a blanket then taken to the crematorium. But in the parts of the camp housing those prisoners who, like Anne and Margot, came from concentration camps in Poland, the bodies were taken outside, a rope tied to their legs and they were dragged, to one of the piles which were growing daily in between and in front of the barracks. There was apparently not enough room to bury the bodies or capacity to incinerate them. So they lay there, a revolting nightmare not even the sickest of minds could have possibly conjured. I still tried to avoid looking at them, to keep Gabi and me inside so we didn't have to look see them, but there were stacks and stacks of bodies and I was haunted by images I could not erase, even when I was under my blanket at night, trying not to think about them.

By this point, I could barely remember a time when I wasn't hungry. It felt like more and more time passed from one morsel of dry bread or splash of soup to another. Stealing food was punishable by death but, as people became ever more desperate, I heard stories about people who saw swede growing beyond the fence of our camp and risked their lives to reach it. Sometimes they'd make it back, not always. There was now little to no water so we were almost always thirsty. When Gabi brought me her enamel cup and asked, 'Water?' I had to shake my head and say, 'Not now, hopefully soon.' I craved water and food, but I also craved some – *any* – drop of solitude. There must by now have been 1,000 women and children sharing a space intended for around 150 people – 300 at most. It was always noisy; the sounds of our suffering never stilled. And so I longed for silence, even just one quiet moment.

Oma was still able to visit us at least and sometimes we would go to where she lived with other women in their sixties and older. She was 67. I watched as her once round face became progressively more gaunt, the puckered, dry skin – another sign of hunger – pressed over visible bone. She was no exception; all of our bodies had been reduced to this but it hurt me to see a face I knew so well transform into something so otherworldly. When Gabi and I went to see her one day towards the end of March, she, who had relished nothing more than a strong cup of coffee with cake at one of her and my grandfather's favourite cafés, had not eaten anything in days beyond a few cubes of bread. We sat at the foot of her bunk and together she and Gabi practised Gabi's counting and we spoke about the chocolate we would eat together at the seaside in Eretz Yisrael.

A couple of days later, one of Oma's friends found Gabi and I in our barracks.

'I have sad, sad news,' she told me.

I instantly understood.

'Your beautiful Oma died overnight. She loved you girls so much, always sharing stories about you. At least now her suffering is over,' she continued. She then pressed a gold ring, Oma's engagement ring, into the palm of my hand. 'It's yours now. May your grandmother's memory be a blessing.'

Mama, Opa, Papa and now Oma. Mama, Opa, Papa, Oma. I repeated it like a chant. *My family's dead.* It was 25 March 1945, exactly one month since Papa died. I hardly weighed anything but still my body suddenly felt so heavy. I wanted to close my eyes, to cry, but all I could do was feel this leaden weight. It was as if I had sunk into the deepest parts of the earth's core. It was now just Gabi and me. I finally felt tears spilling down my cheeks, warm and salty. They reached my tongue. I stared off in a daze.

When Mrs Abrahams heard the news, she and her sister, Mrs Emanuel, rushed over to find us. They sat with us and stroked our hair. Together, we mourned Oma. Mrs Abrahams reminded us we had been family before and were family now. I thought of one of my favourite biblical stories, the story of Ruth. After Ruth's young husband died, she told Naomi, her Israelite mother-in-law, 'Your people shall be my people.'

Mrs Abrahams squeezed my hand.

* * *

In April, it poured with rain. When the skies occasionally cleared, the faintest hint of the fresh smell of springtime penetrated the nauseating smell of bodies and smouldering crematorium smoke. I felt suddenly feverish. My heart dropped. I had feared this. I must not get typhus, I had told myself, repeating the words like a magical charm. But it was everywhere, sweeping our camp and all the camps within Bergen-Belsen. We had learned that there were two varieties of typhus. One was the more deadly variety, referred to as typhus fever, carried by fleas, and the other was a typhus of the stomach. I was nauseous and had terrible stomach pains, so Mrs Abrahams said she thought I had the second kind. I prayed that was the case. I had to stay well enough to look out for Gabi.

'Poor thing, I know you must feel wretched,' said Mrs Abrahams, laying a cool hand on my forehead.

I struggled to leave my bunk. I only got up to use the latrine, and that was with difficulty. Gabi played on the dirty floor nearby and sang songs with Lily Abrahams, Mrs Abrahams's little girl. There was no quarantine by this point, no place to keep her safe from being infected by me or anyone else. During the day, the non-stop noise vibrating in the cavernous barracks made my head pound.

Some of that sound was grief. Mothers grieving children. A sister grieving her big brother. Children newly orphaned, after a father died one week and a mother a few weeks later, or even just days afterwards. Like I'd had to, they were beginning to understand that death spelled a forever loss. For a child, that means the most primal, basic sense of security is stolen – the ground underneath our feet no longer stable.

Overwhelmed and weak as I was feeling, I was keen to follow reports from the IPA that the British and American soldiers were getting closer. I let myself feel a glimmer of hope. But could they reach us in time, so there would be more of us alive than dead?

What would the SS strategy be as their enemy got close to the fences? And I was worried about Anne and Margot and the others from the Polish camps, who were in worse surroundings than we were. I wanted to know what had happened to them but I was too ill to try to find out and there wasn't much I could do. I could only hold them in my heart and pray for them.

Soon, word about trains started buzzing around the camp. That was, apparently, the answer to our question about what might come next. Our camp was to be evacuated. 'Pack your belongings,' we were told. 'You are being transferred. Trains will be waiting.' Transport terrified us the most. The situation we were in was horrendous but surely we could only be taken somewhere worse. Most of us feared that boarding a train meant only death, especially if the talk of gas chambers was true. I looked at Gabi, as usual scampering nearby with Lily. Her honey-coloured hair had grown limp and stringy for lack of washing; her clothes were matted and coated with dirt.

We were told nothing further but a rumour circulated that they wanted to take us to Theresienstadt, a Czechoslovakian concentration camp, where they would then gas us. I consulted with Mrs Abrahams. Was there any way we could stay? Would it be safer to try to avoid getting on the train, in hope the British and Americans would reach us within days? Soon, though, it was clear we had no choice. The orders were for everyone, no exceptions, bar the weakest and those with the worst cases of typhus, typhoid fever, tuberculosis and dysentery, whom it became clear would have to be left behind.

They told us we would have to walk to the train platform, five miles away. But how? Most of us would barely manage a fraction of that. In the end, some of us were brought to the trains by truck. The first group left on 8 April 1945. I witnessed people I had come to know and care for forced to part. Children who had no choice but to leave ailing parents behind, while parents who wanted to stay with extremely sick children were forced at gunpoint to instead head to the train.

Two days later, it was my group's turn to go. Mrs Abrahams helped Gabi and I to pack up our belongings. Once again, I filled the burgundy suitcase I had first packed with Mrs Ledermann two years earlier. Gabi and I had both outgrown our clothes by now but they were all we had. I packed our enamel bowls and cups, one for each of us, and smoothed over the creased cover of my Florence Nightingale book, a reminder of Mrs Goudsmit and the outside world. I had just one thin blanket for the two of us.

It was hard for me to lift our suitcase but everyone around me was also weak and struggled to carry their belongings too. I was worried I might collapse, and then what would Gabi do? Mrs Abrahams was busy with her seven children, all reassembled now that her two boys were with her, along with her husband. I was relieved when we and our bags were hoisted into the back of a truck. We found seats amid the others, mostly children. Looking back towards Sternlager Camp, I thought about how this was the place I had last seen Papa and Oma. Now we were going on without them. Gabi and I had first lost our mother, then our home, then, one by one, the rest of our family. Gabi had been two years old, a baby really, when we were deported and had lived almost half of her life in camps. I tried to push away these thoughts and focus instead on making it to the train. I was exhausted enough as it was.

The gates of our camp opened; the black and red barrier lifted. I could see the tidy barracks and grounds of the SS officers, including their soccer field. A warm spring sun enveloped us. I noticed the SS officers had switched to their lighter, summer uniforms. We bumped over the same uneven road that had taken us to Bergen-Belsen. Strewn along the way were flashes of black-and-white prison garb on skeletal corpses. I shrunk into my seat and fixed my gaze on the green fir trees just beyond the road or the open, washed-out sky over us.

Deposited at the train platform, we waited for hours as other truckloads arrived and those who came by foot straggled in. No one seemed to have much energy for talking. We were given a bit of bread and margarine for the journey. Some had a couple of raw beets and turnips as well. I scanned the growing crowd for Anne, wondering if she and Margot might also be put on our train. I had only heard her voice when we met at the fence. Would I have even recognised her in the crowd, I wondered, shorn of her beautiful hair and as ill and malnourished as the rest of us?

On the platform, one of the German soldiers who had been sent to escort us smiled when he saw Gabi. They had been fighting with the army, not guarding concentration camps.

'Would you like a cookie?' he asked her.

'What's a cookie?' she asked.

In that moment, I saw his face crumple. Something told me he was only just fully comprehending how dehumanised we had been by his people. His expression seemed to say: 'What have we done?'

Gabi ate the biscuit – every last crumb.

As we waited, the sun went down and the sky grew dark. People lay down and slept. Feverish still, I cradled Gabi's head in my lap. Around midnight, we were loaded onto the waiting cattle cars – somewhere around 45 in total. As the soldiers herded us on the trains, I lost sight of Mrs Abrahams, Mrs Immanuel and their families. Gabi and I found a spot on the straw-strewn floor and sat down next to the sliding door. It was open a crack and I thought the fresh air would be good for us both. But once the train started rattling down the tracks, the wind felt punishing and cold. I shivered and pulled the thin blanket close. I lay down, curled together with Gabi. I barely had the strength to sit up any more. The train was dark; no light was allowed for fear it might make the train a more visible target for bombing. I lay back and tried to black out the groans of my fellow passengers. There were no 'facilities'. People had no other option but to urinate in their underwear. I was at least relieved that the breeze from the door made the smells less overpowering.

I was told by other inmates we'd be travelling between two fronts: the Americans and British were said to be north of us and the Russians further south. Sure enough, we could hear the sounds of fighting getting closer. Through the crack in the door, I could also see the fiery glow of what I assumed were the results of bombings and anti-aircraft guns we could hear going on all around us. At one point, our train lurched to a halt at the sound of an air-raid siren. Sometime later the noise stopped but we did not move. Moonlight fell on our edge of the train car, now finally silent. Later still, we were all shaken awake by the crashing sound of a nearby explosion. The sky was growing red. Some thought it was a nearby city on fire from bombings.

In the dawn that followed, people crept out of the train. We were all incredibly thirsty and some set out to look for water once they realised the German soldiers assigned to guard our wretched lot were not shooting anyone who did so. Only a few people had the strength to wander off on such a mission and I was definitely not one of them. Even if I was, I decided I could not risk getting separated from Gabi.

Someone helped Gabi and me get off the train once it became clear we were going to be here for a little while. I looked around at the strange scene. Some of my fellow prisoners had made small fires where they roasted their beets. Others lay in the grass, fast asleep. I took a deep breath: spring. We had stopped in a meadow, with budding flowers and rich black earth.

'Gabi, look. A bird! See the bird?' I said to her. I couldn't remember seeing or hearing birds at Bergen-Belsen.

'Bird!' she shouted. It was so good to see her smile. I shook out our filthy blanket and with the help of one of the women pulled out our winter coats from the suitcase. I tried to make us a little nest to rest in. We lay back, I closed my eyes and felt the wonder of sunshine on my face. Above us was a deep blue sky.

'Back on the train,' rang out the order. My eyes shot open. Around me I saw German soldiers stamping out the small campfires, knocking over the pots of boiling beets. People scrambled to grab their belongings and run or limp to the train. I don't know how but I found the strength to sweep up our things and head towards our train car as fast as I could, all while holding tight to Gabi's little hand. Back on the train, again to our spot by the door, the misery began again. We were still in Bergen-Belsen, I thought to myself, just a mobile version of that hell.

That first stop and frantic order to reboard signalled what was to come. Travel and stop. Travel and stop – sometimes we'd lurch to a halt for an hour, sometimes for an entire day. Sometimes the stops were at station platforms where we'd line up for water taps. I was not always lucky enough to get water to put in our cups before we were again called to get back on the train. My throat felt dry and parched; I imagined it looked like a sun-cracked desert.

At one of our stops, I watched as the German soldiers tied white sheets and flags to the train doors and along its roof. They wanted the British and Americans who were bombing the area to think this was a civilian train, not a military target. When the bombing got too close, the train would stop and we'd be ordered outside again. Would this ever end? Where were we going?

'Get on the ground! Get on the ground!' the soldiers shouted at us.

It was disorienting, this shift from the monotonous forward motion of the train, body vibrating, eyes closed, wondering when all the coughing and groaning surrounding me might come to a merciful end, only to suddenly find myself being hauled out of the train.

'Run into the fields, get away from the train,' a soldier holding a submachine gun shouted at me. 'Get away from the train, fast!'

That's how I found myself lying on the dirt, my body covering Gabi's, the bombs sounding like claps of approaching thunder. We heard the bombers flying overhead. Terrifying booms echoed around us. There was also artillery fire and some people were screaming. I felt entirely exposed, with only my prayers to God to stave off the terror I felt. I prayed for safety, for the bombs to stop, even though I knew they meant the 'good guys' were trying to save us.

'OK, all clear. Get back on the trains now,' the soldiers shouted once they thought a bombardment, which could last as long as an hour and a half, was finally over.

Every day, I saw people in my train car die. We would try to bury their shrunken figures on the side of the tracks. These were hasty burials, but if there was time, one of their male relatives, or a stranger if needed, would stand over the grave to recite the Kaddish, the Jewish prayer for the dead.

The soldiers guarding us were quite passive, many of them older, all of them with weary, lined faces. Some even spoke openly that the war was already over and they just wanted to go home. It was excruciating to see they had provisions when, by now, none of us had any food left. Gabi asked me for something to eat but there was nothing to give her. All we had was gnawing hunger pains as the wind rushed over us from the crack in the door, a barrage of non-stop cool air with no mercy for our chattering teeth and shivering bodies.

The soldiers did not warn us not to escape. In fact, when the train made a long stop they told us we could forage for food in the forest or walk to one of the villages to ask farmers for food. For most of us this wouldn't have even been possible. Skeletal, yellow stars on our ragged clothing, lice crawling in our hair and eyebrows and not strong enough to outrun the next possible danger. Where would we even go? I could not have risked leaving Gabi, even if I hadn't still been sick. So we remained prisoners without the strength, the clothes, the money or documents to even dream of making a run for freedom.

One of the families on our train car were the Finkels, who had seven children. At one point, when we had been stopped somewhere in the countryside for a while, I heard Ida Finkel tell her older son to go and scout for food at one of the farmhouses we could see in the distance.

'Jackie, you have to get food. This is the end. We're on our way to freedom.'

I watched as Jackie and his father jumped off the train car and made their way towards one of the farmhouses to ask for bread, potatoes – anything. Mr Finkel returned with some potatoes, but Jackie was still heading back as soldiers were sliding the massive train door shut. We could see him racing across a field.

Otto and Anne Frank (centre) with other guests at the wedding
of Miep and Jan Gies, 16 July 1941.

Source: Anne Frank House, Amsterdam.

Jewish families rounded up and forced to leave Amsterdam.

Source: NIOD Institute for War, Holocaust and Genocide Studies, Amsterdam.

Dutch Jews board a train to take them to Auschwitz.

Photograph by Rudolf Breslauer, c. 1942–1943.

Celebration of Hanukkah in Westerbork, the Netherlands.

Photograph by Rudolf Breslauer, c. 1942–1944.

Source: NIOD Institute for War, Holocaust and Genocide Studies, Amsterdam.

Transit camp at Westerbork, the Netherlands, *c.* 1940.

Life at Bergen-Belsen, Germany.

Jewish prisoners from Bergen-Belsen in the immediate aftermath of the liberation by American troops in Farsleben, Germany, on 13 April 1945. They had been on one of three trains that set out from Bergen-Belsen towards Theresienstadt concentration camp at the very end of the war. Hannah and her sister, Gabi, were on another of the three trains, dubbed 'the lost train', which meandered for almost two weeks before being liberated by Red Army soldiers.

Hannah and Gabi with their aunt Edith after the war, *c.* 1947.

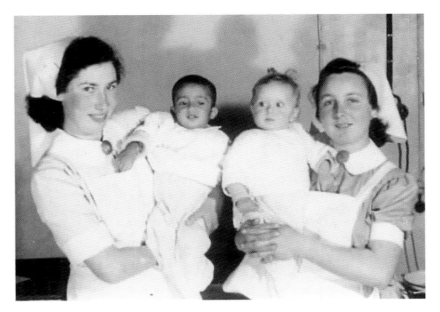

Hannah and a fellow young nurse hold two of the babies
in care at the hospital, Jerusalem, *c.* 1948.

Hannah meets with the actress who played Anne Frank in the first Hebrew production of the play *The Diary of Anne Frank*, 1957.

Hannah with her husband, Dr Walter Pinchas, in Jerusalem after the war.

Hannah with her husband and children, Yochi, Chagi and Ruthie, in Jerusalem.

Hannah at the Anne Frank House, Amsterdam, pointing
at herself in a photo on the wall, October 2012.

Source: Marcel Antonisse / EPA / Shutterstock.

Hannah holding up a photo of her childhood friend Anne Frank in 2022.

Source: Eric Sultan / The Lonka Project.

'Wait! Stop!' Mrs Finkel shouted at the guards. 'My son is still out there; open the door for him! You have to open the door for him!'

I watched her pounding her fists on the train door, screaming. My heart ached for her and the whole family. We could only watch their agony. Her husband tried to console his wife: 'He'll catch up with the train soon, when it stops next. You'll see.'

But the train kept racing along, this time not stopping the rest of the day until nightfall. Poor Mrs Finkel lay on the train floor, moaning, 'Where's Jackie? What happened to my Jackie?'

I didn't know what to say. I prayed silently for God to protect him.

*   *   *

It was dark when our train pulled up to what we were told was Berlin. Berlin! Where I was born, the city my mother and father loved and pined for. But it was now, we could see as we approached its outskirts, at least partially in ruins. I thought about my family's elegant apartment building across from the Tiergarten. I wondered if it was still standing. I stood up from my spot on the filthy, hard wooden floor and tried to peek out for a better look. I saw flattened buildings; a building burned out from one end to the other, the street visible on the other side. Few people were walking around that I could see and most of them were soldiers or firemen sifting through the debris. It was such a big city but so completely broken down, I thought to myself. I felt a foreign emotion well up inside: revenge. I realised I was happy that the city had suffered.

The train cut through Berlin, station by station, until we were again in the countryside. It was getting harder to take a few steps or even sit up as the days passed. At this point I could no longer keep track. Had we been living on this death-trap train for a week? Longer? Why was it taking so long to get somewhere?

Around me, I saw people had begun trading whatever they had for food – the leather jacket of a beloved, now dead, father, or jewels, watches, even pieces of gold. At one of our stops, I dug around the very bottom of my rucksack where I'd hidden Oma's diamond engagement ring. I found it and held it up close to examine it – admiring its smooth, deep gold band with the small, sparkling diamond at its centre. It had been slid on her finger by Opa in the same burned and bombed-out Berlin we had just recently passed.

At the next stop, I pooled the ring with other rings from women in my train car. I walked up to a German soldier and said, 'We'll trade you this for food.'

He returned with a freshly killed rabbit. The exchange was six gold rings for one rabbit. One of the women quickly built a small fire over a circle of rocks and roasted our prize. We gathered around the fire and shared the tough but treasured pieces of meat. I picked apart small pieces and fed them to Gabi. It was important we both eat all of our allotment.

'Eat, Gigi. It could be a while till we have anything else,' I told her. She was not picky that day and ate every last piece.

Back on the train, people were only growing sicker. More drifted off and never woke up, their bodies removed for quick, now almost routine trackside burials. The smell of the train car was as foul as the sounds of its misery: a chorus of moaning, calls for 'Mama' and prayer. Despite being so ill myself, I knew I had to survive because of Gabi. Even as days and nights blurred, it meant willing myself to make it to the next day. I did not want to be a *'Muselmann'* – the word we used at Bergen-Belsen to describe someone who had been reduced to a starving, hopeless lump – void of any spark of life or desire to survive.

As we slowly continued on our way, the earth continued to shake with the sounds of war, buzzing airplanes, the rat-a-tat-tat of gunners and the massive booms of falling bombs. Why are they torturing us? I wondered. If they want to kill us, why are we still alive?

A Hungarian man with glasses, perhaps in his thirties, was sitting next to Gabi and me. I could see he was extremely sick, probably with dysentery, maybe also typhus. He had diarrhoea and had been relieving himself in a bowl. As the train rumbled onwards, he limped over to the slice of open door just above us to toss the contents of his bowl outside. But he missed and the waste fell directly onto our blanket as we lay there together on the floor. It also splattered on us. Frail as I was, I screamed. I cried. I shouted with a fury and volume that startled everyone around us. I was hysterical and for a while just could not calm down. 'How will we ever get clean?' I wailed.

I had tried so hard to keep our one blanket as clean as possible, shaking it off at every stop, doing my best to keep it free of dirt and lice. The putrid stench now clung to the blanket, our clothes. There was no water on the train to drink, let alone to wash ourselves and our belongings.

* * *

On what I would find out later was our thirteenth day of wandering, I woke up. The train had stopped again. I looked around and saw that the train car was empty. 'Gigi, what happened?' I asked but she just shook her head.

'Where is everyone?' I shouted out, suddenly very frightened.

A voice called out, 'The Russians! The Russians liberated us. We woke up and the German soldiers were gone – vanished. Russian soldiers came upon our abandoned train and started speaking to us but no one understood what they were saying. One of the Jewish Russian soldiers who spoke Yiddish told us, "People: you are free now."'

Liberation. I had dreamt of this since being woken at dawn five years earlier from the roar of invading German planes; I had prayed for this day, fantasised about and had almost given up hope of ever seeing it. And this was it? I had missed the triumph of seeing the German soldiers skulk off into the night? I had been deprived of seeing soldiers on our side, our heroes, telling us we were free? Would I not hear the cheers of the people I had suffered with for so long expressing together the deepest sense of relief?

I felt frustrated – robbed.

I dragged myself to the train door and looked outside: where even were we?

Chapter 14

Liberation

I tried to stretch my limbs. They felt limp and heavy. My whole body was leaden. The train floor was scattered with straw and sticky with human excrement, the disgusting smell making me nauseous despite my empty stomach. Hardly anyone was left on the train; most had gone to the nearby village to look for food and shelter. Of the handful of people who remained was Robert Heilbut and his mother. Robert was, I think, about a year younger than me and he'd also slept through liberation, just like I had. Hearing the news that Russian soldiers on horseback had told us we were now 'free', he responded by groaning, 'I've heard that one before.' He rolled over and fell back asleep.

In Amsterdam, the Heilbuts had lived across the street from us and attended our synagogue. Our parents were friendly. Robert's father and two older brothers had not survived, I'd learned. So it was only him and his mother now. A few days previously, I'd seen her trade her dead husband's and middle son's watches for a few tins of canned meat and some cheese from the soldiers. Even so, Mrs Heilbut was still too weak to leave the train. And so was Mrs Finkel, who was very ill. Her son, Jackie, had of course not caught up with the train after it had left him behind, as her husband had tried to reassure her that he would. Both Mrs Finkel and Mrs Heilbut would have to stay behind for now. But we needed to go. I had to get us away from this train and find food.

I dragged myself to the edge of the car. The Russian soldiers had instructed everyone on the train to look for food and to commandeer a house in the nearby village of Tröbitz. So, together with Robert, Gabi and I started to walk in what we hoped was the right direction. But – 'commandeer'? The idea that I could take over a house from German people struck me as absurd. *Look at me*, I thought. I was a rail-thin 16-year-old girl who was finding walking a short distance exhausting. How could I possibly take anything from anyone?

Still, we started down a path through thick woods. Luckily, it turned out the village wasn't far away but we were so weak it took us some time to get there. When we reached a clearing that led into the village, I took in the sight of houses with white stucco walls and red tile rooftops built close to one another along a cobblestone road. White flags fashioned from sheets were hanging from many of the windows.

Others from the train were roaming between the houses. I was transfixed by the jars of preserves and bread they were carrying. Someone we passed told us they'd been looting cellars brimming with food. Even after these long years of war, the cellars told a story of plenty: jars of vegetables, including corn, peas and pickles, jam and loaves of bread, hunks of cheese, meat. The survivors from our nightmare train were loading what they could into sacks that had previously contained flour and sugar. When we walked past the town's bakery, we saw that its windows had been shattered, smashed by people desperate to reach the bread inside. Some people had even found pots of stew and soup boiling on stovetops and gulped them down straight from the pan. I would later learn that many of those who gorged on the newfound paradise of plenty became violently ill and some even died. Faced with food for the first time in so long, their famished bodies were overwhelmed. To almost starve to death only to die from the first meal to break your famine seems desperately cruel.

By now, my hunger outweighed my fear, so together, we walked into one of the houses. I saw cheese and milk in the kitchen but the German woman living there, her eyes round with fear, and very possibly disgust at the sight of us, pleaded: 'It's all my baby and I have left to eat.' Robert and I looked at one another and didn't take it. Instead, we headed directly down the stairs to inspect the cellar. We searched everywhere but couldn't find much of anything left to eat. The house had already been ransacked by the others from the train. We also discovered there were no more houses left in Tröbitz to try to stay in; everywhere was full. The survivors from the train were not 'kicking out' the German residents but sharing the quarters together in uneasy proximity. There was just no room left.

It was so strange to me that the Germans were frightened of us now – although repulsed is perhaps the better word. They looked at us in horror as we wandered about in our soiled rags, bone thin, demanding food. They recoiled from our appearance, and no doubt from the diseases we carried, too. I learned they were terrified of the Russians. One villager told us she was sure that they would herd them into the village church and burn them all. They believed the propaganda their leaders fed them about rampaging, murderous Russians. Later, when I'd had some time to process the scene that day, I wondered: why aren't they mad instead at their government, who did this to us?

I didn't know what to do. It was so frustrating that we'd lost time in the race to find a place to stay. Soon, we saw some Russian soldiers – the first I'd actually laid eyes on. I noticed that, like the German villagers, they also seemed stunned by our appearance. Some of the soldiers wept when they first saw us. They also clearly wanted to keep their distance, not wanting to catch typhus, dysentery or anything else we might be infected with. They instructed us to go to Schilde, a tiny farming hamlet nearby. In Tröbitz, most residents had put up white flags and surrendered when the Russians arrived, but stayed where they were. In Schilde, some residents had fled, leaving empty houses.

Once we made it to Schilde, someone directed us to the house of the village's mayor, an ardent Nazi party member who had taken his family and run away. It was now ours. Our luck was that the cellar had some food, but not too much. So there was no opportunity to gorge on rich foods and inadvertently eat ourselves to death. We mostly found potatoes and some jam. The gas stove was working and so we located a pot and boiled the potatoes on the stove. The warm potato melted on my tongue. Gabi hungrily gobbled up her share. It was incomparably better than what some of us on the train had resorted to: chewing on leaves and even sucking on the bark from trees.

A mother and her daughter claimed the one side of the house for themselves. They promised to make sure to keep the other half for us, as so many were competing for shelter. So we left and made our way slowly back to the train to bring Mrs Heilbut back to this Nazi mayor's house. We found a small wagon, a wheelbarrow of sorts, to transport her back.

By now, our new reality was beginning to sink in.

'Gabi, we really are free,' I told her.

Her forehead wrinkled. 'Free?'

'Yes, free. No more camp, no more train. Tonight we will sleep in a real bed!'

On the walk back to Schilde, the shooting hunger pains calmed by that first meal of luscious potatoes, I let myself feel the warm sun on my skin. It poured through the trees, spilled onto the wildflowers. Even uttering the word springtime – 'This is springtime!' – to Gabi felt like a thrill. I pointed out to her the brilliant blue of the sky, informed her that flowers come in all colours and can give off the most wonderful fragrance. I don't think she remembered there was such a thing as flowers in the world. I let myself take in deep breaths of the clean air, not a trace of crematorium smoke to be found.

I realised with a start: *I am warm, I am not hungry.* I repeated the words as I tried to digest this information.

Back at our requisitioned house, we did our best to clean away the broken glass on the floor, the result of those who had broken in earlier searching for food. Mrs Heilbut, even though she was weak, helped to get us organised. We had to get clean, that I knew, trying to think what my mother would have told us to do next. I perched Gabi on a chair in the bathroom and peeled off our soiled, lice-infested clothes. I sponged her and then myself with the cold water that ran from the tap. I was shivering as I washed my hair but, still, I barely felt the cold. It was exhilarating to wash away weeks of filth and sweat – to remember what being clean felt like again. I was astonished to see Gabi's eyes shine out from her soft, freshly washed face.

I found a dress hanging in a closet, made of red wool with black geometric shapes. It was my size. I presumed it belonged to a girl who lived in the house. It was nothing special, just a regular dress.

But it was a dress without lice. I stepped into it slowly and for a moment let myself luxuriate in the newness of such a sensation. No itching, no stickiness, no stench.

Now that both of us were clean and in clean clothes, I pulled down the white eiderdown quilt on the bed in the room Gabi and I were going to share. I caressed the white sheets, feeling the softness of the cotton, inhaling their freshly washed smell. Their unblemished whiteness felt almost blinding to my eyes. My dream from the barracks of Bergen-Belsen was coming true: a clean, soft bed. Our emaciated bodies sank into the mattress. I pulled the quilt close over the two of us and snuggled into it, totally elated. Gabi giggled. I was also struck that we were alone, in our own private, quiet room! None of the racket from the crowded, ever-noisy barracks.

I looked out from the bed and around the room, noticing that the light green walls were actually wallpaper. There was a repeating pattern of a shape on it. It suddenly took form before my eyes. Swastikas.

I could hardly believe it. The bedroom we were sleeping in on our first night of freedom was covered in swastika wallpaper.

*   *   *

Those first few days were spent mostly in and around the house as we slowly got our strength back. There were six of us altogether in the house: Mrs Heilbut and Robert, Gabi and I, and a mother and daughter named Theresa and Ursula Klau – all of us German Jews who had found refuge in Amsterdam. Mrs Heilbut, stronger every day, was extremely resourceful. She identified a plant growing in the garden that was edible and from it made a nourishing soup for us. She kept reminding us to eat slowly and not too much.

The worst part of being on the train had been seeing Gabi so emotionless. She was like a rag doll, not complaining, nor crying. She was starving, like all of us, unable to do much beyond existing. Our main activity as sisters was picking lice off one another, crushing them between our nails. I felt such relief watching her in our temporary home slurp spoonfuls of soup, the light coming back into her eyes.

The Russian soldiers in their drab green uniforms with the five-pointed red star, the symbol of the Communist party, on their caps pretty much left us alone. There was a language barrier when trying to communicate with them, but they did give us ration cards to buy basic provisions like margarine, cheese, milk and bread in the local shops. They also set up a small field hospital. They forced local German women to retrieve the gravely ill who had remained behind on the train cars. Some they carried on small wagons, others in makeshift stretchers made of blankets.

We were free, but the number of dead still grew. Bodies lay on the ground of both villages, covered in blankets, awaiting burial.

Gabi and I had been separated from Mrs Abrahams and her family on the train but I desperately wanted to find out what had happened to them. Trying to remain hopeful, I started asking around. Information of any kind was hard to come by. But eventually, I found out that Mrs Abrahams, her husband and eldest son had died of typhus the day after liberation. The cruelty of it sucked the breath from my body for a moment. She had done so much for us. How would I have managed without her care for Gabi while I was in the hospital after our arrival at Bergen-Belsen? She let us into her family group and held me when we lost first Opa, then Papa and Oma. She had been our *lamedvovnik*, our quiet human saint.

Much later, I learned the numbers. Of the 2,500 forced onto that train at Bergen-Belsen, 568 people did not survive. Our train had wandered for 13 days as the Russians and British closed in. I could not have said at the time how long we spent on it; it seemed simply a nightmare without end. Though perhaps the planned ending would have been worse than the journey: I later heard from the Finkel family that the train engineer had told Mr Finkel he had received orders to drive our train to the edge of a bridge over a river and let it plunge into the water.

There were in fact two other trains that also left Bergen-Belsen around the same time as ours, headed for the Theresienstadt, or Terezin, ghetto in Czechoslovakia. One made it there; another was liberated by the Allies. Ours would later be dubbed 'The Lost Train'.

* * *

In the mornings, I'd watch the early light start to fill the swastika-covered room. Gabi and I were beginning to adjust, to reawaken to the colours and scents of springtime and life. I could smell coffee brewing in the kitchen, I'd run my hands over clean towels and sheets. It was all a wonder.

The tiny villages of Tröbitz and Schilde felt fully under Russian occupation. We saw the soldiers on foot, on horseback and in trucks, riding through the small streets. Once even a column of their tanks rolled through Tröbitz. They were our liberators. Officially 'Soviet', of course, but we simply called them 'the Russians'. I did not have any negative interactions with them but we knew the Germans in the villages where we were living were especially fearful of these soldiers viewing their women and girls as 'spoils of war'. There was justification for this fear. The Red Army had become notorious on the battlefield for equating their role liberating Europe with behaving as they pleased.

The women in our house were understandably wary of them – and protective of me and Ursula, the other teenage girl living with us. A story was circulating that two women from the train were raped and died shortly afterwards. Women tried different tricks to avoid this danger. There was an 18-year-old who had learned to say in Russian 'I'm only 14'. She said that when she was approached by a group of soldiers this seemed to work and they backed off. Ursula's mother put up a sign in the window with red dots, indicating (falsely) that we were a house with scarlet fever. It may well have worked as I don't remember soldiers trying to enter the house.

So there we were on the edge of a forest, in remote farming villages surrounded by a motley mix of Russians – overwhelmed by the task of overseeing us and who we feared might rape us – and Germans, who loathed us. They hated us, instead of the German Nazis who did this to us. We all desperately wanted to get out of Germany, to return to the Netherlands. But we were told we'd have to wait. A young married couple decided they did not want to wait any longer. At some point, they stole a pair of bicycles and biked all the way – over 400 miles – back home to Holland.

I don't even remember hearing the news of 7 May that Germany had unconditionally surrendered to the Allied troops. Hitler, I'd hear later, had committed suicide on 30 April, exactly a week after the train stopped and we were told we were free.

About six weeks later, towards the end of June, restless and ready to move on, we were finally told by the Russian soldiers to report at 8am the following day with our belongings in the centre of Tröbitz. We were going to be taken back to Holland, with a stop first in

Leipzig, a city 50 miles to the west. This was the news we were waiting for. But it was also painful for those who, like Mrs Abrahams's children, were leaving behind loved ones who did not survive those first days. Mrs Abrahams was buried with several dozen others in a new section of the Tröbitz cemetery made for those of us from the train who had died after liberation.

'We are going back to Holland, Gabi,' I told her. Holland! She knew that was where we were from but had no memory of our lives there. She was now four and a half. I had tried to keep the memory of our parents alive, telling her stories about them, and I also told her about my friends – Anne, Sanne, Ilse, Jacque – and the games we played together and jokes we shared. Now that returning to Holland was within sight, I began fantasising about possible reunions with them. I was so grateful I'd seen Anne. For some reason, I was certain she would have made it. Surely she'd also be on her way back to Amsterdam too, I thought.

I did not have much to pack in the old suitcase from home. The morning we set out, I was wearing my only dress: the black and red wool one I'd found hanging in the closet. We saw a long line of military trucks when we got to the centre of Tröbitz and milling around them American soldiers who, I'd find out, called themselves GIs. Together with Mrs Heilbut and Robert, we climbed onto the waiting trucks. The Americans seemed so different to me from the Russian soldiers. They were in a good mood, no doubt happy to be going home themselves soon. They laughed a lot and tried to speak with us in English.

Bumping along in the truck we travelled through the countryside to Leipzig. So far, apart from my view through the gap in the train carriage, we had only properly seen Bergen-Belsen and the tiny towns of Tröbitz and Schilde, so it was good to see the open fields, valleys and church steeples whirring by. When we entered Leipzig, I saw the rubble and flattened buildings that indicated how severely the city had been bombed. I was beginning to understand just how devastating this war had been beyond my limited view of it.

We arrived at a school that had been converted into a temporary shelter for us. There were long rows of cots and makeshift kitchens where we did our cooking. I saw the Finkel family again when I helped Mr Finkel carry heavy blanket rolls into the school. There were people from other concentration camps being housed there too. I wondered if Anne and Margot might be there and kept scanning the crowds for their faces. We were there just a few days until we were taken on a Red Cross hospital train to the Dutch border.

Gabi looked at me with some hesitation when she saw the train. 'This is a good train, Gigi. Don't worry,' I told her.

It was staffed by friendly American nurses who made us comfortable in soft beds provided for us. Like everyone else, I was still extremely thin. I weighed only 30 kilograms and this was after several weeks recuperating in Schilde, so I still felt pretty tired most of the time.

At one point, the nurses handed out tinned pork for us to eat. I was kosher so I'd never eaten pork before. But I also knew well the principle of *pikuach nefesh*, the Jewish tenet that the preservation of human life overrides any of the Jewish laws. I figured this might be my only chance to sample this meat that everyone found so tasty, which was otherwise forbidden to me.

Oh no, I thought, opening the tin to see the fatty part of a piece of ham, which I understood was not as delicious as the bacon that an even more religious friend than I had received in her tin. I ate it and it wasn't bad. But I always wondered what that bacon tasted like.

The remaining 350 miles to the Dutch border brought us through the Elbe River valley, with views of mountains and farming hamlets, and past the city of Weimar, birthplace of my mother's beloved Goethe and where Germany's first democratic constitution was signed, lending its name to the creation of my father's beloved Weimar Republic. Soon we reached a border province of the south-east Netherlands called Limburg, a rolling landscape now pockmarked by battle-scarred villages and towns. We were on Dutch soil again! I immediately felt a wave of relief wash through me. It hardly seemed real.

Our first stop was an old castle with cherry trees in the garden. 'You are stopping here first for medical check-ups and delousing,' the nurses told us.

As we stepped onto the grounds we were delighted to be met by a pair of local sisters in their early twenties who gave us some sweets, a gesture that moved us greatly. But we then encountered a bewildering scene: a line of Dutch men and women guarded by American and Canadian soldiers.

'Who are they?' I asked.

'Dutch Nazis – the NSB,' someone answered. It seems they had recently been rounded up and were awaiting trial. I thought of my old school friend Lucie's parents – I wondered what the war had been like for her. Would her parents be among the arrested? Their faces grew dark when they saw us. Some of the other Jews who had been on the Red Cross train yelled and cursed at them.

I felt angry and confused. Who thought to put returning Jews and Nazis in the same place, I wondered? We, who all longed for a warm return in Holland, were jolted by the sight of homegrown Nazis, having thought ourselves finally free of them when we left Germany.

There was a long line to get clean clothes. I breathed in the fresh, laundered smell of them – I still couldn't get over the wonder of this scent. I was also given shoes. Leather shoes that fit, that did not pinch my toes! And we were also deloused, which involved being doused in a special kind of powder.

Our next mission was to stand in another line to get registered. It was then I remembered that Gabi and I were officially 'stateless'. We had only ever had German citizenship, but as Jews that was stripped from us after Hitler came to power. I had grown up only knowing Amsterdam as home, speaking Dutch at school. But officially, I was not Dutch. I recoiled at the idea of anyone considering us German. As much as my parents had always felt themselves to be German and I spoke fluent German, my mother tongue, I was scared of the Germans still. The Dutch officials registering us seemed puzzled at what to do with so many of us like this: German-born 'stateless' Jews.

I was happy when the doctor examining Gabi did not find anything wrong with her. 'She's just fine,' he said. Then, turning to me for my exam, he pressed a stethoscope up to my chest and back. I felt a sharp pain as I followed his instructions and breathed in deeply. I told him it was sometimes painful when I coughed.

'I'm afraid your lungs have been damaged,' he said. 'You have pleurisy, an inflammation of the lungs.'

He said he was sending me to a nearby hospital in the city of Maastricht. Gabi, because she was fine, could continue onwards. *What?* We couldn't be separated. We only had each other. I tried to explain. But the doctor said no. Gabi could not stay with me.

I felt panic rising inside of me. I remembered the feeling; it was the same panic I'd felt coming down with jaundice the morning after arriving at Bergen-Belsen. My mind raced frantically. How could I be separated from Gabi? Who would care for her instead? I felt a stab of grief thinking once more of good-hearted Mrs Abrahams.

But again, helpers stepped in. Mrs Heilbut said not to worry, she'd accompany Gabi to Laren, just outside of Amsterdam, and make sure she was fine. There she would be handed over to the care of – I could hardly believe it when I heard this – Mr and Mrs Birnbaum, the 'angels' from Westerbork who had run the orphanage there. Miraculously, they had survived along with their six children and were still performing their selfless work looking after orphaned Jewish children in Laren. It was arranged that the Birnbaum family would care for Gabi till I could be reunited with her.

On 1 July, I gave Gabi a long goodbye hug. I rubbed her fuzzy, freshly shorn head. I was told it was the only way we could get rid of the lice, hopefully once and for all, though fortunately I had been spared that indignity. And so, having kept her hair in Sternlager at Bergen-Belsen, Gabi's head was now shaved.

'We will be together soon,' I promised as she curled herself into me. It felt agonising to part ways. Everything about us was intertwined. We fell asleep next to one another every night; it was seeing Gabi when I woke up in the morning that had forced me to move forward in even the blackest of moments. I had done all I could to keep her alive, which in turn had stopped me from giving up. Thank God the Birnbaums would be waiting for her, or I hardly know what I would have done.

'You'll see, little mouse, I'll come and pick you up as soon as I'm out of the hospital,' I told her as she prepared to board the train to Amsterdam, 100 miles away on the other side of the Netherlands.

My time was to be spent recuperating. When I arrived at the Catholic hospital in Maastricht, a nun was on the front steps waiting for me. I was taken aback by her starched white headdress and black tunic, but her smile helped me relax. What I remember most from my time there is the fresh clean sheets and summer sunlight, long days meant for healing. My lungs needed to clear and I had to gain weight, mostly with the help of large bowls of oatmeal. The nurses and doctors made small talk but no one asked what had happened to me. I did not know yet how to speak about what I'd endured over the past two years. It felt like a dark, impossible dream, but one it was absolutely clear to me even then that I could not wish or imagine away. I'm not even sure I searched for words to make it make sense. In the hushed, clean corridors and rooms of the hospital, the lice-eaten barracks – dark, filthy and endlessly loud – at times felt like an appalling apparition.

A girl named Erica, about my age, who had also been in Westerbork (we had worked together in the orphanage) and Bergen-Belsen, shared my hospital room and we quickly became good friends. It was so good to have a companion as we both recuperated.

One of the first things I did was write letters to the only people I knew I had left in the world: Mrs Goudsmit in Amsterdam, Uncle Hans in Switzerland and Aunt Eugenie in England. I had memorised my aunt and uncle's addresses in the hope I would be able to contact them once we were free but so far had only been able to write short postcards.

I soon heard back, first from Mrs Goudsmit, in a letter she wrote on 14 July. She began, 'It was with joy, but also with sadness, that we heard a little of your fate from your first card. We found your names on a list and then immediately investigated further. Then your two postcards arrived, and today your three letters.'

She then wrote that her husband had seen Mr Frank. I could hardly believe I was reading such words. Anne had seemed convinced he was murdered at Auschwitz. Her words 'I have no one' had never stopped ringing in my ears.

Mrs Goudsmit continued:

My husband met Mr Frank, a good friend of yours. He has returned from Auschwitz, but he does not yet know anything about what happened to his wife and children. The men thought about it together, and he immediately wrote to your uncle in England and in Switzerland, whom he knows well. There's no need for you to worry any more, you'll see, you will be taken care of. Now you just have to wait, but everything will be fine. We and Mr Frank, who seems to be a very kind, good person (I will be meeting him tomorrow for the first time) will not let you down.

I felt so moved by her words. And I was relieved to see a reference to her husband, Paul. I knew that he was Jewish but somehow he had made it through.

She also had fresh word of Gabi, whom she and her husband had visited at the orphanage in Laren! Mr Frank had somehow found out she was there and told them. I felt like my heart would burst with joy reading her words:

She is staying there at the Birnbaums', who have a very small cottage in the orphanage. It was quite a reunion. She still knows who we are. She is as sweet and adorable as she always was, only much smarter and more sensible. She looks very well.

She also gave me the update on dear Sjors. She described him now as 'a big lad' and said that he had come with them to visit Gabi, and the two had played again together like old times. The Goudsmits had brought her stuffed brown bear and other favourite stuffed animals, which they had taken for safekeeping after we were deported.

Reading news of our old world from our old dear neighbours brought me such joy and relief. I found myself wiping away tears reading the letter. She told me to focus on getting better and was so kind to reassure me Gabi was in good hands. My heart hurt with relief to hear she had been able to see Gabi in person.

And now above all, my darling, don't worry about anything. Just think about getting healthy and strong again. Let others take care of you now. I know that everything will be fine. Gigilein is so well taken care of. The Birnbaums are so good, and they are taking care of her, and we are nearby too … And now my beloved Hanneli, take care. All my love and heartfelt kisses.

After two years feeling entirely cut off from the civilised world, the connection and the feelings of warmth, love and hope these words evoked are hard for me to describe, even now.

I rested back on my pillows and tried to imagine Gabi's reunion with her old sidekick Sjors and how Mrs Goudsmit must have wrapped her in hugs and kisses. Then I greedily gobbled up the good news again of Mr Frank's return. I read and reread the letter at least 20 times and told Erica and the nurses about it and all the good news it held.

Within a day or two, I received a handwritten postcard with the return address of Opekta – Mr Frank's office in the building over-looking the canal that I knew so well. It was from Mr Frank! He'd written it on 13 July 1945, the day he had met Mr Goudsmit.

'Welcome to the Netherlands,' it began.

I have asked after you for such a long time, and you can imagine how attached to you I am given our old friendship. If there is anything I can do for you, please let me know. I will be going to Laren tomorrow to see Gabi and I will report back to you. I have written to Uncle Hans twice. I have also asked an acquaintance to visit you and report back how you are doing. It's sad you had to be held back. Beterschap [a Dutch expression meaning 'get well']: *I hope that you will feel better soon. What can you report about Anne and Margot? What did Ilse Wagner tell you?*

He soon sent further word that he'd be making the journey to visit me soon. I had not heard anything from Ilse, so did not know what he meant, but I so hoped I'd be seeing her soon too. Although I still didn't feel strong enough to do a cartwheel like Anne, Sanne and I used to, I did a little cartwheel of joy in my mind to celebrate this wondrous news.

Chapter 15

Beterschap

'Hanneli, you have a visitor,' one of my favourite nurses told me. I was sitting up in my bed, golden afternoon light filling the room.

A tall, gaunt man in a suit appeared. For a moment, I was startled by how changed this familiar face was. But I immediately recognised the deep-set brown eyes filled with kindness.

'Mr Frank!' I burst out.

'Hanneli!' he said, rushing towards me.

I was overcome by how good it was to see him. For a moment, time collapsed. We were back on the Merwedeplein. I was safe, cared for and loved. I felt a surge of strength looking at Mr Frank's face, seeing him stand in front of me, in solid human form. Not a memory. Instantly, I felt less alone.

'It was quite a journey to reach you,' Mr Frank said. 'For the last 14 hours, I've been on a truck!' The roads across the Netherlands, like the rest of Europe, were in a dreadful shape in the wake of the war's destruction, cratered and broken from bombs, key bridges wiped off the map.

When he reached out to hug me, I felt self-conscious at how underweight I was and thanked my luck that, unlike Gabi, my hair was not shorn after liberation. I hoped I was still recognisable to him, even following these three unimaginable years since we last met.

'Anne's alive! I saw her,' I told him. The words poured out of me. I felt so sure and was excited to let him know.

But then, confusion. I watched as his face, so bright in greeting me, crumpled and darkened.

He quietly told me: Anne and Margot were dead.

We spoke for a very long time. In his slow, steady voice, whose competence and fatherliness I felt with every devastating word, he walked me through what had happened. He had been so full of hope for a reunion with Anne and Margot. But as time passed and others returned, or word about their whereabouts surfaced, and there was still no information about his girls, a creeping fear began to overtake him. Anne and Margot had been the single sustaining hope that had kept him alive through the beatings and deprivation at Auschwitz.

About a month after he was liberated in Auschwitz on 27 January by the Red Army, he had found out that Mrs Frank had died a couple of weeks earlier of illness and exhaustion. Had she held on just a little longer, he said, his voice trailing off, she too could have been freed. The woman who told her of Mrs Frank's death had been in Auschwitz with her and had also witnessed Anne and Margot be selected for a transport to another concentration camp.

The family had originally arrived together in Auschwitz, 25 square miles of mass-murdering prison in southern Poland, on 6 September 1944. They were on a transport of 1,011 Jews in sealed, stiflingly hot cattle cars, on what turned out to be the last train east from Westerbork. By now, enough rumours had spread for them to know Auschwitz likely spelled death, but Mr Frank – still then somehow the optimist I remembered him to be – had clung to the hope that the advancing Allied forces might be able to rescue them in time.

Most trains arrived at nighttime, another tool of the Germans to disorient and terrorise their victims. Men and women were immediately separated. His last sight of Mrs Frank and the girls was Margot's shocked face. Those over 50 were normally selected before sunrise to be sent to the gas chambers. But Mr Frank, then 55, arrived healthy and looking relatively well fed after over two years in hiding – that and his almost regal bearing may have been what saved him from that fate. Instead, he was put to work, first outside digging ditches and then inside peeling potatoes – a job that came with an automatic suspicion that prisoners were stealing. Mr Frank received heavy and regular beatings from one particular kapo. But he had a strategy for staying alive that he shared with his comrades, including the other men from the hiding place: to focus on mental survival by avoiding those who spent endless hours imagining and discussing food and to instead sustain themselves and their dignity by talking of opera, the music of Beethoven and Schubert and books.

By November 1944, Mr Frank's resilience ran out and he could hardly stand. He was despondent, subsisting on little food, and the diarrhoea would not stop. A helpful Jewish doctor had him placed in the sick barracks, a move that saved his life. As the Red Army advanced and the Nazis started planning the evacuation of the prisoners, he begged Anne's old friend Peter van Pels, with whose family he had hidden for those years in the attic and who had been transported with him to Auschwitz, to hide with him in the sick barracks. Peter's own father had been gassed in October and he had become like a son to Mr Frank, secretly bringing him extra food every night when he was ill. Now, faced with a forced march ordered of all those still able to walk as they vacated the camp ahead of the approaching Red Army, going into hiding again seemed the best option. But Peter declined, thinking he had a better chance of survival on the march – a decision that proved fatal. He survived the march, arriving at Mauthausen where he was forced to labour in the mines. He had fallen ill and died five days after the camp was liberated by American soldiers.

Mr Frank was the only one of their group of eight who had hidden together in Amsterdam to survive.

He told me that the first Shabbat after liberation, when he was still in Auschwitz, he had huddled together with the other men, like him, still deathly weak, and led them in reciting the Kiddush, the ceremonial prayer for sanctifying and ushering in Shabbat. He knew the words and the tune because of the many Shabbat dinners he had spent with my family in Amsterdam.

It took him a long time to get home to Amsterdam. The journey back home for Auschwitz survivors like Mr Frank, who weighed just 52 kilograms when the camp was liberated at the end of January, began by train to the Polish town of Katowice only in March. He finally reached the Ukrainian port city of Odessa, where he waited for weeks for permission to return to Holland. The war in Europe was still being fought in parts of Western Europe and Holland was not yet liberated. It took until 5 May 1945 for the Germans in the Netherlands to surrender – the week after Hitler committed suicide, and almost five years to the day since they invaded and I hid in my parents' bed as warplanes roared overhead. Two weeks after Holland was liberated, Mr Frank boarded a New Zealand ship to Marseilles and then onwards to Amsterdam.

In Amsterdam, his excruciating limbo continued as he scoured listings in newspapers for names of both survivors and victims. He never stopped asking the Red Cross about the fate of his daughters. Every day, he'd trudge over to the central railway station to search the lists that were posted there with names and information. He also paid for ads in the local newspapers seeking information about his daughters. He reasoned that perhaps they were in a hospital recovering or a displaced persons camp in a Soviet-held area, from where it was even more difficult to obtain updates. He was not alone: Jews and non-Jews in all corners of the globe were desperately trying to find out the fate of their loved ones.

It was on 18 July, just five days after he wrote me that first postcard, that he was checking the Red Cross lists again at the train station and spotted the typewritten names: Margot Betti Frank, Annelies Marie Frank. Next to their names were symbols of the cross, indicating they had been reported deceased. Mr Frank was determined to verify the information and find out who had submitted it. This led him to a young Jewish woman named Lin Brilleslijper in Laren, the same town near Amsterdam where Gabi was staying at the Birnbaum-run orphanage. When they met, she told him how she and her sister had met and befriended Margot and Anne at Bergen-Belsen. She later wrote in her memoir that they seemed to her 'like a pair of frozen birds'. The two pairs of sisters were housed together in the tent camp where I had found Anne on that day in the later part of February. When the storm knocked the tents down, they were rehoused in different barracks. When the winter snows began melting, Lin and her sister saw the Frank girls again, but by then typhus had swept the camp and both girls were extremely ill. Lin said that Margot died first, after rising from her bunk but then crashing to the ground, followed shortly afterwards by a now completely hopeless and hallucinating Anne. It was March 1945, so not long after we had spoken, unable to see one another, through the barbed wire stuffed with straw. Lin and her sister were the ones who discovered their bodies and together they carried them to one of the mass graves for burial.

I could hardly breathe. How I wish I could have reached her somehow. To tell her to hold on. There was hope. She was not all alone – her beloved Pim, as she called her wonderful father, was still alive and would be waiting for her.

'Only those who have lived this can understand what we went through,' Mr Frank said.

Sitting there in this sparse, sunny hospital room, reunited with Mr Frank, but trying to digest that I was never going to see Anne or Margot again, I'm not sure I could understand anything. I was in shock.

I didn't know it for sure then, but perhaps I was already beginning to realise: Anne and Margot were not the only friends who were never coming home.

Mr Frank wanted to know if I'd heard from Ilse Wagner, but I had not since she was deported in the spring of 1943. I'd find out later she was sent to the gas chambers at the Sobibór death camp with her mother and grandmother. Sanne never returned and neither did her parents; all three were gassed in Auschwitz. My boyfriend Alfred Bloch who asked me to wait for him – he was murdered in Auschwitz. The numbers, when it was possible for the authorities to calculate them, defy comprehension. Of the 120,000 Jews who lived in the Netherlands before the war, only 5,000 of us returned from either the camps or hiding.

Mr Frank was one of the tiny minority of Jews over the age of 50 who had survived the Holocaust.

* * *

The doctors and nurses took excellent care of us in Maastricht. And I passed the time in conversation with Erica and others who survived the camps and by writing letters to Uncle Hans in Switzerland and Aunt Eugenie in England. It seemed that getting the travel documents Gabi and I would need to get to Uncle Hans in Switzerland would be extremely difficult on account of being stateless, but Mr Frank said he would help us. I received a much-welcome steady stream of postcards from friends in Amsterdam, like Barbara Ledermann, who had survived living under her false papers, Jacque van Maarsen and Ietje Swillens, one of my (and Anne's) closest non-Jewish friends from Montessori school. I missed Amsterdam so much and asked them to send postcards of Merwedeplein and other images from our neighbourhood.

Every letter and postcard was a gift. In August, I received my first letter from Aunt Eugenie in Leeds. She had found out that Gabi and I were freed by the Russians as our names were on a list published in a London newspaper by the Dutch government on 21 June. She had then looked for us by any means she could think of, it seemed.

'Since then, I have been looking for you in Holland. I have tried so many ways to contact you,' she wrote, noting she had sent telegraphs to a hospital she thought I may have been sent to, reached out to a Jewish nurse she heard of there and even asked a Canadian soldier she had met by chance in Leeds to look for us and bring us chocolate.

Her letter was dated 15 August 1945. She described the day as 'Victory Day in England'. She wrote:

People are very happy that the war has finally ended, with all the terrible things it has brought upon us. Now people are dancing and singing in the streets, a band is playing music and children are bringing all sorts of things to make bonfires with later this evening. For me it would not have been a happy day – I am thinking too much about Opa and Oma and your dear mother and your dear father … I am very happy that you wrote to us and that I know where you and Gigi are and what you are doing … Now, my dearest Hanneli, the first and most important thing is that you get completely better. I am so longing to see you and our adorable little Gigi. So many people have written to say how sweet she is and that she was a joy for everyone who knew her in the camp. But what they all wrote about you, my good Hanneli, moved me very much and also showed me how proud we can be of you: how you cared for your dear father and Gigi under the most difficult conditions and were a help and a consolation to them – I will never forget that. You are my good, considerate and wise Hanneli, whom I love very much. I would like to ask you so many questions, but I don't dare stir up too much from the past, nor do I want my questions to make you feel sad. I want you to be happy and look to the future and we will all help to make the future good for you and Gigi. You are now our dear children, and Uncle Hans and Aunt Edith's too.

She also listed other relatives who had been asking about us, from cousins who had emigrated to Cleveland, Ohio, to some who had found refuge in Boston, London and Tel Aviv. I put the letter down feeling very emotional. It had been so many years since I saw Aunt Eugenie and here she was, my mother's sister, a voice from afar, so loving, hopeful and patient.

* * *

Summer turned to autumn and I was still in the hospital. The arrival of the Jewish high holy days for the first time since liberation came early, in September that year. I and several other Jewish patients asked one of the top doctors not to be served food on Yom Kippur so we could observe the ritual fast and he agreed. But when Yom Kippur arrived, he was not on duty and the nurse in charge of the ward refused to honour our request and made us eat what was served to us, despite our protest. I understood she was looking out for our health; her job was to make us better and the hospital in Maastricht was nothing like the camp, of course. But still my mind went back to the forced shower of our last Yom Kippur. The refusal of the nurse to respect our wishes and desire to observe this, the holiest day on the Jewish calendar, after all we had been through, was an indignation that stayed with me.

I knew Mr Frank was working to get me transferred to a hospital in Amsterdam. He thought it would be better for me to be closer to Gabi, him, Mrs Goudsmit and our other friends. I was desperate to be with Gabi again and I longed to be back in Amsterdam.

By early autumn, I was taken to the Joodse Invalide, a Jewish-founded hospital in the centre of the city. I was still too frail to leave the hospital and explore so had to satiate my curiosity by looking out the window and taking in the scenes outside, getting reports from the outside world by visiting friends and Mr Frank, who by now had told me to call him Oom Otto, Uncle Otto.

I was tremendously grateful to him for helping navigate the mountains of bureaucracy, made only more difficult by Gabi and I being both Jewish orphans and stateless. The Dutch government left it mostly to Jewish organisations to sort out. Both Aunt Eugenie in Leeds and Uncle Hans in Geneva wanted us to live with them, but for now it was decided Switzerland would be best for our health, considering the damp climate in Leeds. But I had made clear to everyone: my plan was to follow my father's dream. Gabi and I would settle in Eretz Yisrael, the Land of Israel. But first we'd need to get visas to British Mandate Palestine, which were still extremely difficult to obtain.

*　*　*

On 11 November 1945, Mr Frank wrote to Uncle Hans in Geneva and Aunt Eugenie in Leeds, reviewing the logistics around our impending departure for Switzerland. We'd be travelling together with Erica Neuburger, my close friend who was still in hospital with me, and her sister Marion. We were two sets of sisters orphaned by the war. Mr Frank, desperate to see his mother and siblings in Switzerland, wanted to accompany us, but because of his stateless status did not yet have travel documents.

His old friend Nathan Strauss Jr, the son of the Macy's co-founder and an associate of President Roosevelt who had unsuccessfully tried to help the Frank family flee the Netherlands, sent him $500 after the war. Mr Frank used part of the funds to help in the effort to resettle us.

His letter, which I saw many years later, provides an insight into my state of mind at the time: how difficult it was for me to talk about my parents and how attached I was to the community of fellow survivors. Mr Frank wrote, apparently in response to a question about my mother's grave: 'I will cautiously ask about Ruth's grave. With Hanneli, everything concerning her parents is a sore point and it all upsets her.' He continued:

It is hard for her to leave here; she has a strong attachment to the past and to the people she was with during those terrible times, and who were good to her... I shall be glad when the children are given a home again, where they can be brought up individually, especially Gigi. Hanneli is worried about her future and about the fact that she doesn't have a penny to her name and will be a burden on Uncle Hans. She so dearly wants to be a nursery nurse.

And then there is always her Orthodox background; she takes it all very seriously. Since her environment is mostly made up of people who have come from the camps, she is still living in that sphere, and it is time for other impressions to enter her life... For me, Hanneli is like one of my children; the Goslars were with us on a weekly basis in the good pre-war days and for me it is a loving duty to do everything in my power for the children.

Three weeks later, Mr Frank arranged for a car to take me, Gabi, Erica and Marion to the tarmac of Schiphol Airport in Amsterdam for our awaiting plane. It was as far as he could take us. I was nervous about so many things, but in the moment, mostly it was about travelling by aeroplane: I'd never been on one before. He handed each of us a necklace with a Dutch coin. On one side, he'd had the day's date inscribed: 5 December 1945.

He looked at us in the eyes and told us: 'I'm giving you these so you always remember, this is the day you embarked on your new lives.'

Chapter 16

Switzerland

Sitting next to Gabi on the plane, I clutched my backpack tightly, as my most treasured possession was inside. It was our family photo album. Mrs Goudsmit had kept it safe at her home all this time. It contained photos of my parents as newlyweds, Gabi and me as babies, family trips to the beach. I hadn't looked much at the pictures yet as it was so painful, but I was so grateful to have it. And I had added a photo. Ietje Swillens had brought it to me at the hospital in Amsterdam. It was taken at Anne's tenth birthday party on Merwedeplein Square. In the image, we are all in a row: Anne, Sanne, Ietje and I, and our group of friends. Nine young girls in cotton party dresses to just above our knees and patent leather shoes – all hairbows, barrettes and smiles. I was the only one of the four Jewish girls in the photo still alive; Anne, Sanne and Juultje Ketellapper were dead. It was very, very hard to look at this photo.

Mr Frank had put ads in the Amsterdam newspaper to try to help me recover family heirlooms and valuables that we had placed with non-Jewish friends, including the heavy silver cutlery engraved with G for Goslar. I still remember that some small ladles for gravy and fish knives were among the items never returned. The rest was in my suitcase. Uncle Hans had written that he encountered a friend who had been given some of our belongings. Uncle Hans said, 'You know the girls came back?' He replied, 'So good they survived, but what the family left with me was stolen.'

The Finkels had tried to retrieve a large silver menorah they had given to a Christian pastor for safekeeping. But when they asked for it back, he said no – his own family had become too attached to it to part ways with it now. However, the Finkels had been reunited with something more precious: their elder son Jackie, who had been left behind by the train, had made it and I heard he was back with the family.

How little people understood what we went through, I thought, reflecting on Mr Frank's words, that only those of us who had lived through that abyss could ever begin to grasp what we had endured. As the small plane bumped through the skies carrying us closer to Switzerland, I wrestled again with making sense of what I had seen, who I had lost.

* * *

Uncle Hans and Aunt Edith were there to meet us when we landed in Zurich. Aunt Edith, whom I knew at this point only through letters, was in her forties, like Uncle Hans. She had been able to flee Czechoslovakia, but her brother and sister had not been so fortunate. Both had been sent to Auschwitz. They survived but her brother, who was beaten badly there, continued to struggle with his mental health. I know that when Uncle Hans looked at us he saw not just Gabi and me, but his absent parents, my Oma and Opa, and Mama and Papa too. Uncle Hans had worked so hard to get us all out and I could see the regret in his eyes that he was unable to bring us to Switzerland before we were deported, mixed with his relief to see us. Both Edith and Hans wrapped us in hugs and kisses.

After we said our farewells to Erica and her sister, who were going to live with their grandmother in Zurich, Uncle Hans and Aunt Edith announced that they had a big treat for us. We were to spend our first night in Switzerland at the Baur au Lac, a luxury hotel overlooking Lake Zurich with a full view of the snow-covered Alps.

We walked up the stairs into the lobby, my feet sinking into a plush white carpet, and I was struck dumb for a moment by the luxury. I gazed up at enormous sparkling chandeliers hanging from high ceilings and took in the sounds of a classical piece being played on a grand piano. Mama would have loved this.

'It won't be like this every night,' Aunt Edith told us, her warm eyes twinkling, but tonight, this first night, they wanted to 'spoil us a little bit'. She told me it had long been a favourite spot for various members of the European royal families. I was 17 now but I felt the old flicker of my and Anne's childhood fascination with the British and Dutch royals.

I felt relieved to be in the presence of our aunt and uncle in their home in Geneva. Like Mr Frank, they were another pair of adults for Gabi and me to anchor ourselves to, a safe harbour in which to rest for a while. My uncle was kind and had a good sense of humour. His rather protruding dark eyes seemed to take everything in. Like his wife, a dentist, he worked hard. He had been unable to get his law licence in Switzerland, so, like my father, he worked mostly aiding fellow refugees. The pay was meagre, the hours long. His free time was devoted to the Zionist cause, like his father before him – and of course like my father, his brother-in-law. Uncle Hans was the vice-president of the Swiss Zionist Federation.

Edith instantly treated Gabi and me like her own family and quickly became a mother figure to Gabi. Her warmth and care enveloped us both. We both blossomed at their dinner table, talking about art and music, revelling in being together. At home, the talk was almost exclusively about culture and day-to-day issues. I don't recall them asking questions about our time in the camps or about the last days of my grandparents or father. After dinner, Uncle Hans and Aunt Edith washed the dishes side by side. I admired their easy interaction and respect for one another.

But our time with them was not to be long. It was decided that I would travel 75 miles north to a Catholic sanitorium for girls and women called Le Rosaire, where I would complete my recovery. I was desperate to catch up on everything I had missed since halfway through eighth grade – my last time in a classroom over three years earlier. So much time had been lost; I was anxious to fully recover as quickly as I could and finally 'start' my life and resume my education.

My aunt and uncle had married later in life than was usual for the times and had no children. They both worked long hours out of the home and so neither were around to look after Gabi, who was now five, and to take her to school. Also, they did not keep a kosher home, as we had in Amsterdam, and, partly on account of my own beliefs and partly for the memory of my father, this was still very important to me. And so the decision was made that while I went north to the sanitorium, Gabi would be best cared for at a nearby Jewish orphanage, visiting Hans and Edith regularly.

At the time, it felt like the best decision. But for Gabi, who did not remember our years at Westerbork or Bergen-Belsen, the time in the orphanage would be the worst years of her life. She had always had a challenging relationship with food, even as a baby, and her trauma from our time in the camps – even if she did not consciously remember it – seemed to complicate that. She sometimes threw up the food she was fed at the orphanage and the caregivers there forced her to eat what she had purged. I can't imagine why you would force a child to do this. I can only think it was an incredibly misguided attempt to teach her to eat and not waste her food. This was a little girl who could not remember her parents and who had spent the majority of her young life at that point in concentration camps. When I think back on this, I reflect on how little her caregivers, like most of the people at the time, understood about what we had endured and how in need little children like Gabi were of informed care.

The sanatorium was set in an emerald-green valley nestled in the Alps among farming villages. I was instantly smitten by the extraordinary beauty and the sounds of cowbells ringing from the local farmers' cows that sometimes grazed nearby. I loved the tranquillity and quiet. But at first it was very hard. I felt isolated and I didn't know anyone, and I was self-conscious of how thin I was, that I looked like someone who had been in a concentration camp. At first, I didn't meet any other Jewish people there. I was placed in a room with a devout Catholic girl a little older than I was. She had wanted to be a nun, but whatever illness she was suffering had stymied that plan. We became quite close, sharing long conversations in our room or when we took strolls on the paths of the well-tended grounds on sunny days as we got stronger. I was now in the French-speaking part of Switzerland and she patiently helped me practise my French. The Jewish community from the nearby city of Montreux sent tutors to teach me Jewish and secular subjects.

Still, I was rather lonely, so I was delighted to get word from Mr Frank about a month after arriving that he had finally secured travel documents and would be travelling to Switzerland to be reunited with his mother, siblings and other family in Basel, and that he would also be coming by train to visit me. On 16 January 1946, I received a telegram from him reading:

EXPECT YOU TOMORROW MORNING ELEVEN
MONTREUX STATION
UNCLE OTTO

It was a brief but wonderful visit. I was happy to be able to show him how visibly on the mend I was, slowly gaining weight and strength. I was hungry for connection to him and anyone from my previous life.

Though one such connection came out of the blue and astonished me. While I was living in Switzerland, Mr Frank broke the news that for the whole time they were in hiding, Anne had carried on writing in her diary – the one we were all so curious about and that Jacque and I had looked for in her bedroom when the family suddenly vanished – and it had been saved. After the Dutch police discovered the inhabitants of the secret attic and arrested them, Miep Gies, who had worked for Mr Frank and helped hide them, had found the treasured diary. She bundled the pages together, unread, and placed them in a locked drawer of her desk. She told herself she'd give it back to Anne when she returned. The day Mr Frank told her that Anne – and Margot – would never be coming home, she unlocked the drawer and handed him the diary. Mr Frank told me that for a while, he couldn't look at the pages – it was just too painful. When he did finally sit down and begin to work his way through it, he was transfixed by its contents. He started sharing excerpts with some family members and friends, including me.

They were a revelation. I lost my best friend Anne when she had just turned 13 and began keeping her diary. In those pages, I felt I was reunited with her. It was such a strange sensation to witness her evolve and mature, all while having a window into her internal life and her life in hiding. The Anne I met in the most terrible of circumstances at Bergen-Belsen was starving and desperate, hardly the vivacious girl I knew. These precious pages allowed me to see her between those two moments. The writing was so rich and vivid I felt like I was right next to her again. It felt both euphoric and heart-shattering.

I ached knowing she had written many of those words while still living so close to me – but all the time I was thinking she was hundreds of miles away, safe. I imagined her trying to mute her coughs when she was sick and her footsteps during the day, always living with the backdrop of fear they might get caught. I was profoundly moved not only by her talent for describing the events and dynamics among the eight in hiding, but her rich inner world – her thoughts and feelings, her observations of others hiding in the attic on Prinsengracht. For all of her maturity, she was a teenager still very much at the beginning of her life. I related to her desire to feel true love, to feel truly understood by someone else and her longing 'to have a good time for once and to laugh so hard it hurts'. She was so vibrant, so alive. I felt scrubbed raw reading her words. I missed my friend more than I could have ever expressed.

I thought about Anne a lot – about our other friends too – but I knew I also had a job to do: I had to win my health back. The snow on the mountaintops began to thaw and the wildflowers bloomed in the valley I looked out over every day. One day, I went on a hike along a river with other Le Rosaire patients. At some point, one of the other girls looked at me and remarked, 'You are looking so well. No one would know you were in the camps.'

I took this as welcome evidence of my recovery but the comment also stung. Would my wartime experiences become invisible, now that I no longer showed the outer vestiges of surviving this other planet called Bergen-Belsen?

*   *   *

I had not wavered in my plan to emigrate to Eretz Yisrael, although I suspect Uncle Hans and Aunt Edith were still hoping I'd stay in Switzerland. Uncle Hans, like my Opa and Papa, had dedicated so much of his time and energy to the cause of a Jewish homeland and believed in it absolutely. But Uncle Hans was older now, at home in Switzerland and perhaps wary of starting over in an entirely different part of the world and in Hebrew, which he could read in prayer books but did not speak. He said that he did hope to eventually join Gabi and me there, but he had been diagnosed with a heart condition and was wary of the extreme heat.

Hans and Edith thought that after all I'd been through, Switzerland would be a draw: a place where life was orderly, calm and – most important – peaceful. We heard reports of the battles that had already begun to take place in the streets of Jaffa and Jerusalem, and elsewhere, between the growing Jewish population and Palestinian Arab fighters over who would control this small strip of land once the British left. The British had at least declared their support for the idea of a 'national home for the Jewish people' but their policy was to do so while not harming the rights of the Arabs who lived in Palestine. It seemed like an irreconcilable situation to everyone.

Unlike Uncle Hans and Opa, Papa's dream had been to move there. He had told me stories of what it would be like and I saw it in my mind as a land of citrus groves and a sparkling sea, where it was always warm, where the holy tongue of Hebrew was spoken in the streets as an everyday language and Jews could never be refugees, could never be made stateless ever again. I thought that Eretz Yisrael would become a Jewish homeland for the Jews, just as Holland was the homeland of the Dutch people and Switzerland the nation of the Swiss. My father's dream of building a life there was now mine.

But first I wanted to get my high-school diploma. I did not want to emigrate until I had achieved it. I hoped to condense my studies and finish in a year. That way, my new life could begin.

So, after about five months in Le Rosaire, I travelled back to Geneva for some family time with Uncle Hans and Aunt Edith and Gabi, who I had missed dearly. But it was important to me to be in a kosher home. So my aunt and uncle found an Orthodox Jewish family I could live with, named the Sohlbergs. They had seven children and I could share a room with one of their daughters. But the catch was that they lived in Basel. It was hard for me to be so far away again from Hans, Edith and Gabi – this time almost 200 miles north, near the German border. But I tried to stay focused on my plan. I could not wait to be back in the classroom, learning and catching up on the knowledge I had missed out on while being held prisoner.

In November 1946, I turned 18. I was officially an adult. It was disorienting. I was fortunate to remember my childhood as warm, protected and full of joy. For all the war had taken from me, I did have those happy memories of my parents, my school friends, our neighbourhood. But I felt like I'd missed out on being a teen-ager. The closest I came to a 'first crush' was Alfred and that was such a short-lived experience. We had both been consumed by our shyness and then he vanished in the night with the other teenagers, called up for 'work camps'. The curfews, the ban on tram riding and socialising with non-Jews put an end to any real exploration of the city beyond our Rivierenbuurt neighbourhood, precisely at the age when we would have been starting to do so. Anne's thirteenth birthday was the last party of boys and girls I remember, then friends and classmates began disappearing, my mother died and I was thrust into the role of being a 'little mother' for Gabi. Now I was an adult, with no parents and no money of my own, reliant on the support of my uncle.

I came from a family where education and understanding was prized. My mind at aged 18 was not on teenage things. I was determined to make up for lost time as best I could and prepare for my new life. At a Shabbat lunch at the Sohlbergs, I met a young man named David. Our fathers had been friends. Romantic interest flickered but he had a girlfriend who had already emigrated to Eretz Yisrael and nothing came of it. (Though amazingly, our paths would cross again far more significantly decades later.) I was focused on school and not much else.

I was studying in Basel, the city where Anne's grandmother, Alice Stern, lived. When Gabi and I had first arrived in Geneva, at our aunt and uncle's home, there had been a wonderful package of goodies from her, which she described as a 'welcome to Switzerland', waiting for us. In the accompanying letter, she wrote:

My dear children, I hope you had a good journey and have arrived with your dear relatives and so I hope to be able to speak to you soon, dear Hanneli, and to say 'güten tag' to you.

Many years have passed since we last saw each other, but my love and devotion to you both has remained the same. Have a good rest, after all the difficult things you have been through … I am sending you a few little trifles to welcome you to Switzerland.

She signed the note 'Yours, Omi Frank', German for Granny Frank.

I would occasionally visit Grandmother Stern's elegant home in Basel. She was a wonderful woman – warm and strikingly intelligent, with white wavy hair – and she made me feel like an extended member of the family, even though I had found her intimidating when I was a child in Amsterdam. But I always felt the stress of the unspoken question hanging over us: *How is Hanneli standing before me and not also Anne and Margot?*

*   *   *

Uncle Hans let me know the Zionist Congress would be meeting for the first time since the war broke out in Basel in December. The congress was the first Jewish parliamentary-style organisation in modern history, founded in 1897, with the aim of laying the groundwork for all that would be needed to create a Jewish homeland.

It was a big deal in my family. My grandfather had started attending as a young man and I grew up hearing about these storied gatherings, which Opa and Papa attended every year. (Though when I was a child, the best part for me was the bars of a brand of Swiss chocolate in their trademark red and gold wrapping that Papa always returned with.) So I was thrilled when Uncle Hans asked me if I wanted to go. He helped procure me a volunteer job as an usher, for which I was given a gold-coloured sash to wear.

It was exciting to think of the congress gathering again for the first time since 1939, but in reality, it was a sobering, even grim scene. Most of the European delegates from previous years were missing, including Opa and Papa, because so many of them had been murdered by the Nazis. The trauma of the war and the Nazi genocide (we hadn't yet heard this new/old word 'the Holocaust'; that would come later) added urgency to their mission but also a huge weight.

Aside from the enormity of the loss that everyone in that room was trying to digest, there was urgent business to discuss that directly impacted my future: how to establish a Jewish state. I listened in, completely riveted, as delegates debated how to best solve the immediate problems involved, including how to address the current hardline British policy against Jewish immigration. The gates were anything but open for survivors of the war like me, so how to move forward?

By the following year, 1947, however, as I was finishing high school, a number of Jewish refugees from Europe were being granted entry. It was my great fortune that somehow my application for a visa from the British was approved for May 1947. I was so determined to go that I had been willing to try to enter Mandatory Palestine illegally, smuggled in as part of a clandestine operation run by Zionist activists. However, my uncle, ever the lawyer and stickler for the rules, had refused to let me. But now I did not even have to consider such means. Of the small number of visas granted, one was mine.

But there was just one, for me alone. Although it tortured me greatly, I knew I could not take Gabi with me. She was not yet seven – I couldn't look after her and establish myself in this new place.

I had a plan: to study nursing and secure a job. Then I would send for her to join me.

But first, on the way to my future in Eretz Yisrael, I had some unfinished business to attend to: I had to say goodbye to Amsterdam.

Chapter 17

Ghosts

It was early May 1947 when I arrived back to Amsterdam, the only home I'd ever really known and a city I loved with all my heart. Almost exactly two years before, people here had poured into the streets to celebrate the end of the war, climbing onto tanks and jeeps, passing out tulips to the liberating Canadian soldiers. I had hungrily gobbled up any news and images I could find of those joyous days, regretting that I couldn't be there to see them with my own eyes.

But the air of celebration was long gone by the time I disembarked from the train, bleary-eyed after almost a day of travel through France, Belgium and across Holland. I quickly grasped that the city I had returned to – a trip for which I had saved up every bit of my allowance from my uncle – was now a decidedly grim place. Two years after the guns had finally stopped and the Nazi killing machine ended, Amsterdam was still emerging from the war's aftermath.

During the final months of the Occupation, amid the freezing temperatures of one of the coldest winters in European history, the Netherlands was plunged into an immediate famine. The Germans cut off their supply lines as retribution for Dutch rail workers' attempts to thwart the arrival of incoming German troops in hopes of helping the Allies. People ate tulip bulbs and sugar beet to survive. Some even resorted to eating dogs and cats. About 20,000 died of hunger. In their freezing homes, they kindled anything to try to stay warm, including furniture, wood blocks stolen from the tram lines and wooden staircases from empty homes in the Jewish quarter, their residents long since deported. The cold was so severe that children cried out in pain from the frostbite they sustained.

Once the Nazis were driven out, the small number of surviving Jews could return. First back were those emerging from hiding spots. Most did not have a clue what had happened to their deported loved ones. For some young children in hiding, liberation was their first memory of stepping outside. Later, the Jews who, like me, had survived the concentration and death camps returned. But it seemed that the Dutch were so consumed by their own suffering and trauma that they had little patience for or interest in hearing the horrors we had endured.

At first, my heart stirred at the familiar scent of Amsterdam in the spring: fresh new leaves, sunshine, that slight mouldy smell that came off the canals and a whiff of sweetness – was it the flowers? Someone making waffles? Spring had always been my favourite time of year. It was when the city, after a long, frigid, rain-soaked winter, was filled with hope. But I quickly understood that it was to be a bitter homecoming. I felt like I had returned to a city of ghosts. Where I once had family, a large circle of school and family friends, neighbours and teachers who knew and looked out for me, I now only had a handful of friends to call on. Walking the bridges and streets, retracing footsteps from the past, I drank in the familiar sights of sun-dappled canals and flowers in wooden pots, all the while scanning faces for some drop of familiarity. But all I saw were the faces of strangers. *How could this have happened?* I silently repeated the question to myself, one I have been asking ever since.

Approaching my old apartment building on 16 Zuider Amstellaan, I felt excited but also deeply weary. I was home but also so far away from home. I noticed the street name had changed to Rooseveltlaan, to honour US President Franklin D. Roosevelt. Another nearby street name had been changed to honour Churchill. But the old poplar trees still lined the meridian dividing the cobblestone street; the buildings looked the same in their pale brown tidy uniformity. It all looked so deceptively stable, I thought.

I rang the bell on the Goudsmit's ground-floor flat. 'Hanneli! Welcome, welcome!' Mr and Mrs Goudsmit cried out. It felt good to be welcomed into their home and I instantly felt a little bit less like a stranger. I smiled as Mrs Goudsmit cupped my cheeks in her hands in greeting. Little Sjors, six years old now, like Gabi, was getting so tall! Though he still had his blond curls.

I did not dare go up the stairs of the building that led to my family's flat. Another family lived there now. I let my thoughts drift back to our belongings, all long gone. The blue velvet sofa, the wicker 'dining room' table and chairs, the porcelain dishes and my mother's typewriter. All of it hauled away into awaiting trucks by the German company that looted Jewish property after deportation. I wondered who in Germany was sitting on our sofa now.

Afterwards, I stopped at the synagogue on 63 Lekstraat. There was an evening service but I did not recognise any of the faces. I almost cried seeing the small group of men, just barely enough for a minyan, ten being the minimum number of men required for group prayer, according to Jewish law. *So many empty seats*, I thought, aching for Papa and Opa.

Outside, the bough of a large tree hung low, just like I remembered. I remembered every street corner, every door that friends and neighbours had once lived behind. I walked back to nearby Merwedeplein Square, to the pavement where Anne and I had played hopscotch and hide-and-seek with our other friends. Other children were running and laughing, their mothers soon enough calling them home for dinner. So very much the same as I remembered. But now I was no longer a little girl, and so many I had known and loved were dead. I did not yet know the word 'trauma', but I think that is the closest word for what I was experiencing as I roamed the neighbourhood.

Later, I met with old school friends, including Jacque. I saw Barbara Ledermann, who appeared inconsolable. She missed her sister and parents immensely. In a letter to Mr Frank around this time, she wrote, 'After two years of struggle, I managed to accept life as others accept religion: without understanding it. It passes over us, takes us a little further with it and then lays us down again. I don't believe I will be particularly concerned about what happens around me or with me … there is so little point in everything.'

There was at least one positive – or at least bittersweet – thing to reflect on during my time in Amsterdam. Anne's diary was set to be published in the Netherlands on 25 June, in about six weeks' time, just after what would have been Anne's eighteenth birthday. Mr Frank had come to believe wholeheartedly that Anne's writing deserved a wider audience than just us – the depleted collection of her friends and family. He wanted her story to be made public, her spirit to live on in print. But at first it had been tough for him to find a publisher. Some rejected it and even a few of Mr Frank's friends doubted it would find an audience. There was little appetite for an account of the wartime experience of a Jewish teenager in hiding, or really for anything about the wartime persecution of the Jews. However, Mr Frank remained stubbornly persistent and he eventually managed to find a Dutch publisher to take it on. My wonderful friend was to become a published writer, just as she had said she wanted to be.

In fact, I had learned that Anne had heard an appeal on the banned Radio Orange in March 1944, the radio station of the Dutch government in exile, in which Gerrit Bolkestein, the former minister of education, implored Dutch citizens to preserve their everyday documents so that, after the war, people would understand what had been endured under German occupation. He referred specifically to diaries, which caught Anne's attention. She had immediately set about revising her diary for publication after the war, making edits and adding details with a writer's eye for drama and context. Knowing this impressed me still further. In my eyes, Anne had truly become a writer while in hiding, one who dared to believe that her thoughts and observations could be important to people in the future.

But from a more personal perspective, I was moved to read that she had been thinking of me, just as my thoughts had often turned to her while I was at Westerbork and Bergen-Belsen. She had even written about the dynamics between us just before she went into hiding in such a mature and insightful way. The disagreement we'd had over some small jealousy before she disappeared had upset me. I was sad it had happened but I was glad to be reassured that our friendship mattered to her as much as it did me. Mr Frank had asked me if I minded if Anne's writing about me was included in the published version of her diary – I'd asked him to please not take anything out.

Anne had written about our relationship in the context of a waking dream she'd had about me in an entry on 27 November 1943, at which time, unknown to her, I was in Westerbork, going into my first winter as a prisoner. In the dream, I was 'clothed in rags', my face 'thin and worn', begging Anne to 'rescue me from this hell'. She used the pseudonym Lies for me, short for Hanneli. It was a nickname that some of my school friends had called me.

She wrote:

All I can do is pray to God to bring her back to us. I saw Lies, and no one else, and I understand why. I misjudged her, wasn't mature enough to understand how difficult it was for her. She was devoted to her girlfriend [referring to Ilse] *and it must have seemed as though I were trying to take her away. The poor thing, she must have felt awful! I know, because I recognise the feeling in myself! I had an occasional flash of understanding, but then got selfishly wrapped up again in my own problems and pleasures.*

It was mean of me to treat her that way, and now she was looking at me, oh so helplessly, with her pale face and beseeching eyes. If only I could help her! Dear God, I have everything I could wish for, while fate has her in its deadly clutches …

Oh Lies, I hope that if you live to the end of the war and return to us, I'll be able to take you in and make up for the wrong I've done you.

But even if I were ever in a position to help, she wouldn't need it more than she does now. I wonder if she ever thinks of me, and what she's feeling?

My eyes clouded with tears when I reached this section and I could hardly see the words. I wanted to reach through the pages in my hand to comfort her, thank her. *Your prayers were heard. I was saved, Anne! Thank you, thank you. I will always, always hold you close,* I thought to myself, hoping, somehow, my words might reach her still.

About a month later, on 29 December 1943, she had dwelled on my fate again, asking, 'And Lies? Is she still alive? What's she doing? Dear God, watch over her and bring her back to us.' She went on:

> *Lies, you are a reminder of what my fate might have been. I keep seeing myself in your place. So why am I often miserable about what goes on here? Shouldn't I be happy, contented, and glad, except when I'm thinking of ~~Hanneli~~ Lies and those suffering along with her? … Thinking of those you hold dear can reduce you to tears; in fact, you could spend the whole day crying. The most you can do is pray for God to perform a miracle and save at least some of them. And I hope I'm doing enough of that.*

Reading through those and other sections of her diary I was dumbfounded. Most people her age do not have the skill or insight to write the way she did. I found it excruciating too – I felt the noose tightening around her and the others hiding through Anne's words, especially in passages like this one, written on 3 November 1943:

> *I see the eight of us in the Annexe as if we were a patch of blue sky surrounded by menacing black clouds. The perfectly round spot on which we're standing is still safe, but the clouds are moving in on us, and the ring between us and the*

approaching danger is being pulled tighter and tighter. We're
surrounded by darkness and danger, and in our desperate
search for a way out we keep bumping into each other. We
look at the fighting down below and the peace and beauty up
above. In the meantime, we've been cut off by the dark mass
of clouds, so that we can go neither up nor down. It looms
before us like an impenetrable wall, trying to crush us, but
not yet able to. I can only cry out and implore, 'Oh, ring,
ring, open wide and let us out!'

Her diary made me realise just how special and unlike anyone else Anne was. This was a deeper, multi-layered Anne, both familiar to me and, in some ways, entirely new. I was reading Anne frozen in time at 13, 14, 15 years old. I was aware that as I grew older, I could only get further away from her, a girl whose flickering shadow I felt I could still catch a glimpse of out of the corner of my eye. But in just a few weeks, anyone in Holland would be able to pick up her book and read these words. It was a strange feeling.

While I was in Amsterdam, I was able to visit Mrs Kuperus, the beloved principal of the Montessori school who had also been our sixth grade teacher. Mr Frank had shared Anne's diary with Mrs Kuperus too, before he found a publisher. It was good to be able to talk to her about it and share our impressions. Together we remembered her, as well as the Jewish students' last day of school in June 1941. Anne was not the only student of hers to have been murdered by the Nazis during the war, so it was an emotional reunion for us both.

Mrs Kuperus said she was taken by the insights into Anne's inner thoughts and feelings, as someone who knew Anne personally but also as an educator. I asked her how she thought it possible for Anne to write so maturely and sensitively at such a young age. She told me her theory that, put in an extreme setting as Anne was, under incredible pressure, it's possible that she developed emotionally and intellectually at an accelerated pace.

*   *   *

My time in Amsterdam was drawing to a close. It felt like a relief to have something to look forward to after all this looking backwards. I returned to Switzerland where I had to make my final arrangements for my immigration to Eretz Yisrael.

On 20 May, my awaited 'Visa for Palestine ... for one journey only', as it was written, came through from the British Consulate in Geneva. It was stamped on a piece of cream-coloured paper attached to my travel document, called a 'Certificat d'Identité', since I was still stateless and therefore could not be issued a passport. I still have it now. In the photo, my cheeks are full again, my skin clear. My thick wavy dark hair is the longest it would ever be, just above my shoulders. I looked healthy and determined.

Amsterdam was a reminder of the terrible lesson I had learned far too early: nothing in life is permanent. A quiet, loving, comfortable existence can be stolen away by the powerful forces of hate. My visit had served to painfully highlight my two distinct selves: pre-war Hanneli and post-war Hanneli. But at the same time, I was already able, I think, to recognise that the love and values my parents poured into me had made me the person I was. They had not been able to see me grow up but they had given me the tools and the moral compass to know how to move forward. It was my father's roadmap I was following in deciding to go to Eretz Yisrael instead of staying in Switzerland, returning to live in Amsterdam or trying to emigrate to the United States. It was the harder path, to be sure. But I felt certain it was the right one for me.

Chapter 18

The Promised Land

I could hardly believe it as the ship steamed out of the French port city of Marseille. I felt I was finally on my way.

For five days I sailed towards the Middle East, cutting a path by sea between the shores of Europe and Africa on a ship called *Providence*. I spent hours gazing out onto the horizon, feeling the distance growing between the before and after chapters of my life with every mile. I was nervous and excited. But most of all, I was ready to get off the boat – especially after the choppier stretches at sea. So when I first heard shouts of, 'Look! Haifa! It's over there,' I rushed to the deck to see for myself. And there it was, my first glimpse of Eretz Yisrael, a yellow smudge up ahead. I leaned against the railing and watched as Haifa took form. Gradually, I could see the green slopes of Mount Carmel and some boxy stone buildings below, by the port. Around me, people were whistling and cheering; some of the young people broke into Hebrew songs.

After we docked, when we were eventually able to get off the ship, I watched as some people kneeled down to kiss the ground.

I was speechless as a British clerk signed and stamped my travel papers with a rectangular purple stamp that read: 'Government of Palestine Migration Department: Permission to remain permanently in Palestine as an immigrant.' The date was marked: 30 May 1947. I stood in the immigration line all alone but Papa was very much in my heart, the two of us in some kind of continuum between his longing to be here and my actual arrival. I inhaled. I smelled pine trees and salty sea air, and smiled.

My bittersweet moment was broken by the throngs of people. They were pushing to get out to the docks for reunions with loved ones, to get their luggage.

Luggage! I thought with a start. I rushed to my suitcases but there was just one instead of the two I had brought. The one Aunt Edith had packed so carefully for me with things I'd need, like a brand-new set of beautiful cotton sheets and towels, was missing. The sheets and blankets had been sent to me from wealthy family friends originally from Berlin who had immigrated to Sweden. It was their generous farewell send-off to me. And now that suitcase including the beautiful bedding was gone. I was near tears.

I knew I wouldn't dare tell Aunt Edith and Uncle Hans when I wrote to them of my arrival. I blamed myself for the suitcase going missing. It would only worry them to know I was now without some key necessities for my new life and I was afraid they would feel they had to replace them. I was very aware of how little money they had. They were already giving me a small monthly allowance and I would have been ashamed to ask for more. I was determined not to be a burden on them or anyone. But my desire to be economically independent in Israel was, in the early years, a constant uphill battle and at times I would be frighteningly short of money.

Despite the stress of my lost luggage, my journey had been decidedly easier than that of many others. In July 1947, three months after I arrived, an unauthorised ship left Marseille on the same route

I took with 4,500 survivors on board. It called itself *Exodus 1947*. The ship was intercepted and fired on by the British with gunfire and mortars, killing two passengers and a member of the crew. The rest were then all sent back to displaced persons camps in Germany, where hundreds of thousands of other Holocaust survivors were still living, having nowhere else to go. The saga made headlines around the world and brought attention to the plight of these refugees.

*   *   *

Shortly before I arrived, an announcement in the newspaper of the religious Zionist movement my father had once helped lead, read, 'Hans Goslar's daughter, Hannah Goslar, is immigrating to the Land of Israel.' I would repeatedly see how my father's name and people's memory of his good works lived on. 'Ah, you are the daughter of Hans Goslar?' people I'd just met would say.

My first stop in my father's Promised Land was Kibbutz Yavne, where he had imagined one day settling. It was founded just six years before my arrival on a stretch of plain close to the sea by a group of young, idealistic German Jews known to my father and my grandfather. I instantly liked it there. It was basic but the people had character and grit, and it was inspiring seeing them so driven by their mission of creating a religious kibbutz.

I spent my first days exploring its citrus groves and fields under the warm sun. The members were kind to me, welcoming me like one of the family. They told me stories about how my father had inspired them. I knew fairly quickly after arriving, though, that I didn't want to stay there. I was 18 already, an adult. So like any adult on a kibbutz, I'd have to work full days, contributing like everyone else to the experiment in collective, communal living. But I didn't even know Hebrew yet. And I wanted to have a profession – I was determined to become a children's nurse.

Through the kibbutz members' help, I found a spot at a youth village called Kfar Hasidim in the north, back up near Haifa in the foothills of Mount Carmel, where I could study Hebrew. Youth villages had been set up in different parts of the country to care for the large number of young Jews who had arrived here alone.

My days were long, starting in the kitchen before the sun was up, chopping up enormous amounts of vegetables to help feed everyone for the afternoon meal. The cook liked me and I sometimes babysat for her children; it was my only opportunity to make any money and I was grateful for it. In the village were other new arrivals from Europe, teenagers and children, some of them also orphaned during the war or otherwise in the country on their own without parents. Between my intensive daily lessons and my sheer drive to be able to communicate, I learned how to speak Hebrew fairly quickly. Some of the language's guttural sounds that were hard for my classmates were easier for me, since Dutch is also a guttural language.

It could get blisteringly hot during the day – sometimes temperatures soared as high as 35 degrees Celsius. But while others around me were complaining about the heat, I didn't. After being so cold for so long in Bergen-Belsen, the heat really did not bother me too much.

Near our village was a small store where we could buy ice cream, which of course reminded me of home, and falafel stuffed in pita bread. This tasted like nothing I had ever eaten back in Europe but I learned to like it very quickly. I was fascinated to meet a man from a nearby Druze village who came to our village to sell vegetables. I knew of course there were Arabs in the country, but had never before heard of the Druze, Arabic-speaking followers of a secretive offshoot of Islam. I was intrigued by their dress: the men wore moustaches, baggy trousers and distinctive round white caps. The women wore sheer white head coverings and long tunics.

The village was a good first landing spot for me but after the Jewish holidays of Rosh Hashanah and Yom Kippur, I was ready to move on. I had been accepted to a nursing training programme in Jerusalem. So I said goodbye to the cook and her children, my Hebrew teacher and new friends, and, with my one suitcase, made my way south to Jerusalem.

It took several hours and bus changes to make the 100-mile journey, passing by open fields, both older and newer Jewish farming settlements and a valley dotted with Arab villages. Finally, the bus climbed up the steep highway towards Jerusalem. I had been given the address for a dormitory for teenage girls on Rashi Street, near the centre of town. The manager there had known my father, so even though, at 18, I was too old to be a resident, he had agreed to let me live there while I studied nursing.

The first thing I noticed about Jerusalem was that all the buildings were clad in the same milk-coloured limestone, giving the city a rather distinctive and timeless look, I thought. Indeed, Jerusalem buildings had been built from this type of stone for centuries, withstanding fires, wars and various conquerors over time. The British then mandated the use of what is called 'Jerusalem stone' on every building. When I asked why, someone told me it was so that at sunset the whole city could appear a dazzling gold. Once I saw my first sunset, I agreed it was a very good rule.

I was the only nursing student at Beit Tzeriot Mizrahi (Hebrew for the Mizrahi House for Young Women); my roomates were all studying to be teachers. I was to spend the next year and a half studying and training at Bikur Cholim, a nearby hospital. Inside its rounded arches, I worked with babies and young children from across the city. I quickly learned firsthand of the great poverty in Jerusalem. I distinctly remember, one day not long after I had arrived, coming across a group of children who looked particularly poor and dishevelled, roaming on their own near the Old City. I don't know if they were Arab or Jewish as I had yet to decode the layers of 'who was who' that locals seem to instinctively discern. But they looked in dire need and it broke my heart.

I missed Gabi desperately and tried not to remember how her face had looked in Bergen-Belsen as I came into contact with the very poorest children in the city. I wrote her letters and sent postcards all the time, reminding her that soon we would see each other again.

I was aware, though, that there were many who had survived the war and were not so lucky to know where their loved ones were. Not only were newspapers here filled with notices of people still looking for one another, but I was intrigued to find out there was a radio programme called *Who Recognises? Who Knows?* where people described family members and friends on air for whom they were still searching. Occasionally, remarkable tales of reunions emerged, like the story of a survivor from Poland who, spotting a soldier walking on a street in Haifa, recognised him as the son she had mourned, thinking he had been murdered. She had not seen him since he was 14-year-old boy, eight years earlier.

*   *   *

A few weeks after I arrived in Jerusalem, I was walking with a friend and heard singing coming from the courtyard of the building that was home to the quasi-government of what was known then as the Yishuv, the Jewish community in Mandatory Palestine. It was 29 November 1947. We ventured closer and saw people were also dancing in celebration. The United Nations had just voted for the Partition Plan which would turn the country into two states: one Arab, one Jewish.

A Jewish state would now become a reality, we thought. My friend pulled me into the dancing circles and we spun around in celebration. Across the city, people poured into the streets, whistling and cheering. Dozens clambered onto an armoured police car as it drove through the streets and they shouted with joy.

The Jewish leadership accepted partition. The Palestinian Arabs, dumbstruck as to why they would have to share a land they saw as wholly their own and within which they were a majority, rejected it. The celebrations only lasted a few short hours. By morning, fighting had broken out between the Jewish and Palestinian Arab militias, intensifying over the weeks to come.

Soon, the sounds of shelling seemed incessant and I felt constantly on edge. Was the quiet, sunny street I was walking along to work safe that morning, or was a sniper lurking on some rooftop? Was I walking towards danger or away from it? When I paused to look through the glass window of a bookshop, might the glass suddenly shatter if a bomb were to go off nearby? However, while I did feel fear and anxiety, it was muted in some way because I was on my own; if I was hurt, only I would be hurt. In the past, I'd worried constantly about Gabi. In later years, I would have a family of my own to concern myself with. But for now, it was just me. Just my safety to think about. However, I knew it would be stressful for my aunt and uncle to hear about the situation from afar, so I tried to write reassuring letters back to Switzerland, until the postal and telegraph services were halted.

By February 1948, Jerusalem was under siege by Arab militia groups. They blocked off the route into Jerusalem from Tel Aviv, making it increasingly difficult to get basic supplies into the city, namely food, water and fuel. We were in a state of war for months. Convoys intended to bring in supplies came under heavy fire and casualties were enormous.

Jews my age were being drafted into the different militias but as a nursing student I was exempt. We were treating not only children now, but also injured soldiers. Most of the Jewish fighters were native-born, although eventually Jewish refugee survivors arriving from displaced persons camps in Europe, some via clandestine immigration operations, began going straight into military service on arrival. I was both proud of them and scared for them, knowing something of what they had been through. Many, I understood, believed it was better to die fighting as a hero to create our new country than to die as a victim and perpetual refugee.

I had just turned 19 and was again in another war. After clawing my way back to life, it felt bewildering to see how cheap life seemed to be again. New acquaintances of mine were losing friends and brothers in battle. I remember going to the funeral of the brother of one of my nursing student friends along with our entire class.

Many of the doctors on staff at the hospital where I worked were from Germany. I recognised the fear I saw in them because I felt it too. I remember one doctor, a woman who I knew had also been in concentration camps, was especially shaken by the fighting. 'It's happening again,' I overheard her saying. The mood was bleak and people were hungry, some suffering malnutrition, including some of the children we were treating.

I was working on Shabbat on a day that the risk of violence had been deemed especially high. There was talk of moving the children to a more protected floor when suddenly we heard a burst of shelling or possibly shooting nearby. I had been feeding a baby at the time and immediately covered her body with my own. Some shattered glass sprayed onto my back but fortunately the baby and I were unharmed.

On 13 April 1948, a large convoy bringing doctors, nurses, patients, others and medical supplies to Hadassah Hospital in East Jerusalem was ambushed on the road by Arab forces, killing 79 people. Later that day, a Dutch man I knew of from Amsterdam came wandering into the hospital ward where I was working. He was searching for his daughter who had been in the convoy, thinking she may have been taken to us for treatment. When he did not find her, his inconsolable wails filled the hallways. I could not shake the sound of them.

On 14 May, as British troops withdrew, we heard on the radio that in Tel Aviv, David Ben-Gurion had declared independence. I had to be told twice, it was such a surprise. A Jewish state had been declared for the first time in 2,000 years. We could now be masters of our own destiny as my father and grandfather dreamed, I thought to myself.

But in Jerusalem electricity was cut off for several hours a day, the sounds of artillery fire were incessant and the armed convoys trying to break the siege to reach us with supplies were under fire. Then, the day after a declaration of independence was read aloud to cheering crowds, and signatures affixed to it by some whom my father had once known as friends, the armies of Egypt, Iraq, Jordan, Lebanon and Syria invaded. This sparked a full-scale war, that lasted until March the following year, with a terrible death toll on both sides, that left Jerusalem divided and some 700,000 Palestinian Arabs as refugees.

*   *   *

I finished my studies and started working as a nurse in a maternity ward before the war ended, but Uncle Hans, unsurprisingly, would not hear of letting Gabi join me until the fighting had ceased. But, good to his word, once the war was over, Gabi was allowed to come to the brand-new state of Israel. We were Israeli citizens, never to be stateless refugees again. By now, she went by the name Rahli, short for Rachel, her first given name.

She arrived in early June 1949, carrying a little red suitcase and a doll as she walked down the stairs of her plane from Geneva. It had been two years since I last saw her and here she was, already nine, a radiant, beautiful girl with soft light-brown hair she wore in a bob, like I did at her age. It was an amazing feeling to see her again. I could not stop staring at her, marvelling at how vibrant and healthy she looked. She spoke a blue streak, both in French and German now. Her mind was quick as always and she peppered me with questions, begging, as I knew she would, to live with me. I wanted that too but the reality was I was living in a studio apartment and working long hours. I barely made enough money to cover my rent. I couldn't yet support her in all the ways she needed.

It had been agreed that she'd join a special programme for children and youth who came to Israel without parents called 'Youth Aliyah'. There she'd live in a communal setting and learn Hebrew and go to school. Soon, she was adopted by a loving family, who of

Czech and German background, had two older children and lived in a suburb of Tel Aviv.

I knew this was the right thing for Rahli but still I felt terribly guilty. Compounding my guilt was knowing how much it pained Aunt Edith to part from Rahli and Rahli from her. She had become a surrogate mother figure for Rahli and they were very attached to one another. But I knew my father wanted us both to be in Israel and I believed her future was very much here, not in Europe. Aunt Edith and Uncle Hans had been talking about emigrating as well and I really thought they would join us.

My sister was part of a massive wave of immigrants now arriving, and not just from European displaced persons camps, but also from across North Africa and Middle Eastern countries where Jews had lived for centuries. The national focus was on the collective project of state building, less on where any individual might want to live in this new country. The Zionist dream had been idealistic, even utopian, focused on justice and peace. The rough-and-tumble reality often saw bewildered new arrivals spending their first months in crowded tent camps, awaiting housing that was still being built.

Not long after Rahli arrived, I met a young intelligence officer in the Israeli army. His name was Pinchas Walter Pick. He had round black glasses, dark hair, full lips and the kind of smile that made me smile whenever I saw him. He'd served with the British army during the Second World War in Iraq and Egypt. Like me, he was born in Berlin, where his father, an expert in ancient Semitic languages, had been a director of the National Library. When he was fired after Hitler came to power, the family moved to Jerusalem, having previously divided their time between the two cities. Pinchas was 11 years older than me and had a voracious mind. He seemed to know endless and in-depth amounts of geography, archaeology, history, music and politics, and I was quickly smitten by his mind, kindness and sense of humour.

I noticed Pinchas was enormously sensitive to other people, especially to those in need or struggling in some way, and this moved me deeply. He was a tremendous conversationalist and, as a shyer person, I was in awe of his ability to connect with others. Soon after meeting, we realised our fathers had known one another in Berlin, travelling in similar intellectual and social circles as religiously observant Zionists. Again, I felt my father's presence in my new life.

Neither of us had any money. Pinchas's small salary went in large part to supporting his elderly parents (his father's pension had been revoked when the Nazis were in power). I was just finishing my nursing school classes and could barely make ends meet, despite babysitting for doctors on the side and the small allowance I was still receiving from my uncle. But nonetheless, we decided to get married.

In lieu of being able to write to my parents with the good news, I was pleased to share it with Mr Frank. His letter to congratulate me on my twentieth birthday and my engagement meant a lot to me:

I hardly need to say how happy I am for you. You know that I am fond of you and that I am interested in your life and your development. I am so pleased that you have now found someone with whom you want to spend your life and who sees in you his fulfilment as his second half. May you both find the happiness you seek, and with God's help, may you establish a home together and build it in good health.

He added, writing about Pinchas:

Seven years of army service is bitter, even if the work is interesting, and I hope he will soon be able to lead a quieter, more personal life and finish his studies. How nice that your parents all knew each other, and you are staying within a circle that is so close to your heart.

He also updated me on Anne's diary. It was soon be published in French. He had yet to find a publisher in the US, though he remained hopeful he would. I was fascinated that strangers were reading Anne's words, written in hiding from the Nazis. I can't remember anyone asking me about my experiences in the war. New arrivals continued to search for missing family members but concentrations camps were not really discussed.

* * *

Although excited that I would soon be marrying Pinchas, I was sad when I thought of all the people I would have once imagined at my wedding who were either no longer alive or too far away. I was grateful for the small community of which I was now a part, mostly drawn from within the German-speaking religious community in Jerusalem.

One of my closest friends was Tova Cohen. Her mother was a godsend. I'd never had much of an opportunity to learn to cook and I didn't have a mother to teach me these things. So Mrs Cohen, a wonderful cook, patiently taught me how to prepare everything from hard-boiled eggs to chicken soup, roast beef, and – Pinchas's favourite – chocolate mousse. On Shabbats when I stayed with them, she'd send me home with sandwiches so I'd have lunch on my long days training and working at the hospital.

Another anchor was the home of Shulamit and Mordechai Levanon, Pinchas's aunt and uncle. They felt a little like surrogate parents to me. We spent many Shabbat dinners in their stone house on a street tucked into a corner of Rehavia, a storied West Jerusalem neighbourhood thick with trees and parks. It was so popular among German Jews that most of the Hebrew one heard in the streets was delivered in a German accent.

In the late afternoon of 17 April 1950, aged 21, I took a deep breath and walked down the stairs of the back patio of the Levanons' bougainvillea-covered stone house and into their garden to marry Pinchas. I was carrying a bouquet of lilies and wearing a long-sleeved organza wedding dress and veil borrowed from a cousin. Pinchas wore his army uniform. We scraped up the little money we had and borrowed some more to help cover the wedding expenses.

Our guests included Pinchas's parents; Aunt Edith, who flew in from Geneva (Uncle Hans was in Australia on business at the time); Rahli, of course, and Lotte Aronheim, one of my grandfather's favourite cousins. Pinchas was a major in the new Israeli army and Chaim Herzog, his boss, the head of military intelligence also came. During the Second World War, Irish-born Herzog had served as an officer in the British army attached to the company that liberated Bergen-Belsen. He had stood on a wooden crate in the camp and shouted in Yiddish before hundreds of languishing, skeletal prisoners: '*Yidden! Yidden! Es leben noch Yidden!*' In English: 'Jews! There are still living Jews!' (Much later, he would become Israel's sixth president.)

* * *

A year after our wedding, our first child, Yochanan, was born, named for Hans, my father. He was a clever child who, like Pinchas, seemed able to retain every drop of information given him, storing up knowledge like a little squirrel stores nuts in his cheeks. I stopped working to raise him while he was small and his siblings who quickly followed. Chagi (short for Chaim Gidon, after my father-in-law Chaim and a young cousin Gidon, an Israeli air force pilot lost when his plane crashed) was a mischievous, big-hearted little brother. A year later, I had a little golden-haired girl who I named after my mother, Ruth. We called her Ruthie for short. I was so happy to have a daughter too. I stayed home with the children until Ruthie started the first grade. I loved watching my children grow and develop, listening to their stories, watching them interact as siblings so close in age. It was an experience I had always longed for.

We lived on the edge of the Rehavia neighbourhood of Jerusalem in a small but sunny one-bedroom garden apartment where Pinchas had lived with his parents. When they died, it was passed on to us. We were in one of several four-storey apartment buildings scattered around a common green area. I loved watching the neighbourhood children gather there to play football or hide-and-seek. It reminded me of growing up on the Merwedeplein. Here too the kids all knew one another and created their own world in a kind of leafy, protected cocoon.

Letters from Mr Frank arrived regularly, full of warmth and questions and always signed 'Uncle Otto'. He loved children and was looking forward to meeting mine. His long-planned trip to Israel was continually delayed, in part because he was so consumed with attending to the business of what had become the astonishing success of Anne's diary around the world. Mr Frank had gone from struggling to find a publisher for the diary to seeing Anne's book soar to dazzling success.

Most Americans first heard of Anne Frank's diary thanks to writer Meyer Levin's extraordinary front-page review in the *New York Times Review of Books*, published in June 1952. He described for readers the anguish of her life being cut off by the Nazi genocide and his impassioned review surely contributed to it becoming a runaway bestseller. He wrote:

> *But through her diary Anne goes on living. From Holland to France, to Italy and Spain. The Germans too have published her book. And now she comes to America. Surely she will be widely loved, for this wise and wonderful young girl brings back a poignant delight in the infinite human spirit.*

Three years later, on 5 October 1955, an adaptation of the book premiered on Broadway. Mr Frank had approved the script for the play but he didn't see any performances. I imagine it was too much for him to bear. The play catapulted Anne's diary to even further heights and soon it was being performed around the world.

In 1957, Pinchas read in the newspaper that the play's Israeli premiere was soon to take place, performed by Habima, Israel's national theatre. He called the newspaper and told an editor I had grown up a close friend of Anne's.

The next morning, I answered the door to a messenger from Habima Theatre with a pair of VIP tickets for Pinchas and me that evening. I was quite excited but also feeling emotional as I entered the theatre. I thought back to how Anne used to say that one day she wanted to be famous. It felt so strange not to be able to talk to her about it now. I wondered what it would feel like to see my childhood best friend interpreted by an actor on the stage. How absolutely surreal.

We were seated next to President Yitzhak Ben-Zvi and his wife Rachel. Out of nowhere, I was surrounded by photographers taking my photograph and radio reporters shoving their microphones in front of me for comments. People pressed in, trying to see who I was, this friend of Anne Frank's. It was a very unsettling feeling.

As the lights dimmed, I clutched Pinchas's hand nervously, moved by the actors on stage but very much aware – painfully aware – these were not the real Franks or the real Van Pels. Afterwards, I met the cast, including the actress who played Anne, and received a tour of the stage. In the days that followed, a trail of journalists from around the world started showing up at my door for interviews.

A few weeks after that first barrage of media coverage, Mr Frank asked me if I would do a speaking tour in the United States to talk about my friendship with Anne and my experience during the war. However, I was the mother of three young children, then all under the age of four. Pinchas was invited to accompany me but we had no parents to care for our children over the several weeks we'd be away. How could we possibly manage it? In those days, overseas flights were not everyday events and it was a demanding tour that would include 18 cities.

I was taken aback, shocked, almost. But as I thought more about it, I saw what an important mission it could be. Despite the difficulties we would have to overcome, I said yes.

In 1957, few survivors were sharing their stories in public. Many did not even speak to friends and family about what they had been through. Or, at least, that was my experience in Israel. The underlying attitude in Israel in those years was tainted with the shameful feeling that Jews had gone like 'sheep to their slaughter'. We didn't understand trauma much then, or how to talk about things that were so painful. The mood was for forward momentum, for building the new state and our new lives within it. Even survivors like myself did not give too much thought to the importance of talking about what we had been through.

I quickly came to understand that the reporters who had so many questions for me saw me as a proxy for Anne. Her writing and her character had captivated so many imaginations that the world wanted to know more. But some of the questions were also about me and my experience. I realised I had an opportunity to inform people about what we in Israel had begun calling the Shoah, taken from the Biblical term for 'total destruction'. It was still some years before the world became familiar with the term 'Holocaust'.

In September, shortly before Pinchas and I set out for the trip to America, a letter on presidential stationery came to the house from Rachel Yanait Ben-Zvi, Israel's first lady.

> *You are doing such essential work, my friend. Who other than you could share the memory of Anne Frank in all her sacredness, the memory of your friend and the many other dear youth we were not able to save. You were among the few who were able to come to the shores of our homeland.*
>
> *I am convinced of [the importance] of raising the issue of the victims of the Nazi Shoah more than we do and I raise the Shoah at every opportunity I can. But I did not experience it first-hand as you did. To my dismay we are already forgetting our tragedy. Still it's a wound that will never heal – a third*

of our people were cut off, lost to us. And now that we have a country we feel their absence even more.

We were 'already forgetting our tragedy'. Here in Israel, the new nation built by Jews. Only 12 years after the end of the war. The words stung.

A couple of weeks later, I found myself in New York, about to speak to a ballroom full of well-dressed Americans, most of them older than me. I noticed the women in white gloves, their pill-box-style hats and pearls. The men were all wearing tailored suits. It was all so much more formal than I was used to in Israel.

My typed speech was in my hand as I approached a large silver microphone on the dais. I glanced over at Pinchas, relieved to see his encouraging wink and smile. We had been practising my speech together. We had joked that I must channel Anne's courage and Papa and Opa's noted oratorial skills.

'I'm very happy to be here tonight,' I said, looking around the room.

I took a breath and began to tell my story. Our story.

Afterword

by Dina Kraft

Hannah never stopped telling that story.

For the rest of her life, even when it was not easy, even as she was growing older and it was harder to find the energy, even though she sometimes craved to change the subject – 'Again, the Shoah?' she'd sometimes ask me with a sigh – she kept telling it.

That first tour in America in 1957 led to another and was followed by a non-stop train of journalists at her doorstep. She spoke tirelessly. She visited Israeli schools and talked to groups who came to Yad Vashem, Israel's Holocaust memorial. After retirement from her career as a community nurse, she would travel abroad as often as four times a year, criss-crossing the globe from South Africa to Germany, the United States to Japan. Hannah would often give as many as four lectures a day – to schoolchildren and sometimes to audiences as large as 3,000 people in a sports stadium. She spoke in London's Westminster Abbey with Queen Elizabeth II present and met with South African revolutionaries turned political leaders, German lawmakers, Queen Beatrix of Holland and Barbra Streisand. In between talks, she'd give interviews to radio and television stations and newspapers.

When the COVID pandemic hit, Hannah – then aged 91 – continued to speak, but now by Zoom. A group of schoolchildren in a small town in the French Pyrenees had read a young reader's biography and she patiently answered their questions. (Those children and their teacher were so inspired that they have raised money to travel to the Netherlands and follow in Hannah's footsteps.) For as long as she could and as much as she could, Hannah responded to letters she received from children from around the world. Even in what would be her final days, emails were still arriving daily from documentary filmmakers, journalists, young German tour guides who worked in Bergen-Belsen – all of whom were hungry to connect and hear more of her story.

Hannah was extremely aware of her role as one of the last living eyewitnesses to the Nazi genocide of European Jewry. She was prepared to answer questions and to tell again and again of what happened to her because she saw it as a mission to educate people about the horror she had endured, to make a reality of the vow of 'Never again'. She saw the Holocaust as the ultimate cautionary tale of where hatred can lead when good people stay silent and it broke her heart that many other survivors, especially in the initial years after the war, were not encouraged to speak – were even shunned.

Hannah understood that her voice held a particular power because of her close friendship with Anne Frank. Anne has become the most famous of the Holocaust's victims, standing for all six million Jewish children and adults who were murdered. But in Hannah's stories, Anne becomes a regular girl again, an energetic child and then a vivacious girl on the cusp of her teenage years, rather than a symbol or a saint. She was so present in Hannah's home in Jerusalem that her three children grew up thinking of her as a member of the family; Pinchas would even half joke that Anne Frank was his 'second wife'.

Hannah hoped that sharing her testimony would help others understand the part of the story Anne did not live to tell, after she and the others hiding in the Amsterdam attic were arrested and sent to Auschwitz and then Bergen-Belsen. This was the fate of Anne and Margot and so many other children like them at the hands of the Nazis, as Hannah continually emphasised, 'only because we were Jewish'. Among the most quoted lines from Anne Frank's diary is this one: 'It's really a wonder that I haven't dropped all my ideals, because they seem so absurd and impossible to carry out. Yet I keep them, because in spite of everything, I still believe that people are really good at heart.'

Hannah told me, 'I'm not sure she'd stand by that after witnessing Auschwitz.'

*   *   *

When I started helping Hannah to write her memoir in the spring of 2022, I knew we were in a race against time. Still razor sharp of mind but increasingly frail of body at 93, she'd get tired after a couple of hours of talking. I'd say, 'That's fine, we can break for today.' But then she'd invariably think of another thread, another story, and I'd settle in and keep recording. She shared with me that she sometimes needed a nap after we spoke; it could be emotionally exhausting to revisit in detail the moments of her ruptured adolescence. I too would have to retreat after our interviews for a rest – or sometimes a good cry.

By the early fall of 2022, it became clear Hannah was nearing the end of her life. Those weeks felt like a split-screen: Hannah, her hand held by her beloved children and grandchildren as she began to fade, while I wrote of her life. She died on 28 October, just two weeks shy of her ninety-fourth birthday.

I read Anne's diary for the first time when I was 13 years old. On reaching the end and reading of her tragic death, I burst into tears. It was like I'd lost a friend. In getting to know Hannah for this book, I felt like I found a new one. Helping her to tell her story one final time has been a beautiful and life-altering task; losing her felt like a terrible blow. Hannah was buried at around midnight on the Mount of Olives overlooking the Old City of Jerusalem. At the cemetery, I quickly scanned the ground for a stone to place on her grave. I collected three instead, one from me, one 'from' her parents and one 'from' Anne and their friends.

Returning to the final work on the memoir after her death was painful but I had Hannah's stories and determination coaxing me along. Alongside all the interviews we did together, I could also return to the many testimonies she had given over the years. With the passing of so much time, some details had proved difficult for Hannah to retrieve. 'If I knew I was going to be asked so many questions, I would have taken notes,' she joked with me. So we turned to first-person testimonies, diaries, letters and memoirs of contemporaries, some of whom she knew personally, as well as historical accounts, to enrich the detail and daily practicalities of Hannah's time in Westerbork and Bergen-Belsen. Hannah was incredibly knowledgeable about the Holocaust as a subject. Her bookshelf in her small sunny living room in Jerusalem was lined with books about it. She explained to me that she had only known her experience in the war and wanted always to learn more about what had happened in other parts of Europe. Of course, I also returned once more to Anne Frank's diary for guidance and insight, as well as consulting her short stories and essays that touch on Hannah and Anne's school days together. Hannah's daughter Ruthie, who knew her mother's story almost as closely as Hannah did, took part in the interviews and was an invaluable source for fact-checking and additional information.

*   *   *

Hannah's story is, inescapably, one of a girl whose family and adolescence were violently stolen from her. But that is not the whole story. It is as much about the life she built for herself afterwards in Israel, first and foremost with her family, whom she adored. I have heard so many wonderful tales of criss-crossing the small country on overnight and day trips when the children were young, visiting family and friends and scouring historical and archaeological sites with Pinchas, the ultimate tour guide and seeker and explainer of knowledge. On Saturday afternoons, after synagogue and lunch, the children would roam Jerusalem with Pinchas, who delighted in the city's storied history. And Otto Frank never faded from their lives. Not only was he a father figure for Hannah, he was a surrogate grandfather to her children. On his first trip to Israel, he insisted on visiting them at home, rather than meeting at his hotel. 'One must get to know children in their own environment,' he told Hannah. He and Hannah corresponded until shortly before he died in 1980.

Hannah returned to her nursing career once the children were in school and was assigned by the Health Ministry to be a community nurse in several villages in the foothills of Jerusalem where new immigrants from North Africa and the Middle East had been settled, starting in the 1950s. Many of these immigrants were new to modern amenities like electric ovens and washing machines, so in addition to inoculating the children and carrying out health checks, it was also Hannah's task to teach their parents how to use their new conveniences and, in general, how to adapt to their new setting.

Hannah, an immigrant and former refugee, relished her work and forged strong bonds with the families. Back in Jerusalem, she organised clothing and toy drives for them, delivering and distributing what she collected, often with her own children in tow. She was ever the caretaker and the warm, healing presence she had been for Gabi – one can't help but think that the legacy of the Florence Nightingale book she read over and over was living on in her work in the villages.

When Pinchas was in hospital dying of cancer in 1985, one of the women from the villages whom Hannah had helped, an immigrant from Yemen with many children, went from hospital to hospital until she found her because she wanted to support Hannah, just as Hannah had supported her. Hannah returned to visit the villages together with her family to mark her ninetieth birthday and people rushed out in recognition and greeting, the older ones sharing their memories of Hannah's contributions to their families' lives.

* * *

A turning point in the rest of the world's understanding of what was done to the Jews by the Nazis came in 1961, when the story of the Holocaust exploded on the world stage with the Israeli capture of Adolph Eichmann, a high-ranking Nazi official who played a key role in implementing the 'Final Solution' to exterminate European Jews. It was Eichmann who organised the deportation of about 1.5 million Jews to ghettos and killing centres.

Eichmann had been living in hiding in Argentina. Hannah didn't know until years later, but her cousin on her father's side, Zvi

Aharoni (the son of Lotte Aharonheim, who attended her wedding and had been a welcoming familial presence for Hannah when she arrived in Jerusalem), at the time the chief interrogator for the Mossad, Israel's spy agency, was part of the team that kidnapped Eichmann. He was the first to positively identify him and to interrogate him when he was captured.

The trial of Adolf Eichmann – on 15 counts, including crimes against the Jewish people and crimes against humanity – became a watershed moment for exposing the horrendous industrial scale of the Holocaust. Crucially, survivors gave searingly personal testimonies of their experiences of the atrocities. For the first time, their voices were centre stage, confirming the importance of the survivor in understanding the story of the Holocaust. It attracted the largest international media gathering in the world to date.

The trial – taking place under heavy security, guarded by armed policemen and surrounded by soaring fences out of fear a Holocaust survivor might seek direct revenge on Eichmann – was held only a few blocks from Hannah's home in Jerusalem, and she was one of many who attended one of the days. An overflow crowd of those who wanted to see the trial but could not get into the courthouse would gather daily in the stone monastery next to Hannah's home to watch court proceedings on a closed-circuit television on a large screen – the height of technology for its time. One day, the crowds grew so large that they broke through a fence, dozens of onlookers stumbling into Hannah's garden.

Hannah lived for the rest of her life in Jerusalem, raising first her own children and then helping to raise Ruthie's children after she was suddenly widowed, leaving her a single mother with eight children from the ages of 15 to a pair of two-year-old twin girls.

Ruthie lived just a five-minute walk from Hannah's home and the children often went there for meals after school, English lessons from their grandmother and regular dispensings of love and Swiss chocolate. Ruthie's children credit Hannah with giving them a sense of calm and order after the tragedy of losing their father, though Hannah had herself been recently widowed for a second time – after Pinchas died, she was briefly married to David Cohen, the man she had first met as an 18-year-old at a Shabbat lunch at the Sohbergs' in Basel.

Hannah built a remarkably close family. Late Saturday afternoons, she'd host *Seuda Shlishit* at her home for the family – the traditional third meal of the Sabbath, usually consisting of salads and light foods. As I worked on the book, I came to know her children and her grand-children and saw for myself how she was the family's matriarch, the revered and central figure. I was so moved by the family's devotion to Hannah. Every day saw a stream of visitors from all generations. Sometimes they'd drop by with homemade cookies or lunch or a child's drawing, which were all welcomed with delight by Hannah, whose eyes would light up with a special smile, especially when the visitor was a great-grandchild.

When her grandchildren were teenagers, they were given the chance to accompany her on her trips abroad. Each trip, Hannah would take a different grandchild as an escort and, as she'd joke, 'schlepper' of the suitcases. Her granddaughter Michal accompanied her on several trips, including to Amsterdam, where they met with Miep Gies, who played a leading role in hiding the Frank family and the others, and who saved Anne's diary. On one of their trips, they visited Theresienstadt concentration camp and ghetto near Krakow, the would-be destination of the 'Lost Train'. They were put up in a

guesthouse that had a view over the remains of the camp – a pecu-
liar choice to house a Holocaust survivor like Hannah. Michal told
me how she once found her grandmother looking out at the view
of the camp and sobbing. It was one of the only times that she saw
Hannah break down and weep. The memory stayed with her. In the
family, one of Hannah's nicknames was 'Jack in the Box' – in every
crisis, she seemed to bounce back, taking control of any given situation. This, however, was one of those rare moments when Hannah's
trauma was laid bare.

I noticed how the cold she had known in the camp in northern
Germany seemed to have stayed with her, settled deep in her skin.
Even on the hottest days of summer, she would wear a cardigan
as we worked together. She gave each of her great-grandchildren a
gift of an eiderdown quilt, 'So they will never be cold,' she told me.
She thought it was wonderful when her sister gave her a doll-sized
bed and blanket for her birthday, in memory of the clean, soft bed
Hannah had so longed for while in Westerbork and then Bergen-
Belsen, and that they finally shared after liberation.

During the pandemic, in 2020, Hannah became increasingly
less agile, dependent on a wheelchair or walker to move about, and
Ruthie moved in with her. But, after lockdown, she'd still muster
the energy to leave the house for Passover Seder with the family
and other occasions that were important to her. Her grandchildren
continued to marvel at her joie de vivre, how she found ways to celebrate everyday delights.

Hannah had a way of bridging the past and present of her
family history, not just through the stories she told them but in the
gifts she gave. For example, she preferred the Frigor brand of chocolate her father had brought back for her from Switzerland; she gave

her grandchildren the *mahzor* (a prayer book for Jewish holidays) for their bar and bat mitzvahs just as her grandfather had for hers; and the coloured pencils made by the Swiss company Caran d'Ache that she gave all her great-grandchildren were the same kind treasured by her and Anne as girls.

In all, Hannah had eleven grandchildren. Just weeks before she died, she was able to meet her thirty-first great-grandchild, her granddaughter Tali's son. Since then, another great-grandchild has been born. Her sister, Gabi (now known as Rahli), also has a large and growing family and is a great-grandmother too. Hannah sometimes called her and her sister's large broods their 'revenge' on Hitler.

*   *   *

I am grateful to have played a role in helping to bring Hannah's story to an even wider audience, to have been able to bear witness to her as a witness. Her and Anne's stories also brought me into the lives of other friends, like Sanne Ledermann and her parents, Ilse Wagner and Alfred Bloch. I felt like I got to know them too and in turn grieved for their lives, cut so short and in the cruellest of ways.

In her lectures, Hannah would mention how it was Anne who had wanted to be famous, Anne who had wanted to travel and see the world. She was now doing that in service to Anne and their friendship, she said.

Hannah's parents, grandparents, Anne, Sanne and her other friends – she carried them with her till the end. She was always searching for an answer to the question of why? How? In some ways, I believe she was still that adolescent, wondering why her pre-war life was stolen away and with it the people she loved most.

Three weeks before she died, with eyes closed, lying in bed, she said in a clear voice, 'Today is Sanne's birthday.' And it was, 7 October.

Hannah's story is set to come out during the week of what would have been Anne's ninety-fourth birthday. May all of their memories be a blessing.

Dina Kraft's Acknowledgments

My main thanks begin, and end of course, with Hannah herself. She was patient with my questions, some of which demanded her to search the deepest recesses of her heart and memory, not an easy task at any age. Thanks also to Hannah's daughter and right-hand, Ruthie Meir, for sharing her deep knowledge of her mother's story. Her dedication to Hannah, and now her legacy, is immeasurable.

Thanks also to Hannah's sons and their wives: to Yochi and Esther Pick for illuminating the details of Pick family life; and to Chagi Pick and Daniella Oren-Pick for opening their home and recollections to me, and who, along with Ruthie, read the manuscript and helped to ensure its accuracy.

I will always be grateful for the stories shared by Hannah's beloved grandchildren: thank you to Tali and Michal, and to Yael, Avi, Orit, Rafi, Beni, Tamar, Harel, Yuval and Chen.

I'm grateful to Rachel Goslar Moses, Hannah's sister, known as Gabi in the book, for sharing her recollections of the post-war years.

On a research trip to Amsterdam, I was kindly assisted by the Anne Frank House, including Ronald Leopold, Gertjan Broek, Teresien DaSilva and Menno Metselaar. Thanks also to Rian Verhoeven and Janny Van der Mollen and Inge Schwaab.

Thank you to Yves Kugelmann at the Anne Frank Foundation for his assistance, and to Sarah Funke Butler and Michael di Ruggiero for their kind help with Hannah's archive.

I am especially thankful to Professor Ben Ravid, Hannah's cousin, whose research into the Klee family during the war was a boon, and to his wife Jane, for sharing family photos and letters with me. Thanks to George Goudsmit for speaking to me about his mother, the courageous Maya Goudsmit.

I owe deep gratitude to the team at Ebury at Penguin Random House for their personal dedication to this book. Special thanks to Andrew Goodfellow, Publisher at Ebury, who conceived the idea of this memoir and for his kind and steady hand. To Liz Marvin, my editor, if only thanks were enough to express how much I appreciated her patience, insight and cheerful guidance. Massive thanks as well to Jessica Anderson, Evangeline Stanford and Liz Connor.

I'm indebted to Joelle Young, who translated Hannah's German language correspondence, for her enthusiasm and dedication. Thanks also to Annamika Singh for her translations of Hannah's Dutch correspondence.

I am so lucky to have friends like mine, who cheered me along and were understanding when I went underground to get the book done. Special thanks to Dani Haas for letting me steal away to the glorious sunny upstairs of her home for weeks of power writing and treasured company.

I am exceedingly fortunate to have an encouraging family, including my cousin Gianna (Hannah) Levinson, born just a year before Hannah. Endless thanks to my parents, Mike and Lisa Kraft, for instilling in me a love of history and for being my steadfast cheerleaders.

I owe a huge debt to my children, Mia and Lev, for their extreme patience and understanding while I worked on the book and for their curiosity about it. To Gilad, my husband and North Star, thank you for everything.

Elegy for Hannah and Anne's Classmates

On Sunday, 14 June 1942, Anne Frank invited her classmates from the Jewish Lyceum to celebrate her thirteenth birthday at her home on Merwedeplein 37. They drank lemonade, ate birthday cake baked by Anne's mother, and had a wonderful time watching a Rin Tin Tin film projected on the wall.

It may have been the last social gathering for the class. Within two weeks, Anne and her family would go into hiding. Others would follow, and many were deported to concentration camps, some as early as September that year.

By the war's end, more than half of the class was murdered by the Nazis.

Betty Bloemendal, who had long, wavy, light brown hair and who Anne described in her diary as doing well in school and being 'pretty quiet', was deported in September 1942 and killed a month later at the age of thirteen at Auschwitz, along with her mother and brother. Her father died two years later.

Jopie (Joseph) De Beer, described by Anne as a 'terrible flirt and absolutely girl crazy', was killed at Auschwitz in November 1943 aged fourteen. His mother, father and brother were also murdered.

Emiel Bonewit, who had a crush on one of his classmates, was deported and killed at Sobibor in April 1943.

Zunia Erlichman, who had fled to the Netherlands from Ukraine during the war, was killed at Auschwitz, at the age of sixteen, along with his mother. His father and two younger brothers survived.

Eva (Eefije) de Jong, an only child, who Anne said was 'terrific' and 'quite the lady', was murdered aged thirteen at Sobibor, along with her parents.

Werner Joseph, who had come to Amsterdam from Poland, was described as quiet, which Anne believed was because he'd moved around a lot. He was killed aged fifteen, along with his two older brothers.

Jaques Kokernoot, a funny boy who sat behind Anne in class, was killed at Auschwitz in September 1943, along with his parents and sister.

Henriette (Henny) Metz, who Anne described as a 'nice girl with a cheerful disposition', was murdered aged thirteen at Sobibor, along with her brother and mother.

Abraham (Appie) Reens, who Anne said was 'pretty orthodox', was murdered aged fifteen, along with his parents at Sobibor, in June 1943.

Samuel Salomon, who Anne notes as 'an admirer!', was 'one of those tough guys from the wrong side of the tracks'. In her diary, she also wrote: 'Do you remember? How Sam Solomon always followed me on his bicycle and wanted to walk arm in arm with me.' He was killed, along with his parents, at Auschwitz aged thirteen in September 1942.

Harry Max Schaap, 'the most decent chap in [the] class', was murdered aged thirteen at Auschwitz with his sister, parents and grandmother in November 1942.

Ilse Wagner, Hannah and Anne's close friend, was described by Anne as 'a nice girl with a cheerful disposition' and 'very smart, but lazy'. She was killed at the age of fourteen in November 1943 at Sobibor, along with her mother and grandmother.

Leo Slager, who also went to Montessori school with Hannah and Anne, was killed aged fourteen at Sobibor in July 1942, along with his father. His mother took her own life the previous year, in Amsterdam, under the strain of the Nazi persecution.

Salomon (Sallie) Springer, who Anne thought was very funny, was deported and killed aged fourteen in June 1944. His two sisters, brother and parents were also murdered.

Nanny van Praag Spiger, who was 'sensible and smart', was killed in November 1942 aged thirteen at Auschwitz, along with her parents and younger brother.

Ru Stoppelman, who was a 'short, goofy boy', transferred in the middle of the year to the Jewish Lyceum and was killed in October 1942 at Auschwitz at the age of thirteen, along with his older sister and mother. His father later died there.

Selected Bibliography

There were many books and sources that helped in the writing of this book. Here are some of them:

For insights and context of Jewish life in Germany for Hannah's family and many others, Amos Elon's *The Pity of It All: A Portrait of the German-Jewish Epoch, 1743–1933* was especially helpful.

A book written in Dutch, *Anne Frank was niet alleen ('Anne Frank was not alone'): The Merwedeplein, 1933–1945*, helped recreate life in Hannah and Anne Frank's neighbourhood in Amsterdam. Another trusted source for helping reconstruct the Amsterdam pre-war years was *Anne Frank: The Biography* by Melissa Müller. *The Hidden Life of Otto Frank* by Carol Ann Lee offered a well-researched and rich history of the Frank family.

Alison Leslie Gold's book, *Hannah Goslar Remembers: A Childhood Friend of Anne Frank,* based on interviews Hannah gave to the author more than 25 years ago, was an especially helpful reference.

The Diary Keepers: Ordinary People, Extraordinary Times – World War II in the Netherlands, as Written by the People Who Lived Through It by Nina Siegal provided understanding of the immediacy of what Dutch people were seeing and experiencing during the war.

The Netherlands and Nazi Germany by Louis De Jong and *Victims and Survivors: The Nazi Persecution of the Jews in the Netherlands 1940–1945* by Bob Moore helped with detail and insight into how the Nazi regime operated in Dutch society.

Anne Frank's diary itself, *The Diary of a Young Girl*, was a significant source, especially the early passages before Anne and her family went into hiding, and later in the diary when Anne reflects on her friendship with Hannah and comes to terms with her own fate. Anne's *Tales from the Secret Annex* was also valuable, particularly her writing that relates to Hannah and their time at the Jewish Lyceum.

Two of Hannah and Anne's friends also wrote wartime memoirs: *My Name is Anne, She Said, Anne Frank,* by Jacqueline van Maarsen and *Holocaust Memoirs of a Bergen-Belsen Survivor* by Nanette Blitz Konig.

Letters from the Ledermanns, a collection published by Afori Publishing, provided me with insight through the lens of the Ledermann Family, both as deportation approached and from inside Westerbork. Barbara Ledermann's interview with the USC Shoah Foundation was also extremely helpful.

Hannah's cousin Ben Ravid's article, 'Alfred Klee and Hans Goslar: From Amsterdam to Westerbork to Bergen Belsen', published in *The Dutch Intersection: The Jews and the Netherlands in Modern History,* edited by Yosef Kaplan, recounts the frantic attempt by Hannah's family to emigrate.

The Footsteps of Anne Frank by Ernst Schnabel and *The Last Seven Months of Anne Frank* by Willy Lindwer were both were good sources for earlier interviews with Hannah.

Night of the Girondists by Jacques Presser, who had been a teacher at Hannah's school, is a novel set in Westerbork and contains interesting details about life in the deportation camp. A book in Hebrew by the Birnbaum Family siblings called *Eitz Chaim Hee* ('The Tree of Life') helped me learn more about the Birnbaum family, especially in Westerbork.

For the chapters on Bergen-Belsen: Renata Laqueur's *Dagboek uit Bergen-Belsen* ('Diary from Bergen-Belsen'), which she wrote as a 24-year-old living in the same section of the camp as Hannah, and Erich Marx's testimony of life inside Bergen-Belsen, entitled *That's How It Was*, were both rich sources of information.

There are many excellent memoirs and testimonies written by fellow Bergen-Belsen survivors from the Netherlands who knew Hannah including: *Their Image Will be Forever before My Eyes* by Jehudith Ilan-Onderovaizer; *Once the Acacias Bloomed: Memories of a Childhood Lost* by Fred Spiegel; *To My Dear Children* by Max Finkel, and *We Knew Not Joseph* by Robert Bar-Chaim.

In writing the chapter 'The Lost Train', I read a transcript of an extensive interview Hannah gave to Israeli researcher Shoshi Ben-Hamo in 2022, for a project called 'Whoever Saves a Life, Stories of Children from "The Lost Train"'.

For the final chapter, 'The Promised Land', Tom Segev's *1949 the First Israelis* was a rich source.

About the Authors

Hannah Pick-Goslar, known as Hanneli to her friends, was born in Berlin in 1928, as the eldest child of Jewish parents, Hans Goslar and Ruth Judith Klee. In 1933, after the election of Adolf Hitler and the Nazi party, the Goslars moved to Amsterdam, where Hannah attended the 6th Montessori School and became friends with a girl named Anne Frank. In Anne's diary, she recounts tales with Hannah, referring to her as 'Lies Goosens'. In 1943, Hannah, her father, her younger sister Gabi and her maternal grandparents were arrested and sent to Westerbork transit camp, before being sent to Bergen-Belsen. Hannah survived 14 months until the camp was liberated in 1945. She emigrated to British Mandate Palestine in 1947, shortly before it became modern-day Israel, and trained as a nurse. Once retired, Hannah enjoyed the company of her 3 children, 11 grandchildren and 31 great-grandchildren. She passed away in 2022 at the age of 93.

Dina Kraft is a journalist based in Tel Aviv, where she lives with her family. A veteran foreign correspondent, she has written for *The Christian Science Monitor*, the *New York Times*, the *Los Angeles Times* and *JTA* among others. She is currently opinion editor for Israel's newspaper *Haaretz*'s English edition and is co-host of the podcast *Groundwork*.